STATION 43

STATION 43

Audley End House and SOE's Polish Section

IAN VALENTINE

This book was first published in 2004 by
Sutton Publishing Limited

This paperback edition first published in 2006

Reprinted in 2010, 2012

The History Press
The Mill, Brimscombe Port,
Stroud, Gloucestershire, GL5 2QG
www.thehistorypress.co.uk

British Library Cataloguing in Publication Data
A catalogue record for this book is available from the British
Library.

ISBN 978 0 7509 4255 3

Typeset in 10/12.5pt Palatino.
Typesetting and origination by
Sutton Publishing Limited.
Printed and bound in Great Britain.

Contents

Foreword

This book is concerned with one of the most secretive and very distinguished military organisations during the Second World War. Although it was a British organisation, called Special Operations Executive, most of the involved volunteers came from the Polish Forces under General Sikorski's command, stationed in Britain. Their mission was to be parachuted at night into Poland and inflict heavy losses, on unexpected targets, against the German war machine operating in occupied Poland.

The author of this book has collected many unique facts about Audley End House. Having worked as the site ranger in the grounds, Ian Valentine began gathering step-by-step information and material on this secret unit, named '*Cichociemni*', which trained at Audley End, called Special Training School 43 during the war. The highly selected agents were trained in handling explosives, sabotage, 'silent killing', radio contact, shooting and many other duties in Underground operations. Out of 316 volunteers who were parachuted into Poland, 108 lost their lives. Important dignitaries, including Commander-in-Chief of the Polish Forces, General Sikorski, President-in-Exile, Władysław Raczkiewicz, and other generals such as Stanisław Maczek, Stanisław Kopański and Stanisław Sosabowski visited Audley End House from time to time.

I congratulate Ian Valentine on this effort in contributing highly towards SOE history and future generations.

Captain Alan Mack (Maćkowiak), 'Alma'

Small-arms, PT and unarmed combat instructor, STS 43, 1942–4; wounded and POW at Arnhem, Operation 'Market Garden'

Preface

Audley End House near Saffron Walden in Essex stands on the site of a Benedictine Abbey founded between 1139 and 1143. High boundary walls once enclosed fish ponds, dovecotes, granaries, a mill and a farm, all providing produce for the refectory table. Lifting a hatch in the anteroom adjacent to the dining parlour, one can still see what is thought to be part of the original monastic walls below. Visitors picnic beside what was once the largest of the monastic fish ponds.

In 1538, after the Dissolution, the buildings and lands were given to Thomas Audley, Henry VIII's Lord Chancellor. Audley either demolished the abbey or converted it into a three-storey house. Thomas Howard, first Earl of Suffolk, began building the house in 1603 and set about the huge construction of new gardens. After being a royal palace for Charles II, the house and gardens gradually went into decline. However, in the early eighteenth century the restoration projects of Sir John Griffin Griffin, First Baron Braybrooke, began. Much of what the visitor to Audley End sees today is the result of the work that Sir John started. In 1763 he embarked on the rebuilding of Audley End. In the same year the great garden designer Lancelot 'Capability' Brown began his plans for redesigning the West Park, in a way that today is considered to be this nation's greatest contribution to European art, a serpentine style often known as the 'English Landscape Garden'. Brown created the sweeping carriage drives and demolished the remaining seventeenth-century garden walls, which opened up the view to the landscape beyond. He remodelled the canal into a serpentine lake and planted belts of trees.

Audley End House is well known for its Capability Brown gardens and its wonderful Robert Adam interiors. However, standing at the foot of the old Jacobean Mount Garden south of the house rests a modest memorial urn dedicated to a group of men and women who make up the secret history of Audley End House. During the Second World War the Eighth Baron Braybrooke's residence was requisitioned and kept under a cloak of secrecy. Visitors walking in the gardens today may notice evidence of Britain's efforts to repel the expected invasion by the German Army in the early days of the war. However, beyond the concrete tank-traps, the pillbox and bridges, in the dark interiors of the house resided a group of Polish soldiers training to be prepared to parachute into occupied Europe. Major A. Nosek, former chairman of the disbanded *Koło Cichociemnych Spadochroniarzy Armii Krajowej* (The Polish Home Army Parachutists' Association), and himself a trainee at Audley End House in 1943, states, 'Audley End House is such a splendid historical place, where kings and queens have stayed. When they looked down from heaven, I expect they were very surprised to see the arrival of young men speaking a strange language, but I'm sure they gave their approval when they saw what these men were doing.'[1] It was this extraordinary work that had to be kept secret. Local people heard explosions in the grounds, and even Lord Braybrooke himself had difficulty in being allowed into his grounds. This book hopes to uncover the part that Audley End House played in Britain's secret war.

Acknowledgements

*Autor najserdeczniej dziękuje tym wszystkim osobom,
które hojnie zaofiarowały informacje i pomoc w czasie
zbierania materiału i pisania tej książki.*

Special thanks to the people who knew Audley End House
during the war and their families who spent time writing to
me, relating their knowledge and generously lending me precious
photographs and documents, including former FANY personnel:
Elizabeth Austin, née Jessiman; Lord Braybrooke, JP; Anna
Menzies Caldwell and her mother, Anne (Maureen) Menzies,
née Booth; Mr J. Cottiss and his son, Mr M. Cottiss; Sir Douglas
Dodds-Parker; Mr A.S. Fensome, Mr P.J. Fensome and Mr and
Mrs B. Lincoln; Mr W. Leney; Mrs J.D. Fisher and her mother,
Mrs Oughton; Mrs R. Harris and Mr and Mrs M. Harris; Vera
M. Long; Captain Alfons Maćkowiak (Alan Mack); Major Antoni
Nosek and family; Captain Antoni Pospieszalski (Tony Currie);
Mrs Elizabeth Reynolds; the Hon. Mrs C. Ruck, OBE, née Neville;
Lieutenant W. (Horace) Sidell and D. Sidell; Mrs A. Watts; Mr and
Mrs Bronisław Wawrzkowicz and Teresa Miszewska; Margaret
Wilson; and Second Lieutenant Kazimierz Zdaniewicz. Also,
those who preferred not to have their names mentioned.

My thanks also to others who gave me valuable information,
contacts and encouragement: Mr W. Bakiewicz; Warrant
Officer (2nd) S.E. Barnes; Cris Betts; Jeff Bines; David Budd;
Captain W. Cole and his daughter, Val Sandes; Emma Crocker,
Curator of the Photograph Archive, and John Stopford-
Pickering at the Imperial War Museum; Martyn Everett;
Zofia Everett for translation and historical advice; Jonathan
Falconer; Alison Fishpool and Geoff Mason at Frogmore Hall;
Rosemary FitzGibbon for information on her uncle, Major

STATION 43

Fergus Chalmers-Wright; John Gallehawk; M.R.D. Foot; Alexander Grocholski for information concerning his uncle, Count Stanisław Grocholski and Sir Peter Wilkinson; Jerzy Grochowski, son of Wanda Skwirut, and his wife, Ann; Matthew Grout for his historical advice; Mr R. Grove; Steve Harris (RAF Tempsford website: www.Tempsford.20m.com); Richard Holmes at the Essex Record Office; Ian Hook, Keeper of the Essex Regiment Museum; Bob Hughes; Roger Kirkpatrick; Ann Martin; Tom McCarthy; R.V.L. Noble; Mrs Pickering; Tim Padfield at the National Archives for allowing me to use information from public records in Crown Copyright; Ted Pretty for detailed post-war information about Audley End House; Søren Rasmussen (www.stengun.dk) for translation and information regarding the Danish section of SOE; Iga Szmidt at the Polish Library, London; John Shaw-Ridler; Roy Rodwell; Mr V. Selwyn at the Salamander Oasis Trust; Decia Stephenson, Archivist of the FANY for useful contacts; Flight Lieutenant T.C. Stevens; Dr K. Stoliński, chairman and Krzysztof Bożejewicz of the *Studium Polski Podziemnej*, the Polish Underground Movement (1939–45) Study Trust (SPP); Mr S. Thompson; Steve and Darren Todd, for putting me in contact with Mr Stevens; Susan Tomkins, Historical Archivist at Beaulieu; Hilary Walford; Teresa Widd; Stefania Ziomek; and Patrizia Zołnierczyk for historical advice.

At English Heritage, Dee Alston, historic contents cleaner, helped in matching rooms with photographs; Marilyn Dalton, the general manager at Audley End House (now retired), gave unlimited support and access to rooms and photographs; Richard Halsey, East of England Regional Director, Val Horsler, Head of Publishing and Alyson Rogers at the National Monuments Records (NMR) kindly granted leave to reproduce English Heritage photographs; Gareth Hughes, East of England Regional Art Curator, gave advice and entrusted the SOE archive to me; I also wish to thank Pat Payne for her photography, and Robin Steward and other staff at the Enquiry and Research Services, NMR. The house staff, room stewards and custodians at Audley End forwarded information and contacts, including Gillian

ACKNOWLEDGEMENTS

Allcock, Jane Appleby, Val Collins, Liz Davidson, Joy Germany, Nicky Hazell, Linda Ketteridge, Vivien Kroon, Gerald Lowe, Matt Meyer, Chris Trigg and Mel Watling.

Those living in farms and halls in the Saffron Walden area who kindly replied to my letters were Mr P.M. Bell, Mrs Bradfield, Patrick Bushnell, Ian Haigh, Chris and Margaret Johnson, A.W. Pyatt, James Scruby, Michael Snow and Michael Southgate.

Thanks, finally, to my late father, who told me about his father's experiences rescuing aircrews with the Sheringham lifeboat during the war. He also informed me of the many nationalities that served with the Allies, recalling one 15-mile flight he had in 1944 with the Air Training Corps in a Dominie flown by a Polish pilot, an experience he described as hair-raising. He took a trip in a Dominie again over fifty years later; as he wrote: 'On Father's Day 1998 I was privileged again to "fly like a wild bird down the long wind" over the skies of East Anglia.'

Abbreviations

AK	*Armia Krajowa*	POW	Prisoner of War
AL	*Armia Ludowa*	*PPR*	*Polska Partia Robotnicza*
CBE	Commander of the Order of the British Empire	*PSL*	*Polskie Stronnictwo Ludowe*
		PW	*Polska Walczy*
CMG	Companion of the Order of St Michael and St George	RAF	Royal Air Force
		RASC	Royal Army Service Corps
CSM	Company Sergeant-Major	RNLI	Royal National Lifeboat Institution
DFC	Distinguished Flying Cross		
DMO	Director of Military Operations	*RSHA*	*Reichssicherheitshauptamt*
		RT	Radio Telegraphy
DSO	Distinguished Service Order	SAB	Student Assessment Board
EU/P	European Poles	SBS	Special Boat Service
FANY	First Aid Nursing Yeomanry	SD	Special Duties
GHQ	General Headquarters	SHAEF	Supreme Headquarters of the Allied Expeditionary Force
GROM	Operational Manœuvre Reconnaissance Group		
		SIS	Secret Intelligence Service
JP	Justice of the Peace	SOE	Special Operations Executive
KCMG	Knight Commander of the Order of St Michael and St George		
		SPP	*Studium Polski Podziemnej*
		SS	Schutzstaffeln
MBE	Member of the Order of the British Empire	STA	Station
		STS	Special Training School
MC	Military Cross	*SZP*	*Służba Zwycięstwu Polski*
NAAFI	Navy, Army and Air Force Institutes	*TWZW*	*Tajne Wojskowe Zakłady Wydawnicze*
NKVD	*Narodny Komissariat Vnutrennich Dyel*		
		UB	*Urząd Bezpieczeństwa*
NSZ	*Narodowe Siły Zbrojne*	USSR	Union of Soviet Socialist Republics
OBE	Officer of the Order of the British Empire		
		W/T	Wireless Telegraphy
ORP	*Okręt Rzeczypospolitej Polskiej* (Republic of Poland's Ship)	*WiN*	*Wolność i Niepodległość*
		ZWZ	*Związek Walki Zbrojnej*

Introduction

In the winter of 2001 I began researching the wartime history of Audley End House. Armed with scraps of information and a few intriguing photographs, I found that the project soon grew. Serendipity helped. The chance meeting with a visitor to the house led to a wealth of first-hand information and a growing feeling of privilege that people were so willing to talk about their experiences.

In periods of lengthy research it was always pleasing when a verbal report of a particular episode could be cross-referenced and agreed upon by more than one source. Memories obviously change and fade over the sixty years since Audley End was a Special Operations Executive (SOE) training school. Consequently, a historical account of this period, partly based on verbatim reports, can never be a comprehensive study. Some parts of the SOE courses at Station 43, as Audley End was known, remain unclear, and I can only apologise if anyone feels that there are inaccuracies or omissions within the text. British servicemen and Polish instructors were at Audley End for a short period of time, and trainees for six months or less – the time it took to complete a course and get a mission. Also, many individuals still felt bound by the secrecy that was imposed upon them at the time they were there. However, I hope that a general impression of the achievements, willingness and bravery of the Polish soldiers, the training undertaken and life at Audley End House has been achieved.

The records of SOE in Poland at the National Archives are part of a fourth set of restricted files to be released into the public domain, and I have disseminated some files that relate directly to Audley End House, including training reports of seventy trainee agents in 1944, and other files that build up a picture of the work undertaken by the Polish Section of SOE.

Many publications have raised awareness of SOE achievements and losses. The Polish nation suffered greatly as a country before, during and after the war, which can only reinforce the efforts of the men and women who fought with the *Armia Krajowa* (Home Army), the largest Underground resistance army during the Second World War.

Although I use the term 'agent' throughout the text, it is important to stress that the Poles were never 'spies'. SOE was not an espionage body, and the majority of operatives were drawn from a military background. Perhaps 'freedom fighters' would be a better description. Although many personnel – for instance, the couriers – did operate in civilian clothes, many of the soldiers worked with the *Armia Krajowa* in Poland in a loosely uniformed, paramilitary and partisan capacity. Their efforts culminated in the Warsaw Uprising in 1944.

SOE trainees had to pass strenuous courses. The courses at Audley End were no exception, and there were fatalities. Owing to the great risks involved, all agents were volunteers, but it was often difficult to find ideal candidates. Agents needed to be physically fit, self-reliant, courageous, disciplined, intelligent, experts in clandestine warfare and, as many would argue, ruthless.

With almost 100 acres to utilise for the purposes of training, Audley End House could accommodate a number of trainee agents. The nature of small-town England meant that local knowledge did know that something was going on in the Big House. Local people once saw some very outlandish behaviour as they looked on from the public road. Baroness Sue Ryder of Warsaw, herself in the FANY (First Aid Nursing Yeomanry), was attached to the Polish Section of SOE, and describes the activities that were seen in the West Park at Audley End:

> No contact with local people in the area of a [training] station was permitted, and cover stories were given, though at times these must have struck the locals as somewhat less than convincing. A group of curious people gathered one day on the road outside Audley End House near Saffron Walden, Essex

(then used as one of the training stations by the Poles), and gazed across the wide lawns as a number of Bods [agents] taking part in a training exercise and disguised as Germans held off an attack.[1]

One British soldier stated that 'although the townspeople were officially ignorant of the activities at Audley End, they must have wondered at the civilian-dressed people in the dead of night moving round the fields'.[2] They knew that there were questions that one did not ask. Other local people recall that they had no idea about Audley End during the war. People travelled considerably less than today, and obviously there were a fraction of the cars that are now seen on our roads. One elderly Essex farmer stated that he was unsure what was going on in the next village during the war, let alone within the private estate.

Despite the obvious secrecy that was imperative to every residence used by SOE, civilians and Regular Army occupied houses in the grounds. Everyone on site had to sign the Official Secrets Act, and some people are still reluctant to talk about what went on at Audley End during the war. Men from the British Army were stationed at Audley End House to guard the property and maintain its guise as an everyday army camp. They stoked the boilers, cooked for the Poles and the British, undertook administrative and quartermaster duties and ran the orderly room; they drove SOE trainees out on exercises and to the 'holding stations', where agents waited for their missions, and airfields when they had finished their training; they played football with the Poles and became their friends – one British soldier found a few of his Polish friends again in tragic circumstances in Germany at the end of the war. Despite the SOE directive that training at the special schools would be autonomous to the Poles, British soldiers taught trainees to drive and ride motorcycles. The British soldiers, local police and Home Guard also took part in training exercises in the Essex countryside. Their job was to stop the Poles completing their given tasks. The Poles treated these exercises very seriously and at times had to be reminded that, although the exercises had to be as authentic as possible, the men who were directed to stop them were allies and not German soldiers. When asked about the Polish desire for authenticity and rough-handedness in field exercises with the local constabulary, SOE trainee Bronisław Wawrzkowicz smiled and said, 'Yes, we were known as "the Polish bandits"'. Their ferocity was caused by the fact that most of them had witnessed at first hand the ravaging of their country and had fought against the might of the German *Blitzkrieg* and Soviet occupation. Many had been in Soviet camps. Some had seen members of their family killed and others had no idea what the fate of their families was and would wait many years to find out.

The central theme of this book has to be Audley End's position in history as the birthplace of many Polish *Cichociemni* agents, dedicated, fierce and resilient. However, it is important to remember the other people who were part of the lives of the Poles while they were in England: the civilians and British servicemen at Audley End and other Polish establishments; the women of the FANY, the civilian and military code-breakers and the men of the RAF Special Duties squadrons who risked their lives flying missions to the limit of their aircraft's range. The missions that the Poles at Audley End undertook were taking place in a war that was pulling their homeland apart.

Ian Valentine
Ely, December 2003

ONE

'Poland is Fighting'

It is easy to get embroiled in the understandably volatile and divided political opinion that still exists concerning British, American, Polish and Soviet relations during the Second World War. Nevertheless, it is important to attempt to look at the background to these views, as this is intrinsic to any document about Polish military involvement in the war. It is also easy to lapse into conjecture about events between the fixed historical dates. However, it is equally difficult to steer away from the vagaries of political double-dealings, polemics, incongruities and betrayal that occurred between the Allied political leaders, when so many Poles still have strong feelings about what happened to them during and after the war.

History can be approached on many levels. Historians draw on many discursive strategies: a fixed period of history can look very different between individual, social, cultural, political and ideological perspectives. An episode in war can be very different for two soldiers standing only yards apart. It is impossible to tidy these very different vantage points and bring them all together, as this leads only to historical reductionism and oversimplification. In this chapter, I am by no means attempting a comprehensive tract about Poland during the Second World War in so few words, only perhaps to express polarised issues about which many people of different generations still have very strong opinions. For instance, British soldiers at Audley End built up friendships with their Polish comrades in arms but could not march with them in any victory parade at the end of the war, a situation that many

1

found difficult to accept. There was no date stamp to mark the end of the war for the Poles, a distinction discussed in the final chapter. Armistice Day marked the end of conflict for most servicemen and women in Europe (with the ensuing loss and bereavement that touched most people), but for many Poles the threat to their lives continued long after the war had finished, when they were tracked down by Communist Soviet–Polish security forces in their homeland. As this book looks at the wartime experiences of a few individual Polish servicemen who trained at Audley End, in what is inevitably a subjective account of the war at an individual and personal level, we should not lose sight of how the conflicts discussed below affected every Pole during and after the war, as well as all the other servicemen and civilians who were chained to political machinations that were out of their control.

Frontiers become ever fluctuating in the tide of history of many nations, changing with the direction of the prevailing political wind. Countries collide on borders like rifts in continental plates, and disputes about territorial ownership create conflicts and wars that still simmer and ignite today. Poland's borders have changed many times in its history. For many hundreds of years Poland has fought to maintain or regain its independence. The country has been geographically landlocked when it was once sprawling and vast. It has been partitioned and divided by neighbouring countries so that Poland geographically no longer existed. Between 1762 and 1796 Catherine II, Empress of Russia, agreed a series of partitions that resulted in the once independent Poland becoming a protectorate of Russia by 1795. On 24 October of that year Stanisław August of Poland abdicated, and the country was partitioned for the third time among Austria, Russia and Prussia.

From 1795 to 1918, after the country had been partitioned three times, there were no 'indigenous' Polish people, only Poles who lived in Russia, Prussia (Germany) and the Habsburg Empire that later became Austria-Hungary.[1] The partitions and the ensuing subjugation of the Poles created exiled communities in Europe. This subjugation created a strong distrust of the Germans and Russians in the collective Polish psyche. Stalin, the General Secretary of the Communist Party of the USSR, advocated overt suppression of the Polish language and culture, but the Polish contempt for the Russians was not always understood by Allied leaders during the Second World War, as cartoons in the newspapers of the day exemplified.

The regaining of territorial loss after the First World War was of great importance to Stalin, and the territorial dominance of the Soviet Union in Poland was central to this. Stalin's ruthless nature and his mistrust of other nations, combined with fear of invasion from the West, help to explain why Polish nationals were executed or imprisoned during the Second World War, despite fighting the common enemy, Germany. Russia has fought many wars, in the East against Japan, in the Crimea, but predominantly in the West. Napoleon's invasion, the First World War and Hitler's invasion, all were fought in the west, and these were the most costly to Russia. To control Poland would help to secure Russia's western border from attack.

The strategic importance of Poland to Hitler and Stalin was immense, and had been to others before them. Invading armies marching towards Russia would pass through Poland. Catherine II realised this and partitioned the country.

At the end of the First World War, Russia was wracked by internal revolution and was militarily weak. Poland was able to regain independence, and with it Russia lost control of an important buffer zone. Stalin's motivation was twofold: to have a buffer against future invasion from the West and the influence of capitalism, and to regain what had been lost during the First World War. In 1920 Poland was at war with Russia, with Poland's independence threatened again. The war, fought by many of the soldiers who passed through Audley End House during the Second World War, culminated in a Polish cavalry counter-attack at the battle of Warsaw that quelled the Red Army, but remoulded Poland's frontiers so that the Lithuanian, Byelorussian and Ukrainian communities were split. The end of the war also reinforced Soviet suspicion that the Poles were dedicated to overthrowing them.[2]

In Germany at the beginning of the 1930s the popularity of the Nazi Party was growing. The word Nazi was drawn from Hitler's NAtional SoZIalist Party. In the Reichstag elections of 1930 the Nazi Party won over six and a half million votes. However, Adolf Hitler was originally prevented from taking his seat owing to his Austrian citizenship. On 30 January 1933 Hitler became Chancellor, nationalist feeling grew and in March the following year the Nazis built the first concentration camp, at Dachau near Munich.

Poland signed a non-aggression pact with Germany in 1934. This was unsettling, as it created the impression to other European neighbours that Poland and Germany were allies with common goals. Lying innate was the German aim to reclaim territory, and the German minority in Poland saw Hitler's rise to power as a step towards this.

By 1938 the threat of Hitler and Stalin was growing. Poland did not accept the German demand to reclaim the port of Gdańsk in Poland, annexed by the Germans and renamed Danzig. Gdańsk had a strong German population, going against the tentative appeasement of the 1934 non-aggression pact. After Chamberlain had maintained that Britain would support Poland's independence, Hitler revoked the peace treaty with Poland. In September 1939 Poland was forcibly occupied by Germany and the USSR, according to an agreement between Hitler and Stalin, which had been signed on 23 August 1939 by German Foreign Minister Joachim von Ribbentrop and Soviet Foreign Minister Vyacheslav Molotov. Hitler's main purpose was to ensure the Soviet Union's neutral stance in an attack on Poland. Reinforcing Poland's weakness within this political triumvirate, the 'sleeping protocol' to the pact was the partition of Poland between Germany and the USSR, tearing up Poland's independence once more.

Two decades of European diplomacy that had sought to prevent another war came to an end. The German invasion of Poland triggered a war that many thought would not last long. British Prime Minister Neville Chamberlain thought the conflict would be over by spring the next year. Hitler's *Blitzkrieg* (lightning war) raged through the heart of Europe. Divisions of Panzer tanks outnumbered the inadequate Polish forces and the *Luftwaffe* destroyed the Polish railway system. However, despite German strength, the Poles fought on but could not withstand Hitler's attacks into Poland from Slovakia and East Prussia. The Polish hope that Britain and France would save them never happened, as there were no military plans to support Poland. Whether this was because of tardiness, deliberation that Britain would not be successful in helping the Poles, or the sheer speed and military superiority of the German advance is unclear, but, whatever the reasons, similar feelings of betrayal because of inertia would be felt by the Poles in Warsaw in 1944.

The Red Army invaded Poland on 17 September, despite Poland's misplaced hope that it would offer the Poles military support against Hitler. The military defeat of Poland led to Polish prisoners of war in German hands and in Soviet camps, where the army officers were put into separate custody. The underlying secret pact between the Soviet Union and Germany was made flesh in the territorial sharing of Poland between the two powers. A further treaty expressed mutual responsibility for squashing Polish resistance. In February Stalin began deporting Poles to Siberia and eastern Russia, where the people who survived the journey worked as slave labour in camps such as the Pechora Lager in Siberia. Over one and a half million citizens of different ethnicities left their country. Polish citizens who were not deported were often put into prison camps in their homeland.

Poland was to suffer terribly under German occupation during the war, and endure a higher proportion of deaths than any other country. Six million Polish citizens were put to death in gas chambers and concentration camps, or executed on the spot. Hundreds of thousands were deported for forced labour. The Nazi intention in Poland was the complete 'Germanisation' of the country: cities, towns and villages were renamed in

German; the Polish language was forbidden in public; members of the intelligentsia were murdered; Polish culture was denied; villages were razed to the ground for the least signs of resistance; and the Catholic Church was persecuted, resulting in priests being sent to concentration camps.

Recolonisation brought with it the Jewish ghettos and Polish resettlement in annexed regions. These Third Reich policies can be amalgamated into the one aim of Hitler: to annihilate the Polish nation so that the country no longer existed. Hitler's ideology tried to persuade those he made powerless that their powerlessness was inevitable. To take away a nation's language is to disempower it. His desire to 'civilise' condoned murder as a means to an end for eliminating people he saw as 'savages'. In July 1942 the Germans began to deport the remaining population of the Warsaw ghetto to their deaths in the concentration camps and gas chambers. In April the Jews in Warsaw had defended themselves for six weeks against German tanks and artillery, with thousands of deaths on both sides. M.R.D. Foot states that a Pole, Witold Pilecki, let himself get arrested so that he could find out what life was like inside Auschwitz. This he did, setting up a resistance organisation within the camp. He escaped, but failed to convince the *Armia Krajowa* about the horrors of life in Auschwitz.[3] As the war progressed, couriers also brought information concerning the camps to the Allies, including Polish courier Elżbieta Zawacka, the only female occupant of Audley End House who parachuted into Poland.

Before the First World War the partitioning of Poland had also given rise to the subjugation of the Jewish population in the country. Anti-Semitism in Poland was not new (it can be said that anti-Jewish prejudice was prevalent throughout Europe, including the British Nazi Party, and anti-Jewish views were expressed by writers such as Rudyard Kipling and G.K. Chesterton). Part of the Jewish population in Poland was concentrated in the lands occupied by Russia. Catherine II hailed Russian Orthodoxy as the only true faith, thus restricting the largest concentration of Jews in Europe to their own settlement and forbidding them to journey beyond it. Persecution and the ensuing Jewish insurrection resulted in a large Jewish emigration before the First World War. After the Polish–Soviet War anti-Semitism heightened, often with its roots in religion. The Polish Communist Party was largely Jewish, which created a hatred of Jews and Russians alike.[4] Between the wars the Depression badly affected the Jewish community, but Jews were often scapegoated as being catalysts to economic decline. Large numbers of Jews emigrated before the outbreak of the Second World War, those remaining coming under the Nazis' inconceivably evil solutions in their death camps.

Racial hatred has its roots in many facets of prejudice. Some experts argue that racial scapegoating deflects an unworthiness of self, a powerful force of prejudice, others that prejudice is caused by an unequal distribution of wealth – economic precursors to genocide. When individuals are prejudiced against the members of a group, they will often encode information consistent with their prejudice.

The Nazi propaganda machine exploited a negative representation of the Jews through their own media and language. The dominant Nazi discourse dehumanised the Jews as it dehumanised other faiths and races, and the more it was repeated the more it reinforced the prejudice. The Nazis knew that economic and other national deficiencies could be used in rallying ill feeling towards certain groups. The propaganda helped individuals justify their hatreds, and much of the German population began to view the Jews as *Untermenschen,* or subhumans.

Many other nationalities with different religions, prisoners of war and anyone deemed unacceptable to the Nazis also suffered or perished in concentration camps. Over eleven million people lost their lives in the Holocaust, in what was called the *Endlösung,* or Final Solution – the Nazi euphemism for mass murder. Six million of them were Polish and half of these were non-Jewish. After the war Polish literature reconstructed the experience of the death camps in literature, including Tadeusz Borowski's *Proszę państwa do gazu,* a collection of short stories

7

about the author's experiences in Auschwitz, beyond the sinister slogan above the camp entrance: *Arbeit Macht Frei*, Work Makes You Free.

Many of the Polish SOE agents would experience at first hand the suffering endured by men, women and children held in the camps. Incredibly, after the citizens of Poland had witnessed the genocide of the Jews during the war, a marked series of violent anti-Semitic attacks began in Poland in the years after the war had finished. Many Poles, often right-wing, saw the Jews as traitors who were Communists who had spent the time in the USSR during the war and worked in the secret police, or thought that most Jews were against maintaining Poland's independence. This is not to say that *some* Jews, of Russian and Polish origin, were free of blame in such activities. One source told me that her father had been in General Władysław Anders's (Commander of the Polish Army) 1st Krechowiecki Lancers Regiment and had been tortured by a Jewish *NKVD* agent. The *NKVD* was the *Narodny Komissariat Vnutrennich Dyel*, People's Commissariat of Internal Affairs, the name used for the Soviet secret police. The *NKVD* man professed a hatred of Christians and a hatred of the priest with whom the woman's father shared a cell. This priest was tortured and murdered along with many other religious believers. Conversely, many Jews (and other nationalities) fought within the ranks of the *Armia Krajowa* (*AK*).

In the face of such cruelty to Jews undertaken by the Nazis, it is sometimes difficult to accept that some Jews were not always the victims – sometimes they were the perpetrators. One has to acknowledge and condemn any kind of torturer or murderer. It can be said that people behave badly, not because they are Jews, or Poles, or Christians, or Germans, or any other group, but because they behave badly as individuals. They would act that way under any banner. Post-war violence was often the result of victim lashing out at victim, but it is easier to view actions collectively in terms of faith or race, as ostensibly it is easier to explain. Consequently, one can say that dangers arise when the acts, or supposed acts, of individuals are grouped together under race or religion, a factor that Hitler exploited. One Polish woman maintains: 'There is also a great success story in Jewish–Polish relationships that has resulted in an indistinguishable common culture in parts: in humour, culture and values. There are areas of great affection and common ground between individuals, as in my family.' Another Polish source cites a different angle on the painful issue of reasons behind anti-Semitism in post-war Poland. The majority of Poles are fiercely patriotic, and for many their country is more precious to them than their lives. Some Poles felt that, although Jews had settled, lived and prospered in Poland, they are a nomadic people and had never identified with the country itself. This way of life often clashed with the Poles when many Jews sided with the invaders of their country, especially after the Second World War. Many Jews were Communists as there was terrible poverty in the shtetls, and Communism offered the chance of a better life. Some of these Jews did perpetrate many atrocities against political figures and intellectuals, causing a great resentment born of patriotism, not religion.

Hitler's concept of *Lebensraum* (living space) referred not only to the reclamation of territories lost in the First World War, but also to the conquest of new territories in the East. Hitler had written about *Lebensraum* nearly twenty years earlier in *Mein Kampf.*

The *Luftwaffe*'s failure in the Battle of Britain meant that the German Navy and invasion force would be vulnerable to surface and air attack. The failure of Operation 'Sealion' meant that Hitler looked towards the Soviet Union and his Operation 'Barbarossa' – part of the 'living space' he believed to be the right of the German people. Hitler invaded the Soviet Union in 1941, and the British Government pressed the Polish Government-in-Exile in London to come to an agreement with Stalin. In July 1941 a treaty was signed maintaining that the Polish Army had to be formed in the Soviet Union. The members of this army came from Poles in Soviet-controlled prisons and labour camps in Siberia.

In the meantime all Poland had come under Nazi rule and a 'Fourth Partition', and easier times were far from forthcoming. In part of his foreword to George Iranek-Osmecki's accounts of the *Silent and Unseen* (*Cichociemni*) soldiers, General Anders seems to lay Polish deaths at the hands of the Nazis. This reflects a censorship that pervaded Allied leadership during the war. While he was under Allied command, Anders can be said to have been constrained to curb references to Stalin's barbarity in Poland for the sake of the Allied effort. One source revealed that he instructed his troops to keep their knowledge, born of recent and bitter experience, to themselves, as the British war effort relied on working closely with Stalin. The Poles who survived the prison camps in Soviet Russia were debriefed in Persia among other places, though their experiences were censored for the above reasons.

The Polish authorities found that more than 15,000 officers taken in 1939, when the Red Army had taken Poland's eastern territories, were missing. Two years later about 5,000 corpses were found in Katyń forest in Russia, and most of these were found to be part of the core 15,000. It was thought that on Stalin's orders they had been shot in the back of the head by the Soviet secret service.

The massacre at Katyń haunted Allied relations. Poland was attracted by the Germans' public charge of Soviet responsibility for the murders, and the Germans' proposal of an international inquiry into the events. Germany and, later, the USSR conducted their own investigations, conclusively blaming each other. The trials of Germans at Nuremberg after the war for crimes against the Poles at Katyń were mentioned in the indictment of Hermann Göring, the *Luftwaffe* commander, and others, but it was decided that the issue should be avoided, and the Soviets did not take the responsibility of clearing themselves of blame. It was only on 14 October 1993, two years after President Gorbachev had recognised the independence of the three Baltic republics, that *de facto* recognition that Stalin was to blame became evidential. Moscow handed secret KGB documents to Polish Solidarity leader Lech Wałęsa, revealing that it was Stalin and his bureau who had ordered the killing of the Polish officers.

It can be argued that Stalin's personality played an important role in the fate of the Polish nation. Ruthless and paranoid, he eliminated any threat, perceived or real. During the 1930s he ordered purges against the intelligentsia and military to remove opposition and potential threats. Consequently, any Pole who was fighting for Poland during the Second World War represented a threat to Soviet influence and control in Poland, and a Pole who had spent time in the West, like SOE-trained soldiers, perhaps even more so. Britain was seen as a liberal, capitalist democracy. Conversely, many in the West considered the Soviet Union under Stalin as a repressive, communist dictatorship. Anyone exposed to a liberal democracy was viewed by Stalin as tainted, a threat to his authority. They would have to be removed.

After Hitler's invasion of Poland, a few Polish units refused to surrender, and General Władysław Sikorski started to organise the Polish Army in France. General Michał Karaszewicz-Tokarzewski was appointed the general commanding officer and secretly began organising a resistance army under the coalition *SZP* (Service for Poland's Victory). Tokarzewski's task was to amalgamate fragmented resistance groups, known as cells, into a unified force. However, in October 1939 Sikorski, from his headquarters in Angiers, France, dissolved the *SZP* as it was outside the Polish Government's influence. He replaced the group with the *Związek Walki Zbrojnej* (ZWZ), the Union of Armed Struggle.

Sikorski's communication with Poland by courier dried up after the fall of France. The exiled Polish Government remained in London, with its military headquarters ensconced in the Rubens Hotel. With marked reluctance it signed the British-driven alliance pact with the USSR. However, this agreement saw the release of some of the starved Poles who had survived the Siberian and Arctic prison camps. General Władysław Anders was released from Lubyanka prison in Moscow and made commander of the army by Sikorski, setting up his command post near the Ural Mountains.

During September some Polish military units and many individuals crossed the friendly borders with Hungary and Romania. All Polish military personnel were interned in camps, where they were guarded by Romanian and Hungarian military. Many internees escaped and headed for France to join Sikorski, and also to Syria, where units were being organised. This organisation led to the formation of the Independent Carpathian Rifle Brigade, which crossed from Syria into British-occupied Palestine after the fall of France. Despite resistance from French Prime Minister Reynaud, Henri Pétain, leader of the pro-German Vichy regime, capitulated to the Germans in 1940, and the remnants of the Polish Army in France then made their way to ports on the Atlantic and then to Britain. One brigade of 6,000 men was sent with the British and Free French to fight in Norway, and two divisions were fighting in France when the invasion took place in May 1940. Other volunteers to fight with the Polish Army had to travel to the south of the Soviet Union on both sides of the Ural Mountains, enduring long distances with little food, comprising 70,000 men until Stalin stopped conscription.

Only parts of the Polish forces were able to be evacuated to Britain from French harbours. Poles made dangerous escapes through Europe. Under Franco many were put into camps in Spain. They were eventually freed and came to Britain, where Polish armoured divisions, rifle and parachute units, bomber and fighter squadrons were beginning to form. There was also the Polish Navy, comprising a cruiser, some destroyers and submarines.

The nature of living under occupation in Poland required a secret army whose members had to appear as civilians, but trained and ready to take up arms when needed. A British 'Most Secret' document from 25 November 1941 reveals the strength of the reliable and devoted 'Inner Cadre' of the Union of Armed Struggle (ZWZ) resistance army remaining in Poland:

The numbers of this inner cadre are 51,250 men, of which 3,500 are officers; the First Reserve consists of 286 officers and 70,000 other ranks. This makes up a total of approximately 121,600 men of whom nearly 4,000 are officers.

Of these, only some 35,000 men are armed and their equipment consists largely of material which was concealed during the autumn of 1939 after the German invasion. It includes a small number of anti-tank weapons and light mortars and a large number of rifles and other small arms.[5]

ZWZ was renamed the *Armia Krajowa* (*AK*) in February 1942. The *AK* has been widely translated as the Home Army. One source feasibly states that a more accurate translation would be 'Country's Army', as Home Army sounds something more amateur and cosy. Indeed, this highly organised army became occupied Europe's largest resistance force, at its peak comprising 300,000 fighting men and women, including the very young and the very old, all equally determined in their common goal, to rid their country of the occupying forces.[6]

'*PW*' was to become the famous military 'anchor badge' of the *AK*. It stands for *Polska Walcząca*, 'Fighting Poland', or more commonly *Polska Walczy*, 'Poland is Fighting'. *PW* was a particularly potent symbol of Polish resistance. It was a graffito that was often seen painted on walls throughout the country during the five years of Nazi occupation. The Germans feared the symbol, and anyone seen writing it was executed. They knew that the physical embodiment of *PW* signified the great unrelenting threat that the *AK* had on their lives. It was a frank declaration of partisan sympathies and loyalty that could not be expressed vocally. The purpose of *PW* was to boost the morale of the civilian population in Poland and to let them know that, although they were under the hammer of the Nazis' liberticide and genocide, the *AK* was still fighting. There were Poles fighting all over the world for them and they too had to fight against the Nazis. *PW* was an emblem of hope in a time of adversity, a symbol that expressed the predicament of the Poles, but predicted a triumph over their oppressors. *PW* was to become a visible presence again in the Solidarity protests in 1980.

The *Biuletyn Informacyjny* was the *AK*'s communication pamphlet. It was first printed in November 1939, and its last wartime edition was on 19 January 1945. The Underground press printed the paper to give factual and reliable information, rather than propaganda information, so as not to give undue hope to a population that knew the war would last years. The secret publication sought to unite a society in difficult circumstances. With these publications, a secret education system and courts of law, a feeling of strength and national cohesion was often felt by a nation that was effectively 'living underground'. Through efficient communication channels *Biuletyn Informacyjny* reached all *AK* districts.

Despite Allied efforts to drop arms and equipment, it was impossible to arm all the *AK*. However, the *AK* resisted the Germans on every level to stop the 'Germanisation' of its country: from overt military action to illegal printing presses and the setting-up of the Underground state, which sought to maintain education banned by the Nazis. Absolute resistance required an incredible amount of organisation. It is worthwhile briefly explaining the system of the seven 'bureaux' that formed the structure of the *AK*, in Poland and in exile in London and throughout Europe and the Middle East. The following has been gleaned from Marek Ney-Krwawicz's *The Polish Home Army, 1939–1945*. Each bureau of the *AK* was also split into its own subsidiary sections. The First (I) Bureau dealt with all the organisational problems within the *AK*, using status reports and constantly updating staff lists. It also contained the Welfare Department, '*Cichociemni*', dealing with matters concerning SOE-trained Polish parachutists sent from England. The Second (II) Bureau was Intelligence and Counter-Intelligence. This bureau was concerned with dissecting all intelligence given to it by agents and then sending it to the High Command. It also contained the Special Combat Detachment for eliminating informers and traitors, and another special cell for liaising with *AK* soldiers. The

Third (III) Bureau was the Operational and Planning Department for a predicted general rising, and dealt with guidelines for insurrection. The Fourth (IV) Bureau was concerned with all quartermaster issues, including ordnance, commissariat, medical, supply columns, veterinary, dispatch and field post office, prison, ordnance survey and construction. The Fifth (V) Bureau was concerned with maintaining all lines of communication, including the Courier Communication Department. Perhaps the most famous is the Sixth (VI) Bureau, the Bureau of Information and Propaganda. The section was set up for publications and the *Tajne Wojskowe Zakłady Wydawnicze* (*TWZW*), or Secret Military Publications Plant, and also dealt with psychological warfare and all matters of life in Poland under the oppressors. The Seventh (VII) Bureau was the Office of Audit and Finance and was also concerned with the printing of banknotes.

Despite the numbers of personnel, the *AK* did not embody an all-encompassing resistance army in Poland, with all Poles fighting under its banner. There was an incredible complexity of resistance units in Poland, dozens of diverse paramilitary parties operating, each with its own political agenda and disaffections towards each other. The *AK* was affected by internal structural difficulties. Political disaffection centring on many issues, including the Polish–Soviet pact, caused splinter groups to be formed. For instance, the Communist Polish Workers' Party, *Polska Partia Robotnicza* (*PPR*), and, at the other end of the political spectrum, the National Armed Forces, *Narodowe Siły Zbrojne* (*NSZ*), were formed. The *NSZ* fought against the Germans, Jews and sometimes the *AK* itself.[7] The *AK* looked to draft post-war reforms to appease and homogenise splintered paramilitary resistance groups, no mean feat with their various political allegiances. There were also arguments between the Government-in-Exile and the *PPR* over restoration of pre-war frontiers, not to mention internal disaffection within the Government-in-Exile.

On 4 July 1943, one month after the massacre at Katyń had been revealed, General Sikorski was killed in an air crash in

Gibraltar after visiting General Anders in Iraq. His death deeply affected many Poles. Rumours of conspiracy still surround the death of Sikorski, although an inquiry into the possible sabotage of his aeroplane revealed nothing. Many blamed the Soviet secret services, and some people vehemently put the blame at the feet of Winston Churchill. As many Poles had been fearing for Sikorski's life before he left Gibraltar, this only accentuated the bitterness felt when news of his death reached the Polish forces. Rolf Hochhuth's post-war play *The Soldiers* rekindled the conspiracy of Churchill being guilty. There were other rumours: some people maintain that *NKVD* officers in Gibraltar at the time were responsible; that a Polish traitor had sabotaged the aircraft while it was in Cairo, before it even reached the Rock; and even that the aircraft could not take off properly from Gibraltar's short runway because it was so overloaded with contraband, including hundreds of oranges and other smuggled goods that washed ashore after the aircraft had crashed.

SOE received reports on a number of occasions that stories were current in the Middle East that Sikorski was to be assassinated on his forthcoming visit. Senior Polish officers were stating this openly. SOE Polish Section history files deny that this was tantamount to a very real threat to the General's life. SOE took this open fear to be a blatant revelation of poor political relations between the Polish Government-in-Exile and the Polish Army in the Middle East. This conflict centred on General Anders's regarding the Polish Government-in-Exile as unrepresentative of his army. Much of Anders's Army had suffered terribly in the Soviet Union and had not experienced life on British soil.[8]

After much debate between the Poles in London regarding who his successor should be, Sikorski's command was split between Stanisław Mikołajczyk, the leader of the Peasant Party, *Polskie Stronnictwo Ludowe* (*PSL*), who became prime minister, and General Kazimierz Sosnkowski, who took command of the armed forces.

When the Red Army began advancing to the West in 1944,

the Polish Government began to think of the fate of post-war Poland. Churchill and Roosevelt failed in their attempt to make Stalin agree to Poland's reinstatement of pre-war frontiers, secretly concluding between them that Poland's borders would be moved so that the Soviet Union could occupy the old eastern territories where the Polish population was scant.

Warsaw was in an area of Poland renamed the *General Gouvernement*, where complete 'Germanisation' was sought. However, in the summer of 1944 the German Army was in a desperate situation as the Red Army reached Warsaw. In the weeks before the Uprising, the *AK* coordinated a series of attacks in conjunction with the Red Army, which liberated towns and villages. There was also coordinated generalised sabotage under *Cichociemni* command. At the beginning of August the battle to save Warsaw began. Thirty thousand men and women from the *AK*, the *NSZ* and the *Armia Ludowa* (*AL*) or Communist People's Army rallied against the occupation. Children were also fighting in the *Szare Szeregi*, 'the Grey Ranks' Scout movement.

Within the first few days of the Uprising, parts of Warsaw were liberated, but these victories were quickly curtailed. The Germans stopped their retreat and set up their forces and reinforcements across the Vistula river ready to fight the approaching Red Army. However, the Soviets also stopped in their tracks, allowing the reinforced German Army to encircle Warsaw and crush the Polish Uprising. Stalin gave various anomalous technical reasons as to why his army remained stationary for six weeks. It can be said that Stalin would have considered the *AK* to be a considerable threat to him in any post-war occupation of Poland. He refused to allow Churchill to use his airfields to supply the *AK*, but after one month eventually let American bombers use Poltava in Ukraine, though many supplies were dropped into German hands. The *AK* wanted the flights to continue, as any drops that safely fell into its hands were better than none. On 1 August 1944 the Allies made desperate efforts to send in supplies, while the Red Army stood inactive across the Vistula. In short, the advancing

Red Army halted outside the city of Warsaw until the retreating German Army had destroyed Poland's stand, with the *AK* desperately manning barricades and anticipating Soviet liberation. The Uprising will be looked at again in Chapter 5, in the context of *Cichociemni* who trained at Audley End House, many of whom were executed by Stalin's commanders as the Soviet troops advanced towards Berlin. Berlin was 'magnetic north' on Stalin's compass, and a march towards Germany's capital meant raking through Europe's heart.

The Polish armed forces fought throughout the Second World War, serving in their own country, in North Africa, Italy and north-west Europe, and helped to overrun Berlin at the end of the war. Polish paratroopers served at Arnhem, and 145 Polish pilots flew in the Battle of Britain, with many others serving in bomber and fighter squadrons. The Polish Air Force gave a marked contribution, including, through *AK* Intelligence, destroying more than 190 German V-1 flying bombs.

The Poles were instrumental in forwarding research into radio development, having a research station based at Stanwell. The Polish Navy took part in most naval operations: the ORP *Piorun* was the first ship to locate the German battleship *Bismarck*, and Poland's merchant navy helped keep the Allied supply lines going.[9]

Allied Command often wished to confine Underground activity in Poland to sabotage, disruption and diversion. However, some partisan activity in Poland was far from diversionary. In the village of Blizna in the Małopolska region of Poland, experiments on V-1 pulse jets and V-2 rockets were being carried out. The *AK* decoded the military plans to the rockets and retrieved a fired rocket and dismantled it. On 15 July 1944 a Dakota transport aeroplane landed in Poland to retrieve technical information and components from the V-2 rocket as part of Operation 'Wildhorn III'. Two Polish scientists had examined the rockets at their base in the south-east of Poland, and messages by cipher and courier had already reached the Allies. Against all the odds the aircraft made it back to Britain with detailed plans and technical information about the rockets that had killed over 2,500 people in Britain. Obtaining information on the rockets from under the noses of the Germans has been described as 'an inspiring example of efficient cooperation between various services of Allied armies. Involved in the operations were *AK* Intelligence, Polish and British Staffs in London, various courier and radio networks, and last, but certainly not least, the RAF.'[10]

Perhaps most famous of all was the work carried out by mathematicians Marian Rejewski and Henryk Zygalski, who were instrumental in solving the German Enigma codes. Their work enabled the British interception of German messages at Bletchley Park, although Rejewski was never allowed into Bletchley itself.

TWO

Cichociemni, 'Silent and Unseen'

SOE

Stories about secret agents have fascinated people for many years. Defections and double-agents were the familiar topics of newspaper headlines in the Cold War. Fictional stories about espionage have always been popular, from Graham Greene to Ian Fleming. However, surviving members of SOE are keen to stress that they were agents and soldiers, never spies. Like its fictional counterpart, SOE has been researched and represented to the post-war public in many ways, and there is no shortage of factual and fictional literature of exploits, despite an estimated 85 per cent of SOE documentation having been destroyed.

There have been cinematic portrayals of SOE's achievements, often concentrating on women agents – for instance, French volunteer Odette Sansom's work linking resistance networks in France taken from Jerard Tickell's book; Violette Szabo in Lewis Gilbert's *Carve Her Name with Pride*, from R.J. Minney's book; and more recently the film portrayal of Sebastian Faulks's best-selling fictional novel *Charlotte Gray*. The effect of cinema and an emotive musical score on an audience has often made SOE a romantic subject. However underplayed on the big screen, there is still the underlying hint at what some of these agents went through in the field and after capture. Biographical and historical accounts of agents have revealed the level of stress that they were often under: from the fear of duplicity and betrayal, their own intransigent actions leading to drastic reprisals to local civilians; to torture and letting down their friends.

CICHOCIEMNI, 'SILENT AND UNSEEN'

It is impossible to comprehend exactly what emotions the agents had in different situations unless one has had the experience. There are many different coping mechanisms that individuals apply to the prolonged stress of weeks and months of living on their nerves.

The Special Operations Executive was instigated by Winston Churchill in July 1940 to undertake subversive and sabotage operations in enemy-occupied countries. As the organisation was to be an unorthodox fighting service, it was removed from the control of the military and placed under civilian command. The executive was thought up by Hugh Dalton, the Minister of Economic Warfare, and eventually run under the guidance of Air Commodore Frank Nelson. Before the end of SOE operations, Frank Nelson was succeeded by Sir Charles Hambro, who was later succeeded by Brigadier (later Major-General, KCMG, DSO, MC) Sir Colin Gubbins. He advocated the irregular guerrilla war tactics that the Irish Republican Army employed.

Before the war, in March 1938, MI6 saw the need to create a new department, which gave rise to Section D. Predicting the rise of Nazi power, Section D was brought about for subversive operations in Europe, or 'stay-behind saboteurs'. When SOE was formed, the executive gained many personnel from Section D for their work.

Agents were trained in their own specialist covert fields: from sabotage and other terrorist acts, propaganda and courier work, to wireless operation and coalescing already established but fragmented resistance groups. Setting up resistance networks in Europe was often difficult because of the political schisms between groups and their different agendas.

Even though it was widely understood that the fall of France meant it was necessary to set up a clandestine organisation, Churchill did not fully embrace the idea of SOE at the start. The Secret Intelligence Service (SIS) was already established, and Whitehall was suspicious and derisive of this new enterprise amalgamated as SO 1, SO 2 and SO 3, the precursor departments to SOE that dealt with propaganda, operations and planning, respectively. Indeed, the rivalry between SIS and SOE lasted throughout the war. However, it was agreed that action had to be taken quickly to hamper the progress of the oppressors in Europe, and SOE was born out of SO 2 in 1940. In his lecture on *Resistance Movements in the War* given to the Royal United Services Institute in January 1948 (published in the *Journal of the Royal United Services Institute*, volume XCIII), Major-General Gubbins states, 'The shock of initial German success was profound, particularly in the occupied territories of western Europe. France, Belgium, Holland, Denmark and Norway lay as if stunned; only the Poles, toughened by centuries of oppression, were spiritually uncrushed. Yet in all these countries there were hundreds of thousands of individuals who refused to lie down in defeat and who prayed for the means to continue the struggle.'[1]

Operations began under the banner of SOE in 1941. However, SOE suffered disastrous losses in Holland between 1942 and 1943 under the German *Der Englandspiel* ('English game') counter-intelligence campaign. A captured SOE wireless operator omitted his allocated security checks and stated in plain language that he was caught. Ignoring this, SOE dropped fifty agents and supplies straight into the hands of an enemy reception. Despite assurances from Major Giskes of the German military Counter-Intelligence *Abwehr* that the agents would be imprisoned, the department was taken over by Nazi *Reichssicherheitshauptamt* (*RSHA*) command, and forty-seven out of fifty-four agents were subsequently executed.

After *Der Englandspiel* many people wanted SOE closed down, and no one more than Sir Arthur Harris of RAF Bomber Command, who had criticised SOE from the onset as amateurish and irresponsible and regarded the use of aeroplanes for SOE purposes as a waste of resources. Throughout the war many high-ranking officials within the Royal Air Force thought that their aeroplanes could be put to better use than dropping solitary agents and cursory supplies.

SOE operations were often fraught with disaster, with the RAF reflecting these losses in aircraft and personnel. Despite criticism of SOE, it was thanks to the tenacity of the RAF Special Duties squadrons that agents and supplies could be dropped to give support to growing resistance forces *in situ*.

One successful SOE operation revealed that sabotage on the ground could be a worthy factor in helping to destroy the Third Reich's war machine. In the autumn of 1943 ninety-four British Lancaster bombers failed to destroy a large industrial centre in the Burgundy region of France. They failed again in a second attack, and caused civilian casualties in both raids. Following the RAF raids, two SOE agents attacked the power stations that gave the industrial region power and destroyed ten transformers, which crippled production.

Churchill maintained SOE's fragile existence, predicting how useful it could be for operations at the time of D-Day (Decision Day), 6 June 1944, when the activities of SOE became more salient as resistance in Europe grew stronger. Small three-man SOE teams called 'Jedburgh' parties were dropped behind enemy lines on the night 5/6 June to coordinate resistance against the Germans. After the Allied landings in Normandy a great surge of sabotage began. When D-Day arrived, it gave hope to the British nation, a hope perhaps partly marred on the home front by the arrival of the demoralising, pilotless V-1s, and with them the face of a new kind of war that SOE also sought to stamp out with the help of the Poles.

SOE was a necessary invention, and represented the best means of attacking a virulent enemy by unorthodox approaches: 'attack his war potential wherever it was exposed and at least create some running sore to drain his strength and disperse his forces and, finally, when invasion of the Continent did take place, to give the maximum of assistance to the forces of liberation.'[2] Debilitating the German 'war potential' meant sabotage of factories, including vital ball-bearing installations, power supplies, radio stations, supply trains, locks on main waterways, trains and railway lines, overhead pylons, mining facilities, shipyards and shipping, bridges and roads.

By 1944 SOE had a huge staff numbering nearly 10,000 men and 3,200 women. Like all big corporations today, SOE required complex administration and staffing on every level. For SOE, this included a staffing structure far more complex than just a collection of agents and their instructors. They needed men and women who were recruiters of agents; technical experts; high-level staff and directors; policy advisers; liaison staff to government departments, national sections and existing security organisations; cipher experts and decoders; drivers; pay clerks and so on.

SOE formulated the following sections: Albanian, Belgian, Czechoslovak, Danish, Dutch, French, German, Greek, Iberian, Italian, Norwegian, Yugoslav and Polish.[3] Agents were sometimes very young – 18, 19 or barely into their twenties. However, as SOE training reports at Audley End House reveal, agents could also be in their late forties and early fifties.[4] Women were also trained as agents, as they were often more unobtrusive and able to move about more freely in occupied Europe. They received the same training as the men, from unarmed combat to weapon handling. Every SOE employee was paid at ordinary service rates with additional parachute pay.

Agents undertook their assignments in situations of great danger and often without the solace of comradeship. It was expected from the start that many of these trained experts would not return from occupied European soil, and agents knew all too well what to expect if they were captured.

POLISH AUTONOMY

Sir Douglas Dodds-Parker describes SOE as 'quite an association, none better than the Poles'.[5] When one thinks of SOE in Europe it is often France that one conjures up: the French resistance, and dropping off agents by single-engine Lysander aeroplanes in small moonlit fields, as portrayed in many black-and-white films after the war. The story for other nationalities could be very different. For the Polish operatives being dropped into their homeland it meant a long, often ten-hour, flight in freezing conditions in an uncomfortable and noisy aircraft. They were then parachuted into a country where the threat was not only from the Germans but from the Soviets and their own Polish nationals. Owing to the great dangers involved in going into action behind enemy lines, the principle of taking only volunteers was adhered to. The call for volunteers to work in Poland via SOE was addressed to the Polish Army, Air Force and Navy, both in Great Britain and in the Middle East and Italy. Jędrzej Tucholski in his book *Cichociemni* reveals that the officers of the Polish Sixth (VI) Bureau of Information and Propaganda travelled directly to army divisions and recruited directly on the spot. Those already selected by their own superiors were interviewed under the condition of army secrecy, and during the interview parachuting into Poland was suggested to them.[6] One prospective SOE candidate, named 'Zenon', describes a mysterious person arriving at his armoured brigade in Scotland from Rubens. Zenon was called into a room to speak to the man. He states, 'it was all about Poland – that I had been picked out for service there. It was a great distinction for me.' He goes on to talk about having to parachute: 'I was thoroughly shaken. First of all, this jump business. I must say I don't mind jumping from trams, for instance, or a diving-board. But from a plane . . .'.[7]

The decision to join was entirely in the hands of the candidate. If a person took up the offer, the agreement had to be in writing. Next an information search was made about the candidate in the Personnel Department and with Polish Counter-Intelligence. The final decision was taken by the Head of the Sixth Bureau. If the outcome was favourable and no suspicious affiliations were found, the candidate was summoned for training. However, as will be seen from the courses undertaken by the Poles at Inverlochy Castle, many soldiers undertaking preliminary courses did not know they were being singled out for Underground work.

The call for volunteers brought 2,413 applications by 1943, among them several women.[8] Volunteers came from diverse places after the Polish non-aggression pact with the USSR: the agreement saw the release of some of the starved Poles who had survived the Siberian and Arctic prisons and Spanish concentration camps where Franco's pro-Hitler regime interned Polish soldiers who had reached Spain through occupied Europe.

Candidates were recruited for specific work from the onset. For instance, those picked for service in military intelligence in Poland were usually selected personally by Colonel Stefan Mayer, commandant of the Polish Intelligence School. Recruitment of aircraft pilots for creating a force that was predicted to support an uprising in Poland was mainly undertaken by the Department of Studies and the Parachute Army. At this early stage neither British nor Polish training programmes were devised, but the first parachute team was getting ready to depart; improvisation was used to train the parachutists who were dropped into Poland.[9]

Christened *Cichociemni*, meaning 'unseen and silent' (*cicho* translates into English as 'quietly' or 'softly', and *ciemny* as 'dark' or 'obscure', and is pronounced 'chihoh-chemny'), the Polish SOE agents were the first of the Allied agents to parachute into their own country on the night of 14/15 February 1941. George Iranek-Osmecki reveals that it is difficult to pinpoint when the term *Cichociemni* was first used to describe the Polish agents. We are the unseen and silent. This name, though queer, has proved to be very apt. It describes those who appear silently where they are least expected, play havoc with the enemy and disappear whence they came, unnoticed, unseen.

'When the name originated, it referred to the peculiar means adopted for augmenting our numbers by men from units in the line. It was born somewhere in the soldier's community, among the Poles in Scotland, in the year 1941, when the first parachutists were already at their posts, in Poland. How it was born is not known, but most probably in jest. Many such names appear spontaneously from nowhere.'[10] George Iranek-Osmecki's father, Second Lieutenant Kazimierz Iranek-Osmecki, 'Antoni', parachuted into Poland in 1940 and 1943. Jędrzej Tucholski maintains that it was first used by training instructors in September 1941.[11] Today, the Polish commando unit *GROM* (Operational Manœuvre Reconnaissance Group) is said to have its roots in the *Cichociemni*.

Tucholski states:

> Only people of very high moral calibre and demonstrating high skill in acquired specialisation were sent into the country [Poland]. They had to have a knowledge that allowed them freely to operate in conspiratorial situations, situations in which they had never met before. In other words there was a need for rigorous selection and training. At first there was no selection for candidates wanting to serve in Poland. Recruiting was based on individuals volunteering and that was enough. However, there was a danger that apart from the individuals of 'high moral calibre' there will be those who would want to go back to Poland because they did not like the situation they found themselves in at present, those who wanted adventure and people with other reasons. Therefore, quite quickly the decision was made to change the method of selection. The principle of initial voluntary recruitment was maintained, but with the addition of applying stringent criteria as far as candidates' moral standing, as well as looking at their psychological predisposition and physical condition. This further selection was applied during the training of agents, which was very strict and vigorous.[12]

SOE training reports from Audley End House reveal the emphasis placed on looking at a candidate's general outlook on life and character. Only every fourth candidate successfully completed the full training expected of them. There were questions from commanders of regular military outfits, who were understandably concerned that they did not want to lose their best officers. In 1942 General Sikorski ended the uncertainty of selection: 'I know that in the interest of their own divisions the leaders are reluctant to lose their best officers.

Nevertheless they need to understand the need of the Country in this and any other issue must have absolute priority.'[13]

The Polish section of SOE, formed in late 1940, differed from all other national sections. As soon as the agents and couriers touched Polish soil they came under the control of the Polish authorities and the *AK*. It is worth clarifying that, although many SOE-trained agents and couriers were passing through the courses at Audley End House, once in Poland they remained under the aegis of the *AK*, severing SOE's jurisdiction.

The first (and last) all-encompassing SOE military mission to Poland was Operation 'Freston' in 1944, which was exceptional in that it contained agents of non-Polish descent. Freston's purpose was a mission to assess the situation within the *AK* during the period of the Uprising.

This does not mean to say that SOE did not receive intelligence from Poland or that Poles solely worked in their homeland. For instance, the couriers worked with *Zagroda* ('croft'), a division of the *AK* that sent information reports by itinerant couriers from different countries back to the Polish Government-in-Exile in London, with information filtering to SOE command via the Sixth Bureau.

There was also the European Poles (EU/P) subsection of SOE that covered Polish minorities outside Poland. A part of EU/P was codenamed Operation 'Monica', which maintained liaison between SOE and the Polish Government regarding the mining and industrial area situated around Lille and Saint-Étienne in northern France, an area that contained a large colony of Poles. The head of the EU/P section was Ronald Hazell, a former English shipping agent on the Baltic Sea, who spoke Polish and German. EU/P was also instigated in 1940, and before D-Day it sent twenty-eight agents to France. Seven of them were killed.[14] Polish agents and supplies were sent to France in 1943 in Operation 'Colony' to support the impotent *Bardsea* conflagration (see p. 156). Polish sabotage groups in occupied and unoccupied France in 1941 were organised into 150 sections and operated in mining, agricultural and industrial areas in Lille, Grenoble, Caen, Montluçon, Saint-Étienne, Toulouse, Valenciennes, Roubaix, Maubeuge and Perpignan.[15]

The Poles and British worked side by side in the EU/P section. For instance, before being assigned to Monica, Fergus Camille Chalmers-Wright was trained by SOE in Scotland and undertook courses in propaganda at Bletchley and codes and general security at Beaulieu. He undertook his first mission with SOE in late 1943. His task was to find out about two non-Communist Polish resistance organisations in France run by the Sixth Bureau. Little was known about them by the British. In an interview recorded for the Imperial War Museum in 1984, Chalmers-Wright stated that sabotage was undertaken in the Lille area by the Poles at the time of D-Day, and also that they were responsible for the reporting of about thirty V-1 launching sites.[16] These reports were reaching SOE after his return to England from his first mission.

Chalmers-Wright successfully completed parachute training at Ringway in 1944. A second mission to drop him back into France, complete with a bicycle so that he could pedal his way to Lille, was aborted.[17] He eventually parachuted into the Belgian Ardennes after D-Day with a Polish wireless operator and some Belgians, his mission being to get back into the Lille area. However, he injured his back badly on landing and made it back to England in January 1945 for medical examination.[18]

He contacted Ronald Hazell, who had established himself in the Polish Consulate in Lille. Much of France had been liberated by this stage, and stimulating sabotage in Lille was no longer required, as the Poles had done it themselves. Consequently, he was entrusted with a different SOE mission back in France. Romanian–Polish funds under British control were to be distributed to victims of German imprisonment and other matters of concern. Chalmers-Wright reported back to SOE on suitable distribution according to individual cases. The reports were accepted by SOE and he began distributing the funds. This work took him up to nearly the end of 1945.[19] He was awarded the Virtuti Militari by the Poles in appreciation of his courage, the most prestigious Polish decoration for courage in war. He was also awarded the MBE at the end of the war. So Monica and Freston illustrate exceptions to the 'all-Polish affair'.

By using a few examples, it is worth briefly continuing to look at activities undertaken by the Poles with SOE in other countries, to illustrate the breadth of Polish activity during the war. SOE-trained Poles worked in France, Italy, Yugoslavia, Albania, Greece, Germany and the Soviet Union.

Early SOE work abroad was run by Professor Stanisław Kot, who sought to coordinate resistance in Polish communities in many countries, including France, South America and Scandinavia.[20] 'The organisation in Scandinavia [1941] consists of 1,000 members of the Polish community in Stockholm and Denmark. Most of the latter are agriculturalists and of no great value as saboteurs, though their sense of solidarity is a factor to be counted with in the event of a general uprising.'[21]

By 1941 there were about one million Poles working in labour and prisoner-of-war camps in Germany with instances of sabotage.[22] There were plans under Operation 'Dunstable' to utilise these workers in Germany. However, there were few SOE operations in Germany under SOE's X Section, because of the great security imposed by the Third Reich. One X Section operation, called 'Clowder', included Peter Wilkinson, who unveiled the memorial urn dedicated to the *Cichociemni* in the grounds at Audley End.

Resistance was twofold in Yugoslavia: partisans with pro-Soviet sympathies under Josip Tito, and Colonel D. Mihailovič's group, who revolted against the Germans but were violently opposed to the partisans. Partisan territory was favoured by SOE as it afforded the shortest route to Poland. However, SOE had had more contact with Mihailovič, and it was possible that the partisans' pro-Soviet stance would impede Polish movement through 'their' territory. The Balkans were also a territory that Stalin considered his concern, and ructions began between SOE and the USSR's leader concerning operations in this part of Europe, as well as Poland.

The Sixth Bureau was aware that Poles had been conscripted into the German Army in Yugoslavia and other parts of Europe.

Some were thought to have been persuaded by the Germans that the real enemy was Communism, not the Nazis.

The Polish Underground managed to infiltrate some German garrisons to root out Poles willing to cooperate. An operation in June 1944 involved evacuation of Poles from the German Army in Greece. Second Lieutenant A. Domaszewicz was appointed to go to Greece on 16 July with other Allied military personnel. He was tasked with establishing contact with the Poles and other non-Germans (*Volksdeutsche* from Silesia) in the German unit that was set to be attacked as part of the operation.[23]

En masse desertion was also planned for Albania. Other national sections were performing similar operations – for instance, 'Clayton' and 'Cateret', which set about sending agents into Italy to contact Czech troops in the German Army and encourage them to join the resistance.

The Sixth Bureau itself had two posts in the Middle East in cities infamous for espionage – Cairo and Istanbul. The Poles set up these stations for overseeing work in the Balkans. Information was gleaned from travellers and from misleading information given to German counter-espionage agents.[24]

Again, unlike any other section, the Polish Section of SOE had a separate general staff headed by Captain, later Brigadier, Harold B. Perkins, who worked in close contact with the Sixth Bureau of the Polish Headquarters in London. Perkins spoke Polish and had owned an engineering works in Poland before the war. He was once seen to bend a poker double with his bare hands.[25]

Perhaps the Polish desire for exclusivity was in part because their Underground work had been started before the foundation of SOE. Autonomy in training also developed out of the natural need for Polish instructors, who were attached to SOE training to overcome any language difficulties. The Poles took care of their own recruitment, although they occasionally utilised SOE's Student Assessment Board (SAB). However, they rarely acted on the advice of SAB, and a conflict existed between what the Poles and the British thought constituted good selection procedures.[26] 'As early as the end of 1940 the principle was established that Polish officers would carry out part, at least, of the instruction of their nationals, and it was therefore necessary to allocate definite accommodation to the Polish Section.'[27]

The Polish Section of SOE was not unique in its autonomy. The Czechoslovakians, Dutch and Norwegians also had *émigré* governments, and, like the Poles, these country sections instigated missions in their home countries, and answered to their exiled governments. Major-General Gubbins states in his lecture:

> they [the governments-in-exile] were of the greatest importance in all SOE work. Above all other considerations, of course, the British Government and people had a high moral obligation towards these occupied peoples. Beyond that, it was clear from the start that the maximum results could be obtained only by the maximum cooperation with those governments, particularly where they still retained and could continue to retain the confidence of their peoples.[28]

Preserving security at every level was obviously of the utmost importance to SOE and each country section. Radio communication had to be top-notch if an operation was to succeed, and the Poles placed utmost importance in gaining intelligence from the field and on building up layers of security. Polish communication networks were impeccable. A survivor of the Auschwitz concentration camp, Józef Garliński, in his book *Poland, SOE and the Allies*, states that the Poles were the only national section that retained the right to use their own cipher for radio liaison because it was so good (until the strict coordination needed in traffic signals when D-Day approached, and even then Churchill relented to their demands).[29] They also maintained their own wireless stations.

Agents chose their own codenames for when they were in Poland, and these were sometimes known only to the Polish authorities.[30] This sometimes caused administrative problems for the British authorities, but appealed to the Polish desire for protective layers of security.[31]

The departmental framework of SOE and the various training and research establishments were always under numbers or abbreviations, so that F Section referred to the Independent French SOE section; RF to the Gaullist French section; MP for Poland, Czechoslovakia and Hungary, and so on. Audley End House was one of many SOE Special Training Schools, serving various national sections and having different purposes. Special Training Schools were abbreviated to STS and listed by number, so Audley End House is referred to in all files as STS 43. Some sources referred to the houses as 'Secret Training Stations', and the training establishments were invariably referred to as 'Stations' or 'STA'.

Staff and agents in the national sections were also referred to by pseudonym or number in correspondence. General Sikorski was 'Ace' and 'Rubie'; Colonel Wilkinson, senior commander in SOE, was referred to as 'MX'; and General Anders was 'Straight' and 'Mean'.

Letters and numbers within SOE files also denote countries of operation, so that Poland becomes I Land; Romania becomes J Land; Russia [USSR] becomes K Land; Slovakia L Land, and so on. Poland was also referred to as '38 Land' and 'Kensal', and the Sixth Bureau as 'Violet'. To confuse the novice researcher at the National Archives even further, Czechs are sometimes referred to as 'Ones', Poles as 'Twos', and Russians as 'Threes'.[32]

The Poles and Czechs were also keen to form their own national section within the RAF's No. 138 Squadron, which served SOE drops of personnel and supplies into Poland, but no section could be wholly self-sufficient. The various country, or national, sections had to rely on British, and, in the latter part of the war, American aeroplanes, supplies and training facilities. With this came conflicts of interest imposed by supplying different missions in different countries, with each national section maintaining that its mission should be the most important and receive priority.

Station 43

MOUNTAIN LOCH AND MONKEY GROVE

SOE files now released into the public domain are not always bursting with revelations about derring-do, but reveal other necessary organisational aspects regarding what training the Poles were undertaking. There are many documents expressing the mundane financial arrangements and wrangling about who should foot the bill for paying agents, allowances, clothing and expenses incurred by section training. The file 'SOE training of Poles/Czechs' contains correspondence between Brigadier C.E.D. Bridge and Major C.H. Cassels regarding expenses of £15 2s 8d incurred at the Poles' first training school at Inverlochy Castle, Fort William, in November 1940. Major Cassels states:

I think you will agree that none of these charges can be met by us and are a fair charge against the Polish Training Grant. Can you please arrange to send me a cheque for this amount payable to Commandant, Special Training Centre.[33]

Brigadier Bridge in reply makes it very clear that he would rather not approach the Poles and ask them to foot the bill:

I am not clear how this matter should be dealt with. If you will look at paragraph 5 of our memorandum 02E.419 of 17 October, you will see that we asked what other financial matters, besides the pay and allowances for the Polish Officers attending, should be involved.

To this question no reply has been received and I am afraid, therefore, that no arrangements to meet any expenses such as those which you detail have been made. I naturally assumed that all such expenses would be borne by the Training Centre.

The Poles have no Training Grant but are dependent for all their funds on the War Office, so in any case it is only taking money out of one pocket and putting it in another.

Perhaps in these circumstances you could arrange for these

bills to be discharged in some other way. I should not care myself to have to go and ask the Poles to pay, especially as I never warned them in the first place that they would have to do so.[34]

General Sikorski later stated that demands for credits to cover expenditures had to be forwarded to the III Bureau of Staff in London. Preparatory arrangements for even the shortest of courses often created a plethora of paperwork, seemingly harmless in terms of security but nevertheless marked as 'Most Secret'. Early Polish training in Scotland gave rise to an rgent request for 60 complete battle-dresses in denim, 60 pairs of boots specially nailed for mountaineering and 120 pairs of socks. A response to the request cited the difficulty in drawing the articles for the course from ordinary military supplies without stating for what purpose the clothing was required and the ensuing correspondence and possible delay. Further correspondence reveals the likely reason behind ordering special boots: the ascent of Ben Nevis.[35]

Specialist instruction in Underground Warfare at a training school in England was preceded by two main courses. The paramilitary courses were mostly held in the West Highlands of Scotland, where SOE used sections of coastline, lochs and countryside for their training. The Highlands was an ideal, rugged location for SOE and commando training. A total of 208 Polish candidates completed their training at STS 25a, Garramor House, one of nine paramilitary schools near the spectacular Loch Morar, Britain's deepest body of fresh water. Garramor, now a popular bed-and-breakfast establishment, renamed Garramore, lies just off the winding coastal road between Arisaig and Morar, on a narrow stretch of mainland between the Sound of Sleat and Loch Morar. Violette Szabo and Odette Churchill also undertook training at the requisitioned lodge. Used to train agents of many different nationalities, the nine paramilitary schools were all located in shooting lodges around Morar, now a popular setting for films and famous for its white sands.

Major Antoni Nosek undertook one such field course near Loch Morar, which he describes as being partisan fighting under the instruction of British officers. Training students in 'physical conditioning' involved learning to survive from the land, PT (physical training), cross-country runs and close-quarter fighting. Iranek-Osmecki states, 'A queer custom existed in the mountain abode which was our quarters. It was not done to enter through the doors and gates. To avoid paying sixpenny fines for all the transgressions of this code we had to vault over fences and climb in through windows. Similar fines were incurred for inaccurate shooting, slow change of magazines, or clumsiness in readjusting jammed weapons. The kitty thus collected paid for the beer during our free Saturday afternoons.'[36] Candidates were also taught to live off the land by snaring rabbits and eating wild food, reflecting the isolation they might encounter in Europe if they landed off course or had to evade capture for a length of time. This course was known to the Poles as the 'Root course', exemplifying the emphasis placed on eating edible roots and plants. Tucholski states that more rabbits, birds and fish were eaten than any roots, but all were caught by one's own ingenuity.[37] After D-Day, when parts of Europe were becoming liberated, it was thought that there was no longer the need to train agents in the rudiments of fieldcraft, and the Morar course was closed in December 1944.

Specialist training was also preceded by a rapid physical fitness course, which included gymnastics, trapeze work and the parachute practice. The vast majority of Polish agents had to know how to parachute out of an aeroplane. Initial instruction took place at the Polish Parachute Brigade training centre in the grounds of Largo House, in Upper Largo, Fife, with a training tower located at the Lundin Links nearby. The centre was also a major training area for the Special Boat Service (SBS).

Largo House was known as the 'Monkey's Wood', 'Monkey Grove' or even 'Monkey Paradise', because students were required to swing from various pieces of apparatus. To practise landings, trainees were hoisted in a 'lowering trapeze' to a great height before the instructor pulled a lever, dropping the parachutist on a wire. 'The exercises are designed to make all movements during a jump completely automatic. It means one keeping one's feet and legs together all the time, as one would have to do during the jump from the plane, the descent and the landing – there'll be no time to think then.'[38]

Training then took place on the high tower, where agents practised jumping from 75 feet, on the command 'Go!', or 'Skok!' in Polish. Some broke their legs and others were dismissed by the instructors, who, to use their apt phraseology, thought them 'too jumpy'. The 'Monkey Grove' was invariably followed by the second stage of training at Ringway Airfield, now Manchester Airport, where many nationalities and units trained, including the British Commandos, Indian troops and Ghurkhas. Other parachute schools were based in Cheshire, Surrey, Hertfordshire and Northamptonshire. Owing to the diversity in nationalities, this sometimes caused a language barrier that hindered training. This was overcome by procuring informative films showing parachuting technique with a running commentary superimposed on the film and spoken by an interpreter.[39]

The Ringway Central Landing School opened on 21 June 1940, and in November it took the first group of Polish jumpers. Jumps often took place at Ringway from a suspended air balloon, and then three jumps from an aeroplane during the day and then two jumps at night. As at Monkey Grove, the training here was not without injuries and fatalities. Iranek-Osmecki details a fatal accident in July 1943 when a parachute failed to open properly. He also describes a final practice jump at Ringway on 10 July 1943: 'The last jump is over. I am a fully fledged parachutist now. My last jump was a very bad one. My knee hurt so much I had to get on the plane on all-fours. Fortunately I had a good landing. My leg hurts like blazes.' Another recruit stated, 'In this sport, once your nerve goes it never comes back.'[40]

Training at Largo House was not always a prerequisite for further work at Ringway. Candidates often undertook their training at one or the other establishment. SOE also had further parachute schools in England, including Milton Hall, near Peterborough. Tucholski states that training at Ringway was short, often only a week, whereas in Scotland the course could last for at least two and sometimes for four weeks, was more intensive and concentrated on fitness and agility.[41]

Parachute training at Ringway was undertaken under the guidance of Group Captain Maurice Newnham, who had won a DFC in the First World War. Newnham wrote about the parachute school in *Prelude to Glory: The Story of the Creation of Britain's Parachute Army*. He describes the basket suspended beneath a practice balloon as 'the rickety cage in which one crouched fearfully, clinging desperately to handles to avoid falling through the hole which took the place of most of the floor . . .'.[42] Newnham describes an exercise in Scotland in 1941, shortly after General Sikorski had inaugurated the 1st Polish Parachute Brigade, which was later to fight bravely in the ill-fated Operation 'Market Garden' at Arnhem, and from which the majority of volunteers for the *Cichociemni* came. Three Whitleys dropped arms containers and thirty Polish soldiers, who then undertook a mock attack. 'I was impressed then and more so on subsequent occasions, at the remarkable realism with which the Poles infused their training. Their discipline and martial bearing were also first-class.'[43] After the exercise, Newnham spoke to Colonel Sosabowski, the commander of the Polish Parachute Brigade, about the difficulties that the Poles had in reaching Britain, and the anxiety they felt for their wives and families, from whom they had not heard for many months.

SECRET POLISH HOUSES

SOE had an overall training directorate known as MT Section at the cover address, 98 Horse Guards.[44] SOE's Student Assessment Board replaced the Preliminary School Group in 1943 in assessing a candidate's appropriateness for work as an agent, using elementary training and psychological testing. SAB was based at STS 7 in Cranleigh, Surrey.

The scale of SOE's assistance to the Poles in Britain is partly revealed by the British manpower used at the Polish institutions:[45]

1. Holding Stations		Station 18	12 British personnel
		Station 19	10 British personnel
		Station 20A	22 British personnel
		Station 20B	17 British personnel
2. Training Establishments		Station 43 (Audley End)	47 British personnel
		Station 46	41 British personnel
3. Polish Military Wireless Research		Stanmore	12 British personnel
4. Training Station		Italy	11 British personnel
5. Polish Operational Base		Italy	33 British personnel
6. Headquarters Staff		London	26 British personnel

The 'stations' were listed by number and were usually requisitioned country houses in rural areas of England. The number of large historic houses used gave rise to the post-war cognomen for SOE: 'the Stately 'Omes of England'.

Many of the houses were used for the specialist training that each trainee agent had to undergo before an operation. As stated, the paramilitary schools were all based in Scotland and were clustered around Arisaig, Movar and Mallaig in Invernessshire. These totalled nine establishments in all, STS 21 to 25c. Other properties requisitioned provided the holding stations where fully trained agentswaited for the call and specialised sections produced forged money and documents. There were other premises requisitioned for military intelligence that were not always given an 'STS prefix' – for example, those under SIS command. For instance, the Royal Victoria Patriotic Building in Wandsworth was used by the intelligence services. A magnificent and unique building (100,000 sq ft) on the edge of the main railway line from Wimbledon to Clapham Junction, it was built in the Victorian tradition of gothic pastiche in 1857. It was originally created as a place of learning and refuge for the daughters of fallen servicemen after the Crimean War. Used as a hospital in the First World War because of its proximity to the main railway line, it became a Catholic school for girls (Victoria Patriotic School) in the inter-war years. It was taken over by MI5 and MI6 and became a detention and interrogation centre, with Rudolph Hess its most famous inmate. It is now used by a private company. David Budd, who works in the building, reveals its wartime past:

> The connection with Churchill's newly formed SOE agents was based on its use as a reception camp for those escapers from mainland Europe who would then be interrogated for weeks before being accepted or cajoled into service with SOE. Later on during the war those agents lucky enough to return home were brought here to establish whether they had turned double agent by the enemy – some welcoming party for a job well done! However, Elizabeth Reynolds, who worked for SOE after D-Day, is keen to stress that the returning agents at RVPB were considered guests, never prisoners.
>
> Shortly after we moved here in 1987, we met some very old ladies who had worked here as cleaners during the war and they had heard of several double agents who had been taken across the road to Wandsworth prison and were summarily dispatched to the Hereafter. HM Wandsworth Prison is reputedly the only prison now left with a set of fully operational gallows – just in case.

The gadgets of 'ungentlemanly warfare' used by agents were mostly made and tested at the Frythe, Station IX, a requisitioned hotel in Welwyn Garden City. Devices included the now infamous exploding dead rats. Even part of the Natural History Museum in London was utilised as a workshop for making the devices.

Many men and women were plucked from civilian life, for their peacetime expertise to be put to use with SOE. For instance, refugees from Europe often received new clothes when they arrived in Britain. SOE utilised their old attire to clothe their agents. However, when demand outstripped supply, tailors and couture dressmakers were recruited to ensure the meticulous attention to detail that was needed to make clothes with the European cuts in tailoring different from those worn in Britain. The wrong button or zip-fastener could give away the real identity of an agent. Other people were employed to 'distress' clothes and the briefcases that contained the radio sets so that they looked old and blended in with the civilian population.

Lord Montague's estate at Beaulieu, now home to the National Motor Museum, and other houses in the New Forest comprised the principal finishing school that honed agents of many nationalities in their final stages of SOE training, coined as 'the Beaulieu course'. Captain Alfons Maćkowiak, physical and weapons instructor at Audley End House, visited Beaulieu, where he trained in the use of invisible inks, recalling that he could see the Isle of Wight from his bed. Although training schools in Britain served different national sections, trainee agents from different countries were grouped together and had their own schools. Keeping nationalities apart aided security and avoided any confrontations regarding differences in political leanings.

The Poles utilised eight main houses for their training programmes and holding stations, with Inverlochy Castle, Briggens and Audley End House being the principal schools over the period of the war. The following stations were used by the Poles: STA 18, Frogmore Park, at Watton-at-Stone in Hertfordshire; STA 19, Gardener's End, Stevenage, in Hertfordshire; STS 20a and 20b at Pollard's Park in Chalfont St Giles, Buckinghamshire; STS 43 at Audley End House; STS 46, Chicheley Hall (home of the Beatty family) near Bletchley in Buckinghamshire; STA 14, Briggens, outside Roydon in Essex; and STS 63, Warnham Court, near Horsham, Sussex, under Major R.H. Egdell (of EU/P Section), used for operations involving Polish minorities in Europe.[46]

Training at the principal schools was under the control of MT Section, the training directorate of SOE. However, Danish, Czech and Norwegian Sections wished for control over their training programmes. Reflecting the Poles' wish to assert control over their establishments and training, and also revealing the considerable influence they had on SOE command, the Polish authorities gained overall responsibility for the training undertaken in their establishments from 1943 onwards. The country sections were not obliged to consult MT in their operational plans. This meant that it was difficult for Brigadier Mockler-Ferryman, the commander of MT in 1942, to plan ahead and prepare for future training commitments.[47]

After initial concerns regarding the lack of huts to accommodate the officer students had been resolved, the first course in sabotage was started by SOE in 1940 at Inverlochy Castle, 2 miles north of Fort William in the Highlands of Scotland. This impressive house, completed in 1866, lies below the rugged and mountainous Nevis Range, capped by Ben Nevis.

The commandant at Inverlochy was British Major Stacey and the mining instructor was Captain Antoni Strawiński from the Polish Engineering Corps. Strawiński was killed during an exercise with explosives in Italy in 1944.[48] Officers were sent to train here from Colonel Sosabowski's Army before the decision was made to change the outfit into a parachute unit. Those selected had been passed as reliable by the III Division of the Polish High Command. They were given passes, as Inverlochy was situated in a restricted area. Every volunteer was warned that the course would be rough and strenuous.[49]

The officers, mostly junior, at this stage did not know that they were being selected for work as *Cichociemni* agents, and continued mine-laying activities, shooting, sabotage and physical training.[50] The Polish authorities made special provision for the training they were to undertake by providing the officers with oil prismatic compasses.

Ben Nevis, Britain's highest mountain at 4,406 feet, was at the forefront of the strenuous demands put upon the Polish soldiers. One young officer, Antoni Pospieszalski, who was to become an instructor at Audley End House, remembers tackling the massif: 'I remember a six-hour lonely trip up and down the mountain.' Not many miles away, 25,000 volunteers trained at Achnacarry Castle, Lochaber, from 1942 onwards. Eighteen miles from the Nevis range, Achnacarry, the Commando training centre, saw soldiers from Britain, France, Poland, Yugoslavia, Norway and America endure the rigours of training on what was called the 'dark mile'. The Commando memorial, sculpted in 1952, is located nearby at Spean Bridge.

Within the run-of-the-mill correspondence between Brigadier C.E.D. Bridge and Major C.H. Cassels, revealed above, lies a hint at other parts of instruction at Inverlochy in 1940. Captain Strawiński's £15 2s 8d bill that was under dispute was itemised by Cassel. It included tools purchased by Captain Strawiński for demolition experiments; purchase of a railway line for instruction in railway demolition; rubber flex and materials for demolition by Captain Strawiński. Possibly the only evidence Strawiński could show for the bill was a lot of twisted metal.

Other correspondence reveals that the following training took place at Inverlochy: high explosives and mining; close fighting, including assaults upon guards and fighting with stilettos (often under instruction by ex-members of the Shanghai Police); English language; physical training, including football and boxing; lectures on enemy organisation, the German Army and their customs; wireless sets; and armament. Armament training involved tuition in a variety of weapons: Bren-gun; Thomson machine-gun; Suomi sub-machine-gun; Webley .32 pistol; German Mauser 7.63 machine-pistol; two types of British repeating rifle; and light infantry mortars. The continuing emphasis that the Poles placed on practical training is revealed in how much time was spent on the subdivisions within the course. A total of ninety hours was given to armament, high explosives and fighting practice, compared to four hours on enemy organisation.[51]

Detailed programmes of work were drawn up subdividing training in the morning, afternoon and evening. SOE files detail the training undertaken between September and October 1940. For instance, on 18 September 1940 the morning's training was a demonstration of grenade throwing; firing Bren-guns, Boyes anti-tank rifles and Suomi and Belgian automatic rifles. Training in the afternoon was bizarrely entitled a 'bathing parade' and the evening's training was to 'kill, butcher, cook and eat lamb'. Training on Monday 30 September involved 'blowing up a large iron-pipe' in the morning; movement through woods by compass with haversack rations in the afternoon; and a discussion on the afternoon's training in the evening.[52]

A course with the innocuous blanket title of 'the second Rifle course' opened on 15 November 1940 in Scotland with four Polish instructors, including Strawiński. A docket to all concerned stated: 'Its participants have to be instructed to keep secrecy about all works being done at the course.'[53] A letter dated 26 September 1940 and addressed to Captain Harold Perkins from Major Stacey stated, 'I hope you will find time to come up here during the course as there are several points which need a certain amount of discussion. The whole party are very keen on their work and a pleasure to instruct.'[54]

The enthusiasm with which the Poles threw themselves into the early clandestine training was not always matched by the British commanders. In a letter marked 'Secret' and addressed to the War Office, Brigadier 'G.S.' states:

The Poles are taking this business of training at the S.T.C. [Special Training Course] and C.L.E. [?] very seriously and have set up a special department at Polish G.H.Q. [General Headquarters] in London to deal with both.

They are probably much too ambitious, and want to run a continuous series of courses for 50 officers at both places with the object of eventually training at least two battalions . . .

I think we ought to let the Poles know as soon as possible what facilities there are, or are likely to be . . . it is difficult to keep putting them off with vague promises, and I should appreciate a definite statement as to what we are likely to be able to do as soon as possible.[55]

The sabotage course at Inverlochy, hailed as a great success, moved from Scotland to Briggens, Lord Aldenham's seventeenth-century house in Essex, at the beginning of January 1941, and became the first centre for Underground Warfare training. Briggens is in a secluded setting within 80 acres of parkland, and is now a country hotel. It was here that all the forged money, ration coupons and documents were made, under the command of Morton Bisset. Specialist training in microphotography also took place here and was completed by fourteen candidates. Briggens started out as a training school, but remained in use as a forgery base for all country sections when Audley End took over as the principal training establishment.

Although Lord Aldenham welcomed the Poles, he was busy with his own business affairs as a banker in London. His wife, however, attended to the temporary occupants with vigour. 'She [Lady Aldenham] looked after their comfort, gave them the best food that could be had, did her best to make their brief spells of recreation pleasant, drove them in and out of the local village, and carried in the boot of her car, hidden amongst piles of assorted objects, the explosives and other gear which it was necessary to keep from public view.'[56] The British commandant at Briggens was originally Lieutenant-Colonel Evans, who surprised Poles on exercise by putting on a false beard and startling the trainees by appearing in the midst of a mock battle.[57] One can appreciate the irony of a respectable banker's residence being the centre for production of forged money, the story being that he only realised this when he looked in his cellar and found boxes of money.

The course at Briggens was run twice and completed by a handful of trainees: twelve on the first course and fifteen on the second, including Antoni Pospieszalski and future commandant Major (later Lieutenant-Colonel) Józef Hartman.

Tucholski reveals other establishments used by the Poles for specialist training. The Polish course of intelligence training, known under its pseudonym as 'The Course for Officers to perfect Army Administration', was located first in Kensington Park Road, London, and later in Glasgow. Here, Colonel Stefan Mayer oversaw a programme of study that included gathering intelligence; a study of Germany; photography; chemistry; lock-picking; driving; and knowledge of languages. This course took six months, and seventy-three people completed it.[58]

Polish courses in armour and anti-tank weaponry, as well as driving, took place at Catterick Camp, and later in Italy. This specialist course lasted two weeks, with forty-three people completing it. Tucholski also details a British-led two-week course on German tanks taking place at Egham, Surrey, near the wireless research station at Stanwell, forty-three people completing it. An eight-week Polish motor and communications course took place in Dundee, with ninety-four parachutists passing through it between 1941 and 1942. The 'London District School of Tactics Street Fighting Wing' course was completed by fifty-eight parachutists and took place in the bombed ruins of Battersea in South London. There was also training in acclimatising candidates to live in a city on their own for a certain period, taking place in Birmingham, Liverpool and Glasgow, described by Tucholski as 'an English practice.'[59]

There were also specialist courses relating to wireless and cipher expertise. Some took place at the radio workshops at Stanmore. Another centre was located in Anstruther, Fife, and later at Auchtertool, Fife. Both schools were relocated to St Margaret's School in Polmont, near Stirling. A British course specialising in 'Eureka' communications used during the receiving of agents on occupied land operated at STS 40, Howbury Hall, in Bedfordshire, and STS 61, Gaynes Hall.[60] Gaynes Hall, near St Neots in Huntingdonshire, became a Norwegian Section station under Major C.S. Hampton (the other two Norwegian Section houses being in Aviemore, Scotland); a packing station; a base for RAF liaison officers; and a training centre for 'Eureka'. Some FANY personnel at Station 43 in 1941 went on to Gaynes Hall when the Poles arrived. After her brief stay at Audley End, Elizabeth Austin, née Jessiman, moved on to Gaynes, where she recalls Norwegian agents who took part in the mission to destroy the hydroelectric complex in Vemork in 1942. This was at the time when air operations to Norway had just begun under 'Cheese', 'Grouse',

'Raven' and 'Cockerel'.[61] Austin was allowed to keep her horse at the SOE house, recalling that one of the Norwegian agents rode the horse after confidently stating that he was a good rider. She states that her horse never really liked men and proceeded to throw the Norwegian. The Norwegians and FANYs relaxed at Gaynes Hall in the evenings by Scottish dancing and watching films.

Chicheley Hall, STS 46, near Bletchley in Buckinghamshire, was used by Czechoslovakians and Poles, before being handed over in 1944 to the FANY to be used as a wireless training centre. A large Polish staff was kept at the hall to keep in touch with conditions in Poland, so that the *Cichociemni* could be properly briefed. STS 46 handled all details of equipping the Poles, and here they were provided with clothing, boots, hats and all items of personal equipment. SOE did part of the tailoring work, but only under Polish direction.[62] British Army driver Alfred Fensome recalled driving Polish soldiers from Audley End to Chicheley several times so that they could take part in exercises in the house and grounds.

Gardener's, Frogmore Hall and Pollard's Park were primarily used as holding stations, and there must have been many others without an SOE number. Gardener's was also used in the latter part of the war to train German prisoners of war who had been converted to the Allied cause to be dropped into Germany as catalysts towards resistance. Allied progress across Europe annulled the operation.

Tucholski states that SOE organised a travelling propaganda course that toured STS 17 at Brickendonbury and the stations at Pollard's. This course was finished by forty-six parachutists waiting for their drop.[63] A solitary student completed a full eight-week 'English communications course' at STS 40, Howbury Hall.[64] He goes on to describe the activity within a holding station. After the newly qualified agents had taken the *AK* oath and adopted pseudonyms, they departed to the holding station (this was not always the rule, as many agents left Audley End straight for RAF Newmarket Heath and Tempsford). Agents were separated into teams of between three and six and received their equipment. The day before the flight, the dispatch of each team took place, when each person was told the destination address, safe house address and contact addresses, as well as passwords and any special instructions. The parachutists countersigned for money belts and post. The leader and deputy leader of the team received two copies of lists of equipment that were to be taken by the aircraft. At the departure session the document ordering the flight was signed by the whole team. The first of the flight procedures took place in a London flat, the next ones at STS 17 and then from Frogmore Hall.[65] Frogmore remained a dispatch station until the end of the flights from England.

Some of the residents at Watton-at-Stone maintained that Frogmore Hall was occupied by military police and, intriguingly, that Winston Churchill stayed there for a time during the war. All that remains of requisition at Frogmore is four spacious air-raid shelters in the grounds and some graffiti cartoons and drawings. Frogmore Hall was also used by the 92nd Light Anti-Aircraft Regiment, Royal Artillery, for training and practice in gunnery. Tragically, two men died there in motor accidents.

Frogmore was taken over by the Poles in the spring of 1942 and could hold around sixteen parachutists at one time. At the holding stations the Poles were usually under the nominal command of SOE. Sue Ryder describes STA 18's main room as having 'a massive contour map of Poland' on the wall. 'While on the other walls hung mementoes from some of the groups – a collar, a jacket, a shirt, each bearing its owner's code-name.'[66]

Sue Ryder talks of activities at Pollard's Park being seen by a civilian.

There was one day at Ops Station 20 when everyone was engaged in small-arms firing practice and an astonished woman advanced through the woods saying: 'I always understood this place to be a transit centre for the wounded.' Station 20 was small and enclosed, holding Polish agents and occasionally a Czech too. This station lay, together with Station 20b, deep in the woods off Nightingale's Lane near

Chalfont St Giles in Buckinghamshire. No outside contact was allowed. A Polish woman dentist who had been thoroughly scrutinised was allowed to visit the station to treat the Bods [agents] and I well remember the drill, which she operated by a foot pedal. She never froze our gums or gave an injection before extracting a tooth![67]

The SOE Polish Section history files reveal that there was a fault in the system, since, owing to the scarcity of air operations to Poland and to the bad weather that prevailed, the men were held in these houses sometimes as long as three months. 'They tended to forget their training, and since the Stations were run on rather luxurious lines, they may also have tended to become slightly soft and not fitted for the arduous work which lay in front of them. If this situation arose again it would be advisable for the holding stations to be run on very much more Spartan and rigorous lines.'[68]

All the above secret establishments have long since reverted into their pre-war functions or have been transformed into new roles. Warnham Court is a school, Audley End is an English Heritage property, Frogmore Hall is owned by a private company, and Chicheley Hall, Inverlochy Castle and Briggens are now hotels. Indeed, Inverlochy has catered for Hollywood film stars. Apart from fragmentary evidence, a paucity of information within SOE files and local assumption that has changed and faded over the years, often little is known. Current owners often raise their eyebrows when they are told what their properties were used for during the war, perhaps a credit to SOE that they left the properties as they found them.

THREE

Station 43

The Sergeants' Mess over the Co-op store
And the old mansion in its yew-tree shade
That served as headquarters of the brigade.

William Clarke

THE GHQ LINE AND REQUISITION

On 3 September 1939 Britain declared war on Germany. An expeditionary force was sent to France, ending in the disastrous British evacuation from Dunkirk. The Battle of Britain commenced in 1940 and implementations began to repel a seaborne invasion by building coastal and inland defences. On 27 May General Ironside was appointed Commander-in-Chief of Home Forces. The Home Guard was formed and a system of defences was constructed to defend 485 miles of unprotected coast from Cornwall to the Humber Estuary. Tank obstacles, mines and barbed wire lined the beaches. Pillboxes that once stood on cliff-tops are now often marooned on beaches, the thick grey concrete and brick gradually submitting to coastal erosion.

Although the east coast was the centre of concern for an invasion, all potential invasion points on the coastline were addressed. Polish infantry units served as an anti-invasion force on the east coast of Scotland, with camouflaged gunnery positions, keeping watch for the first signs of attack. Inland from the coastal line of defence was a second line of road blocks, where the Home Guard's task was to hamper the progress of the enemy by any means possible.

The third line of defence was the General Headquarters Line. This marked an intricate network of defences that began across the eastern and southern flanks of England, with bulldozers carving large ditches to stop tanks. A phenomenal period of construction began, and by midsummer 1940 a pillbox was being created every twenty minutes by the unsung, difficult and speedy work of the hundreds of building contractors who were employed to construct them. Thus, a chain was created to prevent German forces reaching London under Hitler's secret invasion plan of August 1940, entitled Operation 'Sealion'. 'Command and corps stop-lines', like branches from a main trunk, were created to reinforce the main GHQ Line.

On 7 September 1940 300 German bombers and 600 fighters took to the skies. That evening the War Cabinet issued the invasion code word, 'Cromwell', meaning 'Invasion Imminent'. Bridges were destroyed and church bells rang for the first time since the war had begun. However, the meaning of 'Cromwell' was misconstrued, and many people thought the invasion was actually taking place, rather than imminent. This caused many accidents and the loss of seventy-nine lives, many because of land mines.

There are many reminders of the GHQ Line and the 'command and corps stop-lines' in the countryside today. One cannot go far in the rural lanes of Essex before a concrete emplacement comes into view. The gardens at Audley End provide evidence of this chain, which provided defence against land attack from the east rather than protection of the house itself. In 1940, the Adam Bridge, named after its designer Robert Adam, situated on the border of the West Park, had two concrete chambers inserted below the road at either end of the bridge.[1] The chambers today are marked by two man-hole covers in the road. The bridge would then be denied to the enemy force by an explosion at the weakest point in the bridge. Another chamber is located to the left of the Tea House Bridge in the Elysium

Garden. It is difficult to imagine the military significance of this eighteenth-century Palladian bridge designed by Robert Adam. However, this chamber was the detonation centre for all the bridges on the estate. The detonation switches came together and were attached to a battery, ready to blow up the bridges in the event of an invasion.

A more obtrusive feature relating to the GHQ Line is the concrete pillbox in the West Park, built to defend the western bank of the River Cam.[2] Saffron Walden resident Roger Kirkpatrick, who was in the Intelligence Corps during the latter part of the war, states in his booklet *Audley End at War* (Saffron Walden Town Library archive) that a detachment of Royal Engineers set themselves up in the stables and undertook defensive work in the West Park.[3] He also says that a number of trees and shrubs were cut down in the Elysium Garden in order to improve the field of fire.[4]

Further features in the gardens include the large concrete blocks located in front of the Stables Bridge, and two further blocks by the smaller 'Fly Bridge' behind. The reinforced concrete cubes were constructed as 'tank traps' to prevent enemy vehicles from going over the River Cam. There were tank traps either side of the public road on the Adam Bridge, as seen in two photographs taken later in the war. These large cubes of concrete have since been removed. The traps in the grounds at Audley End at the Stables Bridge and 'Fly Bridge' locations had a steel bar cast into the top of the cubes to enable a steel hawser to be attached between the two blocks. Sometimes a mine was attached from the middle of the wire. However, it is doubtful whether destroying these bridges would have greatly impeded the progress of German invasion, as the river is fairly narrow and shallow at this point in its course. A white arrow pointing right was painted on the left tank trap on the Stables Bridge to give drivers a clear warning of the blocks on dark wartime evenings.

After the Battle of Britain the pillbox would not have remained operational. The threat of enemy invasion was receding and the Regular Army units would not have been welcome within the grounds of the secret training establishment. The tank traps remained and ostensibly served as a security measure for any unwelcome visitors. Despite the sensitivity of the site after SOE had arrived, British ex-servicemen have no recollection of guard boxes at either entrance to the grounds, but do recall a guard posted by the wrought-iron gates at the end of Abbey Lane, which leads from the edge of the eastern periphery of the grounds to Saffron Walden. One soldier also remembers a local police presence outside the Lion Gate but that the police were never allowed within the grounds.

Like many cities, towns and villages during the war, Audley End village and Saffron Walden were subjected to bombing by the *Luftwaffe*. It is probable that local bombing was often because of the close proximity of Audley End station and RAF Debden. The *Luftwaffe*'s poor bombing accuracy and navigation in the early part of the war could also have played a part. A damage report shows that Audley End station was bombed on 16 December 1940. The station, built in 1845, was attacked at 8.45 a.m. with high explosives, an oil bomb and machine-gunning. The attack resulted in one slight casualty, a barn set on fire and an unexploded bomb (UXB), also known as a 'ripe apple', residing 15 yards from the main railway line. The UXB was safely disposed of, which allowed the railway to re-open.[5]

Later in the war, Peter Howe, a corporal in the Royal Army Service Corps at Audley End House, stated that a bomb fell one night somewhere over the steep hill behind the Temple of Concord in the East Park. 'A very familiar sound and sight were the squadrons of British bombers at night and American bombers by day, flying over the house, and sometimes limping home with one propeller [not] turning.'[6]

Michael J.F. Bowyer in his comprehensive accounts of air raids in East Anglia reveals many bombing raids in the Saffron Walden Rural District. On 16 August 1940 thirty-six high explosives (HE) and one unexploded bomb were dropped on the town. On another raid bombs exploded in the gardens at Audley End House. On 31 August 1940 a Dornier loosed off

200 incendiaries, 30 HE and 5 UXB in Saffron Walden RD. At the end of November 1940 a report reveals that Essex had considerably more bombing incidents reported than the rest of the East Anglian region, with 120 raids between 9 and 30 September, 400 raids in October and 186 in November. On another occasion a German gunner fired on a farmer ploughing with horses on his land at Debden. The farmer was uninjured but his horses were killed.

Later in the war, on 16 September 1944, when Great Britain was under the threat of flying bombs, a V-1 pulse jet crashed, causing blast damage to the Saffron Walden Isolation Hospital.[7] These German *Vergeltunsgwaffen*, or reprisal weapons, first appeared over Britain on 13 June 1944, when one hit London. They quickly became know as 'doodle-bugs', and were followed in September by the V-2 rocket, whose explosive force could be felt for miles. Although Saffron Walden received damage from bombing, it was relatively unaffected compared to the scale of bombing in many principal cities and towns. One theory is that Saffron Walden lies in a dip in the landscape and any low cloud or fog often obscures the town from the air. This protected the town from any random bombing from German aircrews wanting to loose off any bombs they were still carrying before the flight back over the Channel.

Requisitioning was a familiar experience for many owners of country, town and coastal properties in this period of history. As will be revealed with Audley End, evidence of requisition can occur decades after the army left at the end of the war. For instance, I recall diligently weeding one of my grandmother's flower beds for 'bob-a-job-week' in the garden at Martin Cross on the coast in Norfolk. The large house in Sheringham had once been home to Ralph Vaughan Williams and was split into flats. Digging a little deeper in the rose beds I came across dozens of live .303 cartridges that had been dumped before the army detachment left.

Houses were occasionally donated by their owners, as well as requisitioned, and used for various purposes, including barracks, hospitals, evacuee centres, headquarters and occasionally prisoner-of-war camps. In the months before the war, teams of Ministry men from the Office of Works were employed to survey regional areas for suitable premises. If questioned by the owners of the properties, they were instructed to inform them that they were merely surveying houses in the area (even if a decision had already been made for requisition). This was to prevent protest, thus maintaining national security. The British Government still has the authority to requisition property for defence purposes under the Defence Act, 1842.[8]

After the first few months of war there was little change to Audley End House and the estate: adjustments were made regarding blackout regulations, and non-essential staff were allocated work of various kinds for the war effort. Roger Kirkpatrick in *Audley End at War* states that a group of evacuees from London stayed for a short while in the service wing but found country life too dull, going back to the city when the threat of air raids subsided.[9]

After the outbreak of war, the kitchen gardens were turned over to more intensive food production, and Lady Braybrooke's daughter helped till the garden with the Women's Land Army before she joined the FANY. The area is completely enclosed by walls, and SOE activities could have been kept very separate. However, it is very likely that the soldiers made use of the pear, plum and apple trees in the orchard, and espalier-trained fruit on the walls of the kitchen garden with intriguing varieties of apple, like Sops in Wine, Irish Peach, Hoary Morning, Darcy Spice and Cockle Pippin. Later in the war, soldiers helped out by scything in Audley End's Victorian kitchen garden in return for apples from the orchard. Alfred Fensome stated that he raked, weeded and dug in exchange for fruit.

General agricultural activity in the district began to intensify as the war progressed, and this had its effect on the topography of Audley End estate. Timber was cleared and the East Park was ploughed for the war effort. The lawns to the west of the Cam were also ploughed during the war. The land was still being used for the growing of beetroot in the 1950s. A cricket pitch was set out on the lawn in front of the house. Consequently, when matches resumed after the war, the odd cricket ball smashed through windows in the ground floor. Audley End and Littlebury Cricket Club have since returned to the original pitch opposite the stables.

The Seventh Lord Braybrooke, Henry Neville, married for the second time in 1917 and became a father for the first time in his early sixties. He had three children with Lady Dorothy: the eldest son was Richard, followed by Robert and a daughter Catherine. When war was declared, both his sons volunteered to fight. However, they were advised to finish their education at Cambridge and wait until the authorities contacted them. Only Richard managed to graduate before they were both called up for duty in the winter of 1940.

Henry died in March 1941 at the age of 85. Roger Kirkpatrick states:

> Within a fortnight of his [Henry Neville's] death, and without warning, two civil servants from Cambridge arrived at the house and gave Lady Dorothy notice that she should be out of the house within the week, as it was required for use by the Army. Fortunately she was able to contact, through the family solicitor, a friend who had some influence, and between them they were able to secure some proper notice and a proper contract with the Ministry of Works. This allowed for reinstatement after the war with time to complete the probate valuation and arrange for the careful storage of the valuable paintings. Nevertheless they were out by the end of June, and installed in the Old Rectory at Heydon, which had been the principal private residence of the 6th Lord Braybrooke.[10]

But all too soon, and only a few weeks after the death of Robert Neville, Lady Braybrooke had to move from the Old Rectory, as the property was to be requisitioned by the Women's Auxiliary Air Force (WAAF). After a short stay in Devon she was able to move into a property in Littlebury that the family owned.

Once requisition had been secured, it appears that Audley End had a variety of roles before it came under the cloak of SOE. Kirkpatrick states that early on in the war a battalion of the Rifle Brigade was stationed in tents in the East Park, in the area between the Temple of Concord and Saffron Walden. The tents attracted a German bomber, but damage was slight. However, these troops were soon moved on.[11] Another source states that the Royal Artillery was camped at Sparrow's End, an area of high ground between Saffron Walden and Thaxted, with its base being Audley End House.[12] There was one rare occasion when British soldiers used the grounds at Audley End after the arrival of the Polish Army. In the days before D-Day, one British soldier describes large numbers of troops billeted at Audley End in tents, nobody knowing who they were or why they were there.

It was not unusual for other requisitioned properties to be used by many different regiments over the course of the war. For instance, the *Memories of Jim Bacon* in the Radwinter Rectory archives reveals that Radwinter Manor Rectory, near Saffron Walden, was used as a headquarters for the following units from 1941 onwards: the Anti-Aircraft Brigade; Royal Artillery; King's Royal Rifles; Durham Light Infantry; the Hampshire Regiment; 51st Highland Division; the Parachute Regiment; a unit from Newfoundland; and, finally, for German prisoners of war and displaced persons.

The Braybrooke family were very surprised when the military knocked at their door, as they had previously offered Audley End House to the government as a Casualty Clearing Station at the time of Dunkirk. Kirkpatrick states:

This offer had to be declined on the grounds that it was quite unsuitable, having available only two lavatories for the potential two hundred beds, and no electricity . . . two bathrooms, even with the splendid brass and mahogany Victorian WC next to the Chapel, were quite insufficient for the needs of even a convalescent hospital in 1940. This offer was not widely known, but the declared unsuitability of the house as well as the total lack of sensitivity as to the manner of it, made the subsequent requisitioning that much more of a shock.[13]

This lack of facilities explains the soldiers having to take regular drives to the public baths in Cambridge. A greater shock had been the tragic deaths of both Lady Dorothy's sons during the war. Both Richard and Robert Neville were killed on active service: the younger, Robert, Ordinary Seaman, was killed in action in 1941 when his ship disappeared with all hands. Two years later Richard, the eighth lord, a lieutenant in the Third Battalion Grenadier Guards, died in action in Tunisia. Consequently, the title now passed to the eighth lord's cousin, Henry Seymour Neville.

Wooden screens and panelling were erected to protect the interior of the house from damage. Only one entrance was used, via the north porch by way of an impressive oak door surmounted by, perhaps appropriately, an allegorical carving depicting the rewards of peace. A partition in the Great Hall was erected to close the main Vanbrugh staircase, with access to the other floors by the north stairs. The treads on the stairs and the rails were also covered. Mr Stephen Thompson, my wife's grandfather, was working for the Ministry of Works during the war in the capacity of Engineering Assistant. Living in Cambridge, he was called to work at Audley End in 1941, travelling to the mansion by train and bus. He was tasked with helping to oversee the erection of the tongue-and-groove panelling in the Great Hall and other rooms, and also had a part in installing electricity. Evidence of securing insulators for the telephone wires in the trees can be seen on the trunks of trees to the left as one approaches the Stables Bridge from Cambridge Lodge.

Mr Thompson recalled that it was a long job and they were still working after the British Army had arrived. He worked with Mr Kitteridge, an employee of Lady Braybrooke at Audley End, and eventually went to his funeral, recalling him as a strict but fair man.

Mr Thompson is still living in Cambridge and recently told me that a wooden panel used in the construction of the protective panelling at Audley End now covers over a section of the central-heating pipe in his living room. He had 'a strong pass' during the war, and once found himself in a holding camp full of D-Day troops with blacked-out faces, waiting for the call to go. Many of them asked him for news 'from the outside'.

The photograph showing a Polish celebratory meal in the Great Hall shows the tall protective screens in front of the staircase. The extent of the panelling erected reflects what all servicemen have stated: that only after the war, when they revisited the house, did they fully realise the splendour of the mansion they had been working in. One soldier stated that they saw Audley End as a barracks, with all the majesty hidden by the austere boarding on the walls. SOE trainee Bronisław Wawrzkowicz hardly recognised it owing to its re-established palatial interior. SOE had its own Property Section responsible for the maintenance of buildings: 'The Training Section [Directorate] was responsible to the Properties Section for the maintenance in good condition of all houses occupied by schools, and for the carrying out of all provisions of agreements with owners.'[14]

THE ARMY IN RESIDENCE

Before Audley End House was used by SOE it had been a British military establishment under former Shanghai Defence Force member Lieutenant-Colonel Terence (Terry) Roper-Caldbeck. However, in early 1941, Corporal Walter Leney was Chief Clerk to Colonel J.C. Petherick, who Leney states was the commandant throughout his short time at Audley End. Roper-Caldbeck must have arrived after Petherick's brief commanding role. The British soldiers based at Audley End were from the Bedfordshire, Hertfordshire and Essex Regiments. Ian Hook, Keeper of the Essex Regiment Museum, maintains that there were no units of the Essex Regiment based in North Essex during the war, so men might have been sent to Audley End from the training centre at Warley Barracks, near Brentwood. These were usually soldiers who were medically unsound for action or those who had been wounded. They were responsible for maintaining the security of the house and estate and for general duties, and initially may well have known very little about the nature of the work SOE was about to undertake.

There are written recollections from Corporal Peter Howe and Sergeant Alan Watts, who were stationed at the Jacobean mansion between 1942 and 1944. They were in the Royal Army Service Corps (RASC), and part of the orderly room staff, Watts having served previously at Briggens. Watts, now passed away, was the Chief Clerk, and Howe his assistant. A Private Hawcroft was also recruited to assist in their duties. Howe was one of the last to leave Audley End, another army unit having arrived in 1944. Howe disclosed that before he left Audley End in 1944 he 'appropriated' a standard lamp from the officers' mess.[15]

In correspondence with English Heritage in 1986, Mr Howe and Mr Watts reveal the day-to-day running of the house and the various asides and histrionics with alacrity, but are cautious of divulging the secret nature of the house. Stoking the boilers at the back of the Lower Gallery in the house was not a popular job with the British soldiers. Howe said that he felt very vulnerable stoking in the dead of night, particularly as the other boiler to tend to was in the stables away from the main house. There was always the underlying fear that the Germans might be sent to knock out the unit, and this would be their chance to remove the soldiers on guard duty.[16]

The first commanding officer (CO) was Alexander Kennedy, a Scottish colonel who, strangely when one thinks of security, organised many events in the grounds for local boys. Terence Roper-Caldbeck was the second CO. Howe described him as 'a charming man from the Argyll and Sutherland Highlanders, who was also very popular'.[17] Kennedy did not remain at Audley End for long, his duties taking him elsewhere. The administrative command was taken over by Roper-Caldbeck when Kennedy left. Kennedy is rarely spoken about, and one British serviceman does not remember him at all. After 1942 Kennedy is named as being in overall command of most of the Polish training establishments and holding stations that housed the fully trained agents before operations, and so would probably have continued to visit Audley End. All the SOE training reports from 1944 bear his signature, so administration from the house was still crossing his desk two years later.

Sergeant Alfred Fensome spent time revealing many aspects of his three-year period of home service as an Army Motor Transport driver based at Station 43. Fensome damaged his hearing and broke his knee cap when hit by flying debris and brickwork at Dunkirk, as a result of a Stuka bombing the beaches, actually at De Panne, just over the Belgian border. He also injured his knee in a fall at Audley End House while on guard duty during the necessary total blackouts and was hospitalised at Addenbrookes, Cambridge. This injury continued to be a major part of his lack of mobility before he passed away in August 2003, aged 94. Not wanting to leave the army, he underplayed his injuries, which was made easier for him by the fact that he was a driver.

There were five drivers/dispatch riders at Audley End. Fensome held a driving licence for seventy-five years, during which time he had seventy-three separate licences, including a bus licence. He lived with the other drivers above the 1780s laundry in the service wing, in what was called the 'transport bedroom'.

Bill Harris's family provide another valuable source of information. Born in Pitsea, Essex, in 1920, Emanuel 'Bill' Harris arrived at Audley End House from Tilbury Barracks, after sustaining injuries from being accidentally shot in the foot. Bill was based at Audley End between 1941 and 1944. He was eventually demobbed at St Neots in Huntingdonshire.

Bill's widow Ruby met her husband while he was at Audley End. She was at a teacher training college for women at Mount Pleasant, Saffron Walden, which is now the Bell Language School. She recalls that Bill was one of the few who enjoyed the stoking duties.

Other staff included Company Sergeant-Major (CSM)
Bradley and CSM Kelly. Owing to many incidents involving
another unnamed CSM, Fensome's pent-up anger resulted in
him 'thrashing him around the Guard Room'. Even Colonel
Roper-Caldbeck stated, 'If I'd been younger, I'd have liked a
few rounds with him.' This comment from a senior officer very
much surprised Fensome. Bill Harris said that the CSM had the
habit of sending the soldiers on long route marches through the
Essex countryside. He would then arrange for an army 'liberty
truck' to pick him up half-way round and then take him back
to Audley End. After it had dropped him outside the grounds,
he would run in as if he had arrived first, leaving his men
straggling behind. Roper-Caldbeck eventually found out about
this obsequious scam, and ordered him to meet him by the river
in the West Park. Pointing toward the Cam, Roper-Caldbeck
ordered him to 'walk in that direction until your hat floats'.

Peter Howe described a succession of three adjutant-quarter-
masters.[18] The first two went to jail, one for stealing rations and
the other for dipping into the mess funds. The third adjutant
was a man called Captain McGowan. Peter Howe described
him as a man who had come up through the ranks. He referred
to everyone as 'what's his name' and was the first man to start
shooting at the ducks on the river, with the rest of the orderly
room staff joining in after him. The orderly room staff often
'stirred up the ducks' on the river and the ploughed field on
the other side of the Cambridge Road. Occasionally one or two
of the staff would go into the grounds and allow the others to
shoot 'wide' of him.[19] All the British soldiers spoken to have
fond memories of their period of home service at Audley End
House, and, despite a few altercations, agreed that the military
establishment operated in a relaxed fashion despite the strict
level of secrecy. This level of secrecy had to be adhered to by
civilians and the women of the FANY at Audley End. Civilians
lived on site during the war and also had to sign the Official
Secrets Act. Mr Kitteridge, the housekeeper, was quite ill when
the house was requisitioned, and was allowed to live with his
wife in Bull Lodge near the Cambridge Gate. Walter Leney

states 'it used to be fun to watch Mr Kitteridge wind the clock (in the South Turret room), which was not allowed to strike in war time as that was a sign of invasion.'

Ethel Spicer lived in Lion Lodge with her mother. Ethel was the daughter of one of Lord Braybrooke's employees, and had lived on the estate since 1913, when her father was a coachman. She eventually moved into Lion Lodge, where she was employed as a dairy maid and game processor. The Polish commandant had the unfortunate experience of being attacked by a flock of geese kept by Ethel. She was sometimes as fierce as her geese, but could be equally generous, especially when dishing out her home-made wine. Ted Pretty, who was plumber and then Area Foreman of Works at Audley End, and was connected to the house from 1958 to 1996, recalls Ethel's excellent wine. She always poured large glasses and the wine was invariably very strong. It appears that how she made the wine was as closely guarded a secret as anything under the auspices of SOE.

In less racially sensitive times Ethel, like Guy Gibson of Dam Busters fame, called her black Labrador 'Nigger'. Ruby Harris recalls visiting the house not long after the end of the war. She remembers Ethel collecting the tickets and seeing her dog with duck eggs carefully in its mouth. Ethel kept an eye on the army and reported any problems to Lady Braybrooke, who would then take it up with the CO. After the war, a Polish officer came back to Audley End to visit Ethel. Mrs Pickering, who worked at Audley End House as a room steward from the 1960s to the 1980s, states that Ethel was given the day off work so that she could meet the man, now married. Mrs Pickering thought that the Pole had lost a leg in the war.

The other transitory residents at Audley End were the FANYs. There were a few FANYs who worked at Audley End, but not in the numbers in which they were employed in the holding stations. There was never a hint of impropriety at Audley End, something that the Poles were very proud of. FANYs looked after SOE agents and often gave the base a relaxed atmosphere, despite some practical jokes being played on them. Antoni Nosek stated that occasionally a FANY would have a small pencil time-bomb slipped into a pocket!

The FANYs played an important role within the structure of SOE. They worked as drivers, secretaries, interpreters, coders and staff within the training schools and holding stations. It must be remembered that they also worked as agents and suffered the same consequences of capture.

When requisitioning by the wartime Ministry of Works began in 1941, arrangements were made to safeguard Audley End House and store its contents in the state rooms and the chapel. Ministry of Works and Buildings plans, dated 9 May 1941, show the proposed usage for each room on the ground and first floors. A plan of the second floor, where SOE lectures later took place, does not exist. Additional text and crossings-out on the plans relate to a burglary at Audley End in the early 1950s, when the Saloon and Lord Braybrooke's Sitting Room were broken into on the first floor. It is possible that the plan would have been reused, as wartime rationing of paper was still in place. The Great Hall was to be used as a lecture room, later photographs showing that it was also the dining hall for Polish officers. The Bucket Hall was used as an orderly room, as it remained until derequisition. The former Museum Room was proposed as a mess room for students, which hints that some form of training was going to take place in the house. The Butler's Pantry and former Butler's Bedroom were also proposed as mess rooms. The public lavatories in the open courtyard, used by visitors today, were used for 'wash up' and as 'ablution showers'. A note on the ground-floor plan states, 'If additional lecture rooms are necessary it is recommended that the stables block be adapted rather than the library and large dining room.' However, this was later rejected. The Adam Library (old dressing room) was used as a bedroom by Roper-Caldbeck. Room 17 next to the Museum Room was used as a mess for other British ranks, most of the British staff being non-commissioned officers or rank-and-file.

Guarding the house and grounds, coupled with the SOE

training in a wide variety of weapons, called for a large number of arms and munitions to be stored in the house and explosives to be stored in the stables and at hidden locations in the grounds.

According to Peter Howe, the Old Muniment Room was where guns and munitions were stored. Presumably this refers to the Audit/Strong Room. However, the Ministry of Works and Buildings requisition plan reveals that the Museum Room were 'not to be requisitioned if avoidable'. Arms and equipment were also stored at the top of the stairs by the chapel. The narrow room leading to the wine cellar below the Butler's Pantry in the basement of the north wing reveals very well-preserved evidence of its location as an armoury. The Polish weapons instructor said that these were the weapons used for SOE training, rather than guarding the house:

Webley .455	No. in store	6
Smith Wesson .38	No. in store	5 + 1, Tot. 6
Colt A. .32	No. in store	2
Colt A. .22	No. in store	2
Sectional Grenades	No. in store	8

A cupboard in the same ancillary room contains the following information pasted to the inner side of the door:

Dummy	.300	135
"	.303	35
Oil Bottles	.303	16
Pull Throughs	.300	16
" "	.303	4
Eye Discs		13
Grouping Rings		3

The Colt Automatic was the small firearm that agents generally carried into occupied Europe. Students were taught to fire two quick shots. Pull throughs refer to barrel cleaners, and grouping rings are the roundel paper targets used in firing practice. Ted Pretty remembers the pungent, oily smell that still permeated the room because of the lack of ventilation, years after the army had left. Pretty also spoke of an unconventional use for a machine-gun bullet. The bullet was revealed in one of the cisterns in the toilet block that visitors to Audley End now use. He said that a cast-iron bell in the cistern was held up by a large bullet to allow circulation of the water. One wonders what still lies in the fields and barns around Audley End House that has not seen the light for over sixty years.

On the upper floors of the house, the Picture Gallery on the first floor was used as a storage room for the Braybrookes' possessions, and was locked, so that access to either side of the house was through the Lower Gallery. Only the guest rooms at both ends of the house were allocated to the commanding officers. Lady Braybrooke's Sitting Room was proposed as an officers' anteroom.

SOE lectures, language training and other courses were all located on the second floor. Some rooms on the second floor were used as 'examination rooms', and one room was used for making documents that the agents would need in Poland. The North Turret Room was where authentic Polish clothes were tailored. This is feasible, as the room affords the best light during the winter months. An SOE trainee at Audley End House, Bronisław Wawrzkowicz, said that even the thread in the clothes had to be of Polish origin. Mr Fensome said that he walked up flights of steps to collect things from the Turret Room on occasion. This raises the issue of the level of liaison between the Poles and the British, which is discussed below. Fensome said that he often had to drive out to places to collect civilian clothing to bring back to the house for the agents to use. The Turret Room was thought to have contained many Polish signatures and intricate pencil drawings of aircraft. Unfortunately, the signatures have since been painted over. Sergeant Watts stated that the bedrooms on the north side of the second floor were used by the Polish instructors. Sleeping quarters for the rest of the Polish occupants were also on the second floor.

Another of the old servants' bedrooms of 1787, now numbered 11, was believed to be a British sleeping quarter, with mattresses on the floor. Peter Howe thought that this was the British sergeant-major's room. Howe maintained that Room 12 in the north wing was his bedroom. The small room numbered 14 was the adjutant quartermaster's office, with the commanding officer's office, Room 13, next door. Room 10 was Mr Watts's bedroom. Soldiers accessed the roof from here, where they sunbathed. The Old Nursery, Room 5, was the orderly room. An illicit .22 rifle and ammunition (for duck shooting) were kept in the room, and an open fire was in use. There were remnants of the outlines of maps of the British Isles on the walls, but these have since faded. Perhaps exemplifying a change in room use over the war years, one former *Cichociemni* agent, revisiting the house after many years, was adamant that his bed was in the Old Nursery on the second floor, pointing to the space on the floor where it had been.

The outbuildings and service wing behind the 200-year-old box and yew 'cloud hedge' were turned into clothing and food stores, another tailor's room and a shoemaker's workshop.[20] The training directorate of SOE was responsible for checking with Hartman and Roper-Caldbeck that all forms of 'barracks and accommodation' stores and supplies were maintained.[21] Stores for STS establishments mostly came from a central source – SOE's Camberley Reception Depot in Surrey.[22] Mr Fensome recalled many supply runs.

According to Mr Howe, the service wing also afforded the overspill of sleeping accommodation for the British soldiers. Although it is perhaps coincidental, it is interesting to note that a tea plate with a Polish mark underneath was found by Chris Trigg in the plumber's store, behind the service wing, after clearance work during the winter of 2002. Mr Fensome stated that this store and the old game larder were either used as general stores for 'odds-and-ends' or were empty. The ground floor of the service wing was used as British sleeping quarters, with Mr Fensome stating he slept above these rooms.

FROM ROYAL PALACE TO SPECIAL
TRAINING SCHOOL

The Polish volunteers were not the first irregular warfare recruits to occupy the house. An SOE adviser at the Foreign and Commonwealth Office, Duncan Stuart CMG, maintained that the house was used as a holding station, with only minor 'finishing' training being carried out. By June 1941, Audley End's first role was indeed as a holding station for agents from various national sections, including Dutch and Belgian. M.R.D. Foot mentions a Belgian gypsy, Alphonse Delmeire, alias 'Canticle', and Harry Rée, English agent ('César') and instructor, being at Audley End House.[23]

Kirkpatrick reveals a 'clandestine removal' from Audley End at this time to add to Peter Howe's standard lamp. The Hon. Catherine Dorothy Neville had by that time joined the FANY Corps. 'Her first posting was to SOE Station 61 near Huntingdon, where "N" Section, the Dutch, had moved from Audley End. She found one of the wooden settles in the mess strangely familiar, and her subsequent enquiries confirmed that it had in fact been "lifted" from her family home when the section moved. Later, she returned to Chicheley when it was commandeered by the FANY.'[24]

Elizabeth Austin, née Jessiman, served as a driver with the FANY after work with the WAAF (Women's Auxiliary Air Force). Before being stationed at Gaynes Hall, she was sent to Audley End House for a brief period of five weeks in 1941. She drove SOE operatives first to Newmarket Heath and then to Tempsford, when it had been set up for SOE flights. Although not told anything about the occupants of the house, she thought that there were Dutch and either Danish or Norwegian soldiers within the holding school, originally mistaking the Scandinavian accent for Welsh. However, until the 'Heavy Water raids', dispatch to Norway was not from England by air, but from the Shetlands Base by sea.

Mrs Grierson, known as Auntie G, was in charge of the FANY while Austin was there, recalling that her bed was in one of the old bathrooms. Her friend 'Golly' Fowles suffered concussion after an accident on the Adam Bridge, which resulted in her being sent back to London headquarters.

Anne Menzies, née Booth, also served at Audley End before the Poles arrived. Always known as Maureen, she married Jean-François George Mennesson, an SOE agent. Naturalised English, he later changed his name to James Francis George Menzies. Captured in France in 1945, he was tortured and eventually killed in Flossenbürg prison at the age of 30. Anne Menzies states:

I went to Audley End House at the end of September 1941 until early November. I was only there for about six weeks because I married a man in the SOE and there was a rule that you could not stay on in this particular job if you did. I met Jean at Brickendonbury. He went on to the usual places, not Audley End House, which in my day was a last stop *en route* to Cambridge Airport. The men were mostly Belgian and French and possibly Dutch, but no Poles, they must have come later. We knew few names and the only one I heard was 'Metrat'. We did mostly housework, cooking and serving and would go for walks and occasionally dance in the evening. I felt sorry for the agents because the weather was awful and sometimes they were with us for several days waiting for their mission. It must have been upsetting for them.

Menzies stressed that, as a FANY, she did what she was told without question or query. Indeed, Elizabeth Austin did not know that STS 61 was actually called Gaynes Hall until after the war. Menzies says, 'We really did not talk about people we met and saw. I had been at Brickendonbury for about a week or ten days when a fellow FANY took me for a walk and said that she expected no one would have told me anything, and she then told me what was going on.'

As discussed, the German *Englandspiel* operation was disastrous for the Dutch Section. Roger Kirkpatrick states the possibility that some of the agents captured during Der Englandspiel debacle gave full details of their training establishments: 'It is almost sure that the role of Audley End as a centre for clandestine operations was known to the Germans by early 1942.'[25] It is worthwhile going into these events in a little more detail. After landing by sea had been deemed impracticable, from July 1941 it was decided that parachuting agents was the best method of infiltration in Holland. Agents began parachuting into Holland from September 1941. The first drop to secure intelligence on the ground and general conditions was undertaken by two agents in Operation 'Glasshouse' on the night of September 1941.[26] Nothing was heard of the agents until January 1942, when 'Catarrh' operatives presumed one had been lost and discovered that the other had been successfully brought out of Holland to Britain by trawler.[27] However, Operation Catarrh, 8 November 1941,[28] was to have serious repercussions for SOE. Two agents were dropped, one codenamed 'Timmer' and his wireless operator, 'Looman'. Tasked with finding out about the Glasshouse team and organising sabotage groups, Looman was arrested by *Oberstleutnant* (Lieutenant-Colonel) Giskes when transmitting back to London. Henceforth Looman was persuaded to work for the Germans. 'In fairness to Looman, it must be added that he endeavoured to attract the attention of London HQ to the fact that he was controlled, by omitting to give identity checks when sending his telegrams.'[29] Timmer was captured after an attempt to rescue one of his group from German captivity. He refused to talk at first, but when he was convinced that the cells were all uncovered, he gave details of his mission. 'His soldierly behaviour was described by Giskes as exemplary.'[30] In April 1942, 'the Plan for Holland' confidently began outlining recruitment aims, lines of communication, training and sabotage.[31] However, all tenets of the grand plan were known to the Germans:

In reality, as is evident from the fate of the agents dispatched during 1942, the position was that the German so-called '*Ast-Niederlande*', under the direction of *Oberstleutnant* Giskes, had control over the whole of our organisation. Through that control, they were able to carry out large numbers of arrests throughout the country, thereby stifling the development of resistance in general.[32]

Consequently, the 'turning' of Looman signified the general collapse of work in Holland, its secrecy shattered by Giskes and aided by the blinkered ineptitude of SOE command, culminating in agents walking from their parachutes into the hands of the Gestapo.

In the early days of Audley End's clandestine status it appears that it was given the number STS 61, the same as Gaynes Hall. Mrs Ruck states that this was the number given to her family home while she was there with the FANY. Søren Rasmussen, a Danish researcher studying Operation 'Chilblain' and the Danish copy-production of the Sten gun, takes up the issue. He maintains that Jørgen Hæstrup, a Danish historian, calls the place STS 61. However, in another book about the successor to Danish agent Bruhn, as the chief organiser of operations in Denmark, STS 61 is applied to Gaynes Hall. Consequently, it appears that Gaynes Hall took over the number when the Poles arrived at Audley End. If Station 43 was known to the Germans at this time, the Poles would obviously have approved of the change.

Søren Rasmussen reveals the Danish presence at Audley End in 1941:

I have seen the information about STS 61/Audley End in several statements. The most interesting is in an interview with Commander Ralf Hollingworth, who was in charge of the Danish SOE section. The interview [which shows a photograph of Hollingworth taken outside Audley End House after the war] is in Danish and dated 27 December 1966 – 25 years after Chilblain, the first Danish SOE operation. He describes the last few days before the first Danish SOE team took off on their mission. I am rather sure that Bruhn and Hammer were the only Danes at Audley End House.

Operation Chilblain took place on the night between 27 and 28 December 1941. Its purpose was to set in place a chief of SOE and a wireless operator in Denmark to coordinate operations. Rasmussen has translated extracts from Per Andersen's interview with Hollingworth in the Danish *Berlingske Tidende* (*BT*) newspaper:

> The atmosphere in Denmark was resigned. However, this was not the case for the four men around the dinner table in Audley End House, near Saffron Walden. Two of the men were British, Commander Ralf Hollingworth, Chief of the SOE Danish Section, and Archibald Rose, commanding officer at Audley End House, which was now called STS 61. The two other men were Danish doctor Carl Johan Bruhn and First Engineer Mogens Hammer. The meal they had served was something special in the 'food-lacking' England – it always was when secret agents were going to go on a mission.
>
> A typical English butler, Mr Kitteridge (from the happy days before the family residence of Lord Braybrooke was seized), looked with a lofty air, and ordered the FANYs in their duties. This was the third time the two Danish parachutists had had their farewell dinner, where they waited after having finished their training at several secret schools. The first two times the operation was cancelled. Tonight it should be.[33]

The article goes on to reveal:

> In some of the many fireplaces in the house there was fire, but it was not cheerful. The walls were bare. All paintings had been removed or covered with boards in order to protect the ornamentation.
>
> Bruhn insisted on having a fire lit in the fireplace in the room he shared with Hollingworth. Bruhn was chosen by Hollingworth to be the chief organiser of the deadly dangerous work in Denmark. Indeed, Hollingworth thought he had made the right choice since he had met Bruhn in the

summer of 1940. As the years passed they had become close friends to the extent that Bruhn was going to be godfather of Hollingworth's first child.

At the dining table Bruhn asked a FANY to cut his hair, but not his beard, and so she did, to the great amusement of everyone around the table. Then the four men got up from the table, got dressed and went to the car at the front door. The car was waiting with the lights covered and another FANY behind the wheel. She knew where they were going and without any road signs she could find her way in the darkness to Stradishall, a Royal Air Force base about twenty minutes' drive away (all later Danish agents were sent from Tempsford, some 75 kilometres further west). In the car nobody talked about war, Denmark, or the dangerous mission.[34]

Tragically, after jumping from a Whitley bomber, Bruhn was killed when his parachute failed to open.

Mrs Pickering talked to a British ex-serviceman who said that he had stayed one night in the house in December 1941. A British commando, he was brought to Audley End at night with other soldiers and piled up the back stairs into a room on the top floor. He said that although it was very dark he was sure that it was Audley End, remembering the army truck driving over the hump of the Adam Bridge. The next day he set off on the raid by Nos 3 and 4 Commandos on the oil installations at South Vaagso, Norway, on 27 December 1941. The German garrison was destroyed, along with fish-oil factories and 18,000 tons of shipping. Another ex-commando, who preferred his name to be kept out of the text, agreed that Audley End House was where they were briefed before the Vaagso raid, and also the attack on the coastal batteries at Dieppe on 19 August 1942. They were ushered into the building and taken upstairs, where they were briefed with maps by the high command. However, he stated that they had left the house almost straight away for the mission in hand, and he obviously had no idea of what the house was being used for by this stage of the war.

In October 1941 Audley End was also being used as an SOE

packing station for the shock-absorbent containers that were used to drop supplies with the agents. Main packing operations then moved to Gaynes Hall in April 1942, with containers still being packed for dispatch to Poland at Audley End House in 1944.

It is unclear why the Poles moved from Briggens to Audley End House, especially as Briggens appeared to offer more topographical security. As Roger Kirkpatrick states in *Audley End at War*, it is perhaps surprising that SOE picked Audley End for their its training:

> Audley End is built on an Abbey site, with all the characteristics which make for a security nightmare. The site is overlooked from all sides – often from cover or from public roads. It is bounded by a village and a hamlet; both closely integrated with the Estate, whose inhabitants, sometimes by right and always by habit, were used to criss-crossing the park. Three roads skirt the park, one a major north–south route. The wall marking the boundary is of very uneven height, and easily scalable at several points, giving on to cover from which the house can be observed. As mentioned, various retired servants and estate workers continued to live in the grounds throughout the war, even though the family had been evicted from the main house. It was the last place that one would have thought suitable for secret operations of any sort.[35]

Perhaps by the very nature of its relative openness, and by the fact that trainee agents wore military uniforms, SOE could give the impression that Audley End was just another big house taken over by the Army, which undertook manœuvres in the grounds. There was one leading factor that made Audley End an appropriate choice. The size of the property meant that it could accommodate a lot of personnel. This was ideal, as thirty or forty Polish candidates were allotted to each of the two training courses taught at the house, and with the British personnel this could total over 100 soldiers.

There is an insidious incident that could have contributed to SOE wanting to move from Lord Aldenham's residence. Roger Kirkpatrick details the following story, which, as he states, cannot be factually traced and must remain as conjecture, as there are no written details, only verbal reportage.

A detachment [of the Home Guard] from Bishop's Stortford and the surrounding area had taken up a night guard in a barge or narrow boat somewhere down the Stort-Lea in the neighbourhood of the locks, sluices and railway bridge at Roydon. Probably after the twelve-o'clock or two-o'clock patrol went out, the chimney of the stove heating the guard post became blocked. The blocking of a chimney is a practice well known in the plains of central Europe – particularly towards the Ukraine. Sometimes it was done with a serious motive, as a ploy perhaps to evict a troublesome tenant, but often as a prank. The acrid fumes of a wood fire, or even a domestic coal fire, would very soon drive out the inhabitants – coughing and spluttering, and no doubt extremely angry – from the house. A point would have been made, perhaps, but no real harm done; just a bit of horseplay. Unfortunately the Home Guard was burning coke in their closed stove, and the coke burning under these conditions gives off an invisible, odourless, cumulative and deadly poison gas – carbon monoxide. When the 'prowlers' returned from their patrol they found their comrades dead.[36]

Kirkpatrick goes on to state that it was definitely an accident in that the result was never intended, and there is no certainty that the Poles from Briggens were responsible – the source being from a verbal report from a son of one of the victims, who maintained in the 1960s that the Poles had been responsible for his father's death.[37] Antoni Pospieszalski states:

The charge that the Polish inmates of Briggens had been guilty of causing death of several people by blocking a chimney seems to me singularly far fetched. I was one of the dozen or so Poles at Briggens at the time and cannot visualise any exercise, or mischief, that would involve blocking a chimney. The reason why training transferred to Audley End was that Briggens was too small. The house was still inhabited by Lord and Lady Aldenham and we occupied only a few rooms in the house.

On 1 May 1942 SOE's Underground Warfare course was officially operating at Audley End. In April, to accommodate the arrival of the Poles, additional British servicemen were brought in, including the cooks and orderly room staff from Briggens. The Scottish Major, later Lieutenant-Colonel, Kennedy took over from Lieutenant-Colonel Evans at Briggens and briefly served at Audley End, as discussed. Many of the Polish instructors began arriving at Audley End, including the famous figure of Major Józef Hartman, who had taken over from Captain Koprowski as Polish commandant at Briggens.[38] To many Poles, Hartman was seen as the 'Father of the *Cichociemni*'.

Audley End House was given the name STS 43, and here, under Roper-Caldbeck, Major, later Lieutenant-Colonel, Józef Hartman set up his training headquarters. Although the Polish Section remained autonomous in its training of agents, occasionally using British training instructors (perhaps less than at Beaulieu), each national section training school was placed under a British administrative commandant.

These officers took no part in the training but were concerned with the commissariat duties and the provision of technical equipment. They were also formally responsible for discipline, and for this purpose they had authority over the Polish course supervisors. In theory this arrangement might have led to friction and misunderstanding, but in practice it never did, as the British officers, who were senior in both age and rank, showed the utmost tact and friendliness and did all they could to help the work along.[39]

Station 43 was used as an operational training, holding and dispatch establishment by SOE until the summer of 1943, at which time it was placed exclusively under Polish control. However, it remained for administrative purposes under Roper-Caldbeck until SOE left at the end of 1944.

Hartman, who was in his forties by the time he arrived at Audley End, was prevented from undertaking operations himself as he was a well-known military figure and would certainly have been known to the German authorities back in Poland, where he had been aide-de-camp to Marshal Józef Piłsudski, a prominent Polish leader before the war. The Germans had photographs of all the Poles who had held civilian and military positions of distinction and were marked out for imprisonment or execution. However, Hartman did take part in two commando raids on the French coast, and joined in with the training at Audley End.[40] He was a popular figure and very well respected.

The house became in effect a finishing school, where all the training, except the prerequisite parachute and paramilitary courses, was undertaken. The Finishing School at Beaulieu could also provide the training necessary for a candidate to 'jump', but students did not have to visit there, as other establishments could provide them with the combined skills that they needed. Students also visited other Polish establishments for training days.

SOE training reports, and the verbal accounts of those who were at the house during the war, reveal that a wide range of training took place at Station 43. Two of the most important courses were located here: that in Clandestine (Underground) Warfare, under Major A. Mackus, and the Briefing, or Dispatch, course, under A. Wejtko and afterwards Colonel Wieroński. Typically, thirty or forty candidates were allotted to each course. The training had to instil self-reliance and discretion, as well as building up excellent physical fitness. If a certain level of expertise was not reached, or if the candidate's character was not thought to be suitable, the trainee agents would be marked 'unfit for Underground work' on their training sheets and would be returned to their regular military outfits.

Polish volunteers arriving at Station 43 had already been pre-selected, having passed the paramilitary, root courses, physical fitness and parachute courses. It appears that some trainees had to make their way to Essex cross-country by covert means as part of the initial training. One trainee decided to hitch a lift in the sidecar of a motorcycle and was promptly driven to Saffron Walden police station and arrested as a German spy.

The 'High School of falsehood', as Iranek-Osmecki has it, took place in 'comfort' at Station 43 and many other places in England where trainee *Cichociemni* lived and ate relatively well considering food rationing. However, they were subjected at any time to 'interrogation' by visiting inquisitors, and they had to have the right answers. 'Our replies always had to consist of lies, but very plausible ones, especially as in the next room another commission questioned the man we'd been to town with yesterday.'[41]

The Polish SOE recruits underwent training in various specialist activities detailed in the Underground Warfare course, below. There was no set order and content to the courses, as they varied to fit the needs of each group of men, depending on what their work was to be on occupied soil. These intricacies of training included the sabotage courses teaching the students how to blow up bridges, factories, pillboxes and telegraphic installations, and also how to dispose of small groups of the enemy. Many Poles specialised in microfilming and microphotography and radio liaison. As a general rule an agent was required to become an expert in two specialities.

THE INSTRUCTORS

Training instructors often underwent training at Station 43 themselves, and not only as a matter of leading by example. Many went on to fight with the *AK* as instructors or were dropped on other missions in occupied Europe. Nearly all the instructors within the Polish Section of SOE were Polish themselves, and instruction was usually in Polish. Hartman was responsible for the type of the training. However, refinements to the syllabus occurred after suggestions from the instructors themselves and by communication with the overall training directorate:

> All syllabuses of training were in the first place prepared by the Training Section, but many of the subsequent developments arose out of the suggestions of the Commandants and instructors of the schools. The Training Section remained, however, the central coordinator of all instruction, keeping the schools informed of the latest developments in material and technique, and considering any modifications proposed by school commandants before their inclusion in the syllabus.[42]

As stated, this depended on whether the commandants chose to liaise with central command. The sharing of new developments (for example, in foreign weapons) across the country sections took the form of one-off exercises or lectures and instruction by 'guest' instructors – for instance, S-Phone instruction (see p. 103) at Gaynes Hall and the travelling Propaganda course at Brickendonbury and Pollard's.

One such temporary British instructor at Station 43 was Major John Oughton. A public-school master in French language, Oughton was conscripted into the Royal Artillery as a gunner in May 1940. He had started his army career by digging trenches in the Colchester region as preventative measures against German invasion. A language graduate and fluent in French, he answered an advertisement in a newspaper calling for people within the armed forces who could speak a foreign language. This small advertisement led Oughton down the corridors of SOE and into F Section, under Colonel Buckmaster. Oughton recalls a sergeant-major who was continually asking him to get his hair cut. But he passed his training and went on to become an SOE instructor himself in 1941. Now a sergeant-major, Oughton was based at the Beaulieu school, where he also ran the local cricket team. He also travelled the countryside on a motorbike to other SOE establishments to train agents, including Warnborough Manor, Guildford and the Poles at Station 43 in early 1942. It is thought that he instructed in 'strategies for coping with interrogation'. His SOE file reveals that he was in charge of external security in the Hertford area between October 1942 and February 1943.[43] When passing Audley End House in a car with his family long after the war, he casually stated that he had been there, and at a time when the Poles were *in situ*. He remarked, like many others, how cold it was inside the house.

The following list, translated from Polish, details the Polish instructors at Station 43. It has been taken from Jędrzej Tucholski's *Cichociemni*.[44] However, instructors changed over the years, and course commanders were replaced.

Instructors (*Instruktorzy*) in Command of Training at Audley End House (STS 43)

Name and Rank	Alias	Training (*Szkolenie*)
Col T. Roper-Caldbeck		In command of British Administration (SOE)
Maj Józef Hartman	'Sławek'	In command of the Polish Instructors

Officers (*Oficerowie*)

Name and Rank	Alias	Training (*Szkolenie*)
2/Lt Alfred Wiśniewski		Microdot photography, invisible printing and false identity documents
Lt Leonard Łysz		Invisible inks and photography
2/Lt Albin Bratek		False documents
Lt Mieczysław Różański		An artist in various fields, handwriting and false documents
Lt Klemens Gajdowski		Photography
Lt Z. Budyn		Shooting, driving instructor and locksmith
Lt Witold Dąbkowski		Partisan sabotage and guerrilla warfare
Lt Eugeniusz Janczyszyn		Expert on creating 'legends' for agents and espionage
Lt Tadeusz Starzyński	'Ślepowron', 'Narcyz',	'Legend' expert and German affairs specialist

	'Gzyms', 'Stasia'	
Lt Antoni Pospieszalski	'Łuk'	Radio communications expert (telegraphy and radio) and German language
Lt Tadeusz Sapalski	'Sarna'	Communications expert (telegraphy and radio) and German affairs expert
Lt Aleksander Ihnatowicz	'Ataman'	Expert on all firing weapons
Lt Alfons Maćkowiak	'Alma'	Shooting (pistols, rifles and machine-guns), fitness and ammunition storage
Capt Mieczysław Jaculewicz		Sabotage and night-drop specialist
Capt Maksymilian Kruczała		Mantraps, mine traps and uses of heavy explosives
Lt Jerzy Lemme		Combat fighting and conspiracy; expert in German language
Capt Adam Mackus	'Prosty'	Conspiracy and tactics
Lt Leon Wujek		Tactics of fighting the enemy in conspiracy

Other Ranks (*Szereg.*)	**Training/Duties**
Pte Kaz Bilewicz	Workshop, stores and motorcycles
Cpl Julian Czarnecki	Tailor for special clothing
Cpl-cadet Zenon Jankowski	Land mines and booby traps
WO Wład Krajewski	In charge of Office and Library
WO Wład Krzanicki	In charge of Office and Library
Cpl-cadet Boh Kurkowski	Chief of Science in conspiracy and interpreter
Sgt Bronisław Lesiuk	Administration
WO Adam Opolski	In charge of Administration Office
Pte Bern Swoboda	In charge of stores with uniforms and expert in German language
WO Gabriel Zając	Locksmith, breaking into buildings, driving instructor in foreign transport, e.g. German and French vehicles and motorcycles

Captain Alfons Maćkowiak (Mack) and Captain Antoni Pospieszalski (Currie) provided information about the nature of the Underground Warfare course. They were often referred to by their chosen anglicised names. Alfons Maćkowiak (who anglicised his name to Alan Mack) arrived at Station 43 in 1942 and replaced a British PT instructor who was thought to be too tough in his approach. Maćkowiak also become Ihnatowicz's assistant. Ihnatowicz was an expert in all firing weapons, specialist in night shooting and was very distinguished and well liked. Antoni Pospieszalski states that his *nom de guerre*, 'Ataman', was a Ukrainian word describing 'a war leader'.

Before he arrived in England Mack had already escaped capture twice. First, he jumped from a moving train after being captured by the Red Army at the beginning of the war and made his way to France. He states that these trains were taking the Polish officers to their execution at Katyń. He was only able to squeeze through the bars preventing escape because of his small stature at 5ft 5in.

Interned in a prison camp near Strasburg after fighting with an artillery battery near the Maginot Line, he escaped on his own at night with no one inside the camp knowing. Incredibly, he made it to Paris after twelve days of walking. In the latter stages of the journey he managed to steal a requisitioned bicycle under the noses of the Germans. As it was summer he slept undisturbed in bombed buildings and corn fields that had yet to be harvested. Having no identity papers was obviously a problem. He needed new clothes as his were in shreds, and decided to knock at a door. Incredibly, the lady inside was a widow whose husband had been Polish. Complete with clothes and an identity card, he headed towards Paris, where he arrived with barely the soles left on his boots. Evading capture, he secured lodgings with a sympathetic landlady. Mack speaks five languages, and his ability to speak French was crucial. In Paris, he sold postcards and carried bags for people at railway stations. The landlady put the money he earned into an account and eventually converted his money into sterling, which came to the grand sum of £50 for the next part of his journey towards Britain.

Travelling with two others, Mack was stopped in Spain by a guard who spotted their movements at night. The only course of action was to remove the man who had seen them.

Consequently, Mack knocked the man out in a fashion that he would later teach his students at Station 43. He found out later that he had killed the guard and the police were searching for him. Consequently, he was unable to go directly from Spain to Gibraltar, and had to make his way to Portugal. After waiting in Gibraltar he made it to Liverpool. Mack trained in tanks in England, and after three months a circular came round asking for volunteers to be paratroopers. He took up the offer straight away. While he was training in Upper Largo, parachutists were given the chance of being dropped into occupied Poland. Volunteering, Mack found himself at Briggens and then Station 43. Completing his training courses, he was ready for his mission. Three days before his mission he was called into Hartman's office, where he was told that he could not go to Poland as he was required to remain as an instructor. The instruction he gave at Station 43 is detailed below.

Mack has an incredible and well-distinguished service career, having been awarded fourteen medals, including the Croix de Guerre. The citation for the medal states:

Outstanding officer: distinguished himself by his exceptional bravery and his qualities of a soldier throughout the campaign, and especially 2nd and 14th June 1940 at Fremestroff, 15th at Alberstroff and 16th at Dieuze, where he did not cease commanding the fire of his battery, in spite of the violent shooting of the enemy's artillery, giving the best example to his gunners. On 17th June he dispersed an adverse company which was attacking the positions and on 18th forced the enemy to evacuate Embermenil, which they had just taken. The present mention includes the award of the War Cross with Brass Star.

Mack states that they attacked German tanks at very close range, and only two out of the original seven men in the battery survived the fighting.

Antoni Pospieszalski was codenamed 'Łuk' and had previously been with the Parachute Brigade. He escaped Poland to Britain via Slovakia, Hungary, Yugoslavia and France with Tadeusz Jaworski, who also worked as the *Cichociemni* agent 'Gont'. Jaworski was killed in Buchenwald concentration camp in March 1945. Pospieszalski trained in Scotland when he first joined SOE, and was married there in February 1942. After undertaking the first part of his training at Inverlochy, he was asked whether he was prepared to go on operations, at which point he said that he would. Pospieszalski was later based at Briggens, where he trained with Hartman, Andrzej Świątkowski and Marian Jurecki. The latter two agents were later to serve posthumously as an inspiration to candidates at Station 43, becoming known as 'the Saints'. Świątkowski was nicknamed 'Afghan'. Because of a navigational error, they were dropped into Poland by parachute near a railway station in an area heavily occupied by the enemy, and were shot in the ensuing battle. Pospieszalski recalled his time with 'Afghan' at Briggens, and described him as a colourful character who had known some shady characters in his travels. He was given the *nom de plume* 'Afghan' as he was in Afghanistan at the outbreak of the war. Very keen to go on missions, he saw war as an ideal opportunity to fuel his desire for adventure. When he thought that a mission was imminent, he would spend all his money, and then when the mission did not come to fruition he had the habit of going to Pospieszalski to borrow money: 'He still owes me a pound.' Captain Mack states that Świątkowski and Jurecki were the real creators of the *Cichociemni*, as the seeds of the unit came from this operation.

Pospieszalski, nicknamed 'the Prof', anglicised his name to Tony Currie, and was stationed at STS 43 from May/June 1942 until training ceased in 1944. Currie thought that his marriage prevented him from going on one early mission. He took part in Operation Freston in 1944, which is discussed in Chapter 5. Currie said that there was a very good atmosphere and high morale at Audley End during training. There was an overall feeling that they all had important work to do. His bedroom was near to the lecture room on the second floor of the south wing. Pospieszalski was an ideal choice for teaching the students the German language as he had been born in Berlin to a German mother and it was his first language. His parents moved to Poland, where he found it easy to learn Polish.

THE UNDERGROUND WARFARE COURSE

Trainee emissaries, almost all of them officers of all ranks, were selected to perform commanding, instructional or specialised functions within the Underground Army in Poland. Officers were preferred by the *AK*, as they wanted men who could assume positions of command. Exceptions to the rule were those selected as wireless operators or saboteurs with special skills.[45] However, being a leader of a section of the *AK* was not logistically easy: 'To lead a detachment of a hundred men, with the required measure of safety, in the vicinity of a large town was not an easy job. It has to be remembered that the men making up the detachment lived their ordinary lives with their ordinary daily duties, and were called to arms only for specific tasks.'[46]

The *AK* and the Government-in-Exile were hoping to concentrate resistance that was to culminate in a national uprising led by *Cichociemni*, who were training and recruiting *AK* members in Poland. An emissary could be placed in one of three groups, all receiving training related to tasks that awaited them. Jędrzej Tucholski states that the largest group were those needed for current actions, such as specialists of reconnaissance, sabotage and communications, and staff officers. Within this group were included rare specialists such as experts in technical sabotage, microphotography, sea reconnaissance, 'black propaganda' or false documentation. The second group were couriers, political emissaries for the Ministry of the Interior in Poland. Some were involved in army conspiracy and were often nominated from leaders of parachute divisions. After completing their missions, they did the tasks allocated to them in the role of a courier. The third group constituted those who were to play the major role in preparations for uprising and in re-creating military power within Poland, and were therefore instructors, officers of communication and armoured divisions, leaders of divisions and even doctors.[47] Further instruction often took place in Poland with the *Kedyw* or the *Kierownictwo Dywersji* (Special Operations Directorate), where more was learnt about German weapons, radio, railway diversion and assault training. The Secret Military Publications Plant produced booklets aimed at military instruction for commanders and section leaders.

There was an unrelenting demand in Poland for personnel to be sent from England. Only part of the Polish officer corps had remained in Poland after 1939. From February 1941 to December 1944 the *AK* had its numbers reinforced by SOE – 316 in total. Many became wireless operators who kept in contact with the exiled government or other sections in Poland, but others fulfilled important roles within the departmental complexity of the Polish bureaux. Thirty-seven undercover agents who were intelligence experts were assigned positions in Warsaw or district departments.[48]

In the years leading up to the Uprising, the Key Command of the *AK* indicated the demand for *Cichociemni* by sending telegrams. Jędrzej Tucholski reveals the following messages sent from Poland to the Sixth Bureau in London. A coded message in January 1942 read: 'I am requesting the following order of dispatching: 1. leaders and sabotage-experts for east; 2. trained reconnaissance officers for the east; 3. staff officers and specialists in local command.'[49]

The *AK*'s division of technical legislation (*Techniczno-Legalizacyjny*) was part of *Komenda Główna*, or the General Command, and codenamed 'Park'. 'Park' had a lack of specialists knowing the latest methods of falsification of documents. For instance, there was a request to the Sixth Bureau, 'Please send two officers specialising in legal issues and with knowledge of photochemistry and engraving. They must know German language, with desirable knowledge of Russian and Ukranian. I need them to operate a legal cell.'[50] These sound like rare individuals indeed, but in response to the telegraph cadet officer Witold Strumpf, alias 'Sud', and Wilhelm Pluta, alias 'Pion', were sent for specialist training in Glasgow. They then parachuted into Poland and were assigned to 'Park'.

Before the operational season of 1943–4, a request was sent for 189 *Cichociemni*, including 17 diplomatic officers, 68 communications experts, 40 aircraft pilots, 4 seamen, 15 reconnaissance officers, 15 armoured personnel and 30 saboteurs. The request could not be fully met, so that only 136 personnel were sent between autumn 1943 and summer 1944.[51]

The training programmes in Britain were being perfected since the first courses at Inverlochy, and would change again when the courses were condensed in southern Italy. The training was influenced by information sent back from Poland, which was studied in great detail. The most pertinent was the information sent by the first *Cichociemni* agents dropped in the trial period of 1941–2. Suggestions were made, including that all *Cichociemni* should be first-class drivers of cars and motorbikes, a plan adhered to by Major Hartman. It quickly became apparent that knowledge about German weapons was also inadequate. Tucholski states that, apart from a few corrections, the main training remained the same, not too much theory, but a great deal of practice: non-stop physical training; perfection in the use of weapons; cultivation of self-reliance and the ability to be included in and to work within a small Underground cell; and the sending-back of maximum information about the situation in Poland.[52]

Parts of the Underground Warfare course could easily be mistaken as a curriculum for criminals of every persuasion: close combat; robbery; setting booby traps; assassination; breaking into houses; sabotaging trains and industrial buildings; picking locks; forgery; quick evasion in different types of vehicle; mine-laying and, in a final honing stage, the ability to be a seamless liar. Breaking into houses would have been simpler during the 1940s than today with modern burglar alarms, double-glazing and CCTV. However, the operation still required skill, especially if an agent wanted to leave no evidence of entry.

There is no doubt that every agent received grounding in set basic courses with defined modules set out in the training reports. However, agents would often have had their skill honed in a particular area if a particular mission or type of work in Europe was known – for example, wireless operators, instructors in the *AK* or couriers. The only fixed training that every candidate had to have was the parachute training and the Briefing course.

The main Underground Warfare course had to be completed before the final Briefing course. It was split between basic, specialist, topping-up and practical. It lasted between four and eight weeks, and gave each candidate basic and specialist training. However, the final Briefing course included candidates who could well be at Audley End for six months, especially when the summer months did not provide enough darkness for the long flights to Poland. During this 'holding time' constant topping-up training was undertaken and fitness maintained. Lectures and language courses were taught in a room on the south wing of the second floor.

Emphasis was placed on PT and skills in shooting, as well as using personal arms in unexpected situations, for instance, firing quickly from the hip, orienteering, hand combat and ju-jitsu. As at any stage of the training, a candidate who did not complete the course for reasons such as serious injury or fractured limbs had to abandon all further training.[53]

Seventy SOE training reports written between March and August 1944 at Station 43 have survived and give an insight into the Underground Warfare course.[54] Courses were completed on 25 March, 30 June, 31 July and 26 August. The reports, all signed by Lieutenant-Colonel Alexander Kennedy, also state the ages, health, character, employment and military backgrounds of the Polish candidates. As stated, Kennedy had left Station 43 by the time these reports were written, but he signed them, presumably as students' administration and documentation were still the responsibility of SOE's training directorate, irrespective of the Polish autonomy in the training programme itself.

Despite the general opinion that most of the Poles who volunteered and were selected were very young, the reports show that they were aged between 19 and 51. Indeed, twenty of the candidates were in their thirties, and thirteen were aged between 40 and 51. With two of the candidates' ages unknown, the average age of the seventy Poles listed in the reports is 30 years. The general health of the students was varied: from 'very good', 'good' and 'satisfactory' to 'heart trouble', 'lung trouble', 'not very strong' and the strangely phrased 'addicted to malaria'.

The reports list sixteen specialist areas of instruction: physical training, fieldcraft, close combat, weapon training, explosives and demolitions, communications, reports, map reading and sketching, intelligence, SS work, irregular warfare, sabotage, combined operations, political and general, advanced technical training, and driving or riding. However, scoring and comments about 'particular standard or ability are made only in regard to the following: physical training, weapon training, explosives and demolitions, communications, irregular warfare, and driving or riding. Further specialist training took place at other Polish establishments, at special training days at Audley End under 'outside' instruction and at the Beaulieu course.

Many of the Poles were selected as wireless operators after their training in communications. However, if we accept that a 'blank' on this part of the report reflects a certain gap in instruction, not all candidates were taught in this particular field. Some reports state 'no training for communications', but most candidates seemed to have passed with 'has learned the use of R.T. (radio transmission) sets'.

The reports also express the instructor's opinion in what capacity, if any, an agent should be operating: as an instructor in the field, a wireless operator, a 'regular' in an *AK* section, or a section commander. Some of the final 'commandant's remarks' on the reports detail Kennedy's suggestions for other specialist work, as well as whether the student had passed or failed. The following concluding comments were taken from some of the reports and reveal the level of scrutiny and the difficulty of the course: 'Suitable for technical and administrative jobs', 'Has not finished the course satisfactorily, not suitable for underground work', 'Has completed the course successfully.

Inspiring as a leader', 'Not suitable as wireless operator', 'Has not completed the course satisfactorily. Not suitable for work in conspiracy', 'Not inspiring as a leader, inexperienced but physically tough', 'Not being a wireless operator he has a very limited knowledge of the Morse code. A short test, however, carried out during the course showed that in his capacity of wireless engineer he is equally unreliable. Recommended for work as an ordinary member of a guerrilla group', 'Recommended as organiser of a smaller area', 'On the whole he is not a guerrilla fighter. Recommended as a subordinate member of a guerrilla group', 'Character unsettled, very youthful, dislikes admitting any shortcomings of his own. Undeveloped as a leader, but may be inspiring'. Twenty-two-year-old Władysław Kościukiewicz's report states, 'owing to his character can be used for risky jobs but should be carefully guided'.

Further scrutiny was applied to a trainee agent's character. For instance, 32-year-old Kazimierz Kaznowski's character was deemed 'reliable, and nervous but self-controlled, talkative, conscientious, intelligent, laborious, possessing a sense of humour'. Another report reveals a trainee's character to be thought of as 'reliable, self-confident, apparently calm, lazy, daring, strives to be self-controlled, not intelligent but cunning'. Another appraisal is less than inspiring: 'Good man but not intelligent enough.' As is a former police officer's summary: 'Not reliable, very nervous, dull, not hard-working.'

Apparently a sense of humour was valued, as 'good sense of humour' and 'no sense of humour' appear throughout the character reports. The character appraisals are sometimes lengthy, contradictory and vague, detailing a string of appraisals linked to a missing rubric – for example, 'weak, confident, physically tough'. Only aplomb comes to the fore as a favourable trait for Underground work. The reports from the instructors and the commandant's final summations and comments are often more telling.

It appears that candidates could receive further training if a particular level was not reached, as comments on the reports reveal. Twenty-five-year-old Aleksander Wichert's report on 31

July 1944 states: 'Has completed the course satisfactorily. Can be a leader but should have additional training completed and should take the work seriously.' Other reports state: 'After an additional training can be leader of a guerrilla section', 'Can be a private soldier of the Underground Army after additional training'. Many of the reports state that after two or three months of technical training candidates could be wireless operators.

Most of the candidates who passed the course were categorised as H, I, F1, D, D1 and B. Candidates who needed further training were given categories D1 and H, and H and I. The letters refer to the work that the trainees were deemed to be suitable for: the higher the letter the more suitable the task.

One of the seventy students successfully completing his training was Bronisław Wawrzkowicz. Long before his arrival in Britain, he had been arrested, as a student, by the *NKVD* and taken from Lwów in Poland (now Ukraine) to Siberia for anti-Communist activities. After two years of slavery under the Soviets in Siberia, Wawrzkowicz travelled from Egypt, Tehran, Brindisi, to the Polish Latiano unit at Ostuni, where he was detached to a parachute unit and trained in jumping from Italian aircraft.

While in Italy, Wawrzkowicz was selected by Major-General Okulicki, *'Niedźwiadek'* (Bear Cub), for special operations. Wawrzkowicz jumped with the general in Italy and remembers him as a fantastic man. Okulicki approached Wawrzkowicz and told him about the work he was being asked to do, stating, 'Son, do you want to go with me to Poland?' Wawrzkowicz replied, 'What, today?' Wawrzkowicz eventually arrived in England in 1944. Wawrzkowicz arrived at Station 43 in early 1944 from his regular unit in Scotland. The 22-year-old corporal began the Underground Warfare course and RT training, his specialist field being disabling and repairing enemy tanks.

From the seventy men taking the courses, Wawrzkowicz states that they were grouped into sections. He said that he was one of twenty-eight, and out of these only two were dropped into Poland. Wawrzkowicz successfully passed the course on 26 August 1944. His SOE report states that he was in good health and physically tough. He was described as 'reliable, steady, reserved, conscientious, clever, and hard-working'.

Candidates were set the most fantastic of tasks. Local police in Essex were warned they might be subjected to sudden attacks, not necessarily owing to enemy action. Such operations included attacking the nearby railway station, the auxiliary RAF airfield and the post office. If the candidate was caught and could not account for himself satisfactorily, he was dismissed and sent back to his unit. Another report of a 'special mission' undertaken was a raid on a railway signal box on the line near Audley End. The Polish trainees approached the hut and used clinker from the track to break the blacked-out windows of the station, frightening the operator so much that they found him cowering in the corner. These agents were thought to have been reprimanded back at Station 43 but not returned to their 'normal' units.

Dressed in dirty overalls and a beret, with a sooty face and a shovel over his shoulder, Bronisław Wawrzkowicz was instructed to get as much information as possible in an afternoon about an electric power plant without being exposed by any of the employees of the plant. He had to describe to the SOE officers what machinery there was and how many people worked there. Wawrzkowicz said that no one took any notice of him and he was able to move freely and get all the information that he needed.

Before he was asked to become an instructor, Captain Mack was given the task of raiding the post office at Roydon as part of the course. The postmaster was told of the raid only an hour beforehand, and was instructed never to mention that the raid was set up or to tell his staff. Mack thought of an unusual approach. Knowing that women could move about less obtrusively than men, he asked if he could dress as a woman. Wearing a wig and a dress and with a pistol tucked into the top of his stockings, he was dropped from a van, with three others, near the post office. Strolling into the office, Mack jumped onto the counter and pointed his gun at the clerk, stating that it was a raid. A second man was instructed to take a telegram form with a post office stamp as proof that they had undertaken the task; a third stopped other people from walking in; and a fourth stopped anyone escaping from the shop. The raid was successful, but must have left unsuspecting people shocked and never to know that the stick-up had been an SOE ruse.

Józef Garliński states that field exercises were not without their problems:

> These nocturnal alarms and excursions were an excellent means of final training, but they were risky, too. The police and Home Guard could not tell who was attacking them, and defended themselves for all they were worth. Usually the chasing, uproar and exchange of shots ended with a drink in some local pub, and there was much laughter over the absurd situations that arose, but on other occasions heads were broken and serious fighting took place in which people were maimed; in two cases the casualties were fatal.[55]

Walter Rodwell was in the Home Guard, 12th Battalion, at Saffron Walden. SOE used the local Home Guard, as it was given the task of guarding key places that German agents would target for sabotage. These included the railway tunnel on the Cambridge–Liverpool Street line. Rodwell's son, Roy, recalls his father talking about an exercise between the Poles and the Home Guard that ended in a scuffle, with one particular fiery Pole having to be restrained.

Corporal Cottiss states that the British drove the Poles out into the middle of the Essex countryside at night. Dozens of Home Guard and police were employed in an SOE exercise at one time. Placed at strategic points throughout the Essex and Cambridgeshire countryside at night, they acted as 'German soldiers' looking out for the Poles, who were dropped miles from Audley End, having to get back to the house without being caught.

Bronisław Wawrzkowicz recalls these exercises. SOE candidates were asked to study a map during the day and then sent out at night tasked with getting to a certain location without being seen by a team that had been sent to search them out. Wawrzkowicz was taken to a spot just outside Newport to begin the exercise. At one point in the dark night, he was crossing the road when he heard someone approaching on a bicycle. He dived down by the side of the road and lay still to avoid being spotted, covering his white hands. The cyclist, who had nothing to do with the exercise, stopped right by him and proceed to urinate over Wawrzkowicz's head into the bushes. It soon became too much for Wawrzkowicz to have someone peeing in his ear. He stood up quickly and shouted at the man. The petrified cyclist mounted his bicycle and fled as quickly as he could. Wawrzkowicz went on to complete the exercise successfully.

Tony Currie thought that the police and Home Guard did not take kindly to 'evasion and infiltration' exercises involving the temporary residents at Audley End, as it created additional work for them that they thought should have been directed elsewhere. Currie agreed that many of the soldiers could adopt rough tactics and there were scuffles during training, but it was necessary as that was what they had to be trained for if they were going to be efficient agents.

Tiptofts Manor, Sewards End, near Audley End, is a very old house, built around 1300. A moat surrounds the manor, forded by an arched brick bridge. During the war Mr Ian Haigh lived at Tiptofts Manor, where his father was a tenant farmer. Haigh's father was asked if the farmhouse could be used as a 'safe house' as part of SOE training. Agents would often set up these places to hide if they were being pursued. Once this had been agreed, the exercise went ahead as follows: several British Army soldiers would approach the farm and state that a Pole would come to the house. Mr Haigh had to lay a sack over one side of the main approach bridge so that it was clearly visible, as if he was drying it out. He then had to remove it an hour later as a signal that it was clear for the man to approach. The Polish soldier in civilian clothes would then approach the farmhouse and ask, 'Is your son at home?' Mr Haigh had to reply, 'No, he's in Cumberland.' Passwords exchanged, he would show the trainee into the farm office. The agent would remain in the farmhouse for twenty-four hours planning a route at night cross-country to some designated destination, often up to 8 miles away, where he would 'cause a disturbance' and then return safely to the farm. Ian Haigh said that he thought that army camps were often used as targets. On the agent's return, British soldiers would approach the farm and demand that the agent 'give himself up'. Mr Haigh had to play the game and state that there was nobody in his house. The British tommies often got bored of 'these ridiculous war games'. Haigh maintains that a soldier was nearly hit when the Polish agent shot at him through a window. Driver Fensome said that he was not surprised that British servicemen were bored, as the British were a secondary consideration to the work that the Poles were undertaking; thus, it seems there was often a feeling of inertia among the British at Station 43. Indeed, Saffron Walden was known as 'Suffering Boredom' to many of the soldiers.[56] It was during a period of long and boring guard duty in the Bucket Hall that Peter Howe sustained an injury when he accidentally made contact with a stone column while shadow-boxing, and received treatment in hospital.[57] Also, a chink in the stone floor in the Bucket Hall is thought to have been caused by a bullet from a discharged rifle.

Wimbish Hall and Shortgrove Hall were used for training activities. Shortgrove was used as an area for cross-country runs but also as an ideally concealed spot for practice in laying mines and explosives. Local farms were also used by SOE. Sticks of gelignite used for blowing out tree roots were found in a cupboard of a shed at Rectory Farm, Littlebury. The newspaper reported it as being for the 'blowing up of trees', but some locals maintain that it belonged to the Poles. This is doubtful, as the explosives used by the Poles were home-made and called 'thunder flashes'. Stansted airfield was used by SOE for practising the procedures for sabotaging airbases and installations.

Although not naming the station that served as the training base, Iranek-Osmecki describes the type of activities he undertook:

> We used to leave this course [the high school of falsehood] to go to various towns, to mingle with the population and carry out prescribed tasks. Some of the exercises were short, others lasted several days. They were all done in mufti [civilian clothes]; picking out and following persons whose descriptions we'd been given, or shaking off the sleuths put on our scent, were among the easiest of the lot. The observation of troop rail-movements at railway junctions, the counting of ships sailing to and from ports, the following of day-to-day events in the docks, making contacts with unknown persons, were among the more difficult. All this had to be done discreetly, without attracting the attention of uniformed police or of security agents. Some, however, were not successful in this and found their way to the nearest police station. When such a thing happened one was not allowed to give the game away, to divulge that these were special exercises. When arrested, one had to lie one's way out of the unpleasant predicament. To show one's cards and own up disqualified one for service with the Underground.[58]

Physical training was the backbone of many aspects of the Underground Warfare course. Its importance was twofold: to keep candidates supple and in good shape to withstand the demands of a parachute drop and the unarmed combat training; and also to build up stamina, which ensured the good level of fitness needed to travel long distances quickly and increased the chances of escape in urban and rural areas. Lieutenant Eugeniusz Janczyszyn, and later Captain Mack, were responsible for keeping the trainees fit at Station 43. In a speech at a reunion at the house, *Cichociemni* agent Antoni Nosek states: 'They [the *Cichociemni*] were all strong and fit men and Alan Mack, who is here today, made sure everyone was in top form.'[59] Mack set up an assault course in the wooded area north-west of the house,

Audley End House from the West Park, late afternoon, 18 February 2003.
(© *English Heritage. NMR*)

Polish flag flying on the Jacobean Mount Garden for the 'SOE–Polish Section Reunion' at Audley End House, 24 May 1998.

Below left: Concrete cover to the detonation chamber in the Elysium Garden at Audley End. (*Author*)

Below: The detonation chamber beyond the Ionic columns of the Tea House Bridge. (© *English Heritage. NMR*)

Above: Orderly Room Staff, 1944: Cpl Howe, Pte Phillips and Sgt Watts. (*Reproduced by permission of English Heritage. NMR*)

Right: Sgt Watts in 1944. (*Reproduced by permission of English Heritage. NMR*)

opposite, top left: Cpl Howe, Pte Phillips and Sgt Watts standing [by] the south wall of the stables in 1944. (*Reproduced by permission of English Heritage. NMR*)

opposite, top right: Cpl Howe, [S]gt Fensome and Sgt Watts on the [fro]nt lawn in 1943. (*Reproduced [by] permission of English Heritage. NMR*)

opposite, bottom left: Cpl Bill Harris, [PT] and wrestling instructor, in July 1944. (*Ruby Harris*)

opposite, bottom right: Captain A.H. [M]cGowan, Adjutant and Quarter-[m]aster, in 1944. (*Reproduced by [pe]rmission of English Heritage. NMR*)

[ab]ove top: British soldiers transferred [fr]om Briggens to Audley End in [Ap]ril 1942. Sgt Maj Dobbs (back [ro]w, fourth from right), Sgt Watts [fo]urth from left in the same row). (*[R]eproduced by permission of English Heritage. NMR*)

[c]entre: British soldiers on exercise [ne]ar the Adam Bridge in 1944. [Cp]l Harris (foreground) and Capt [M]cGowan (kneeling). (*Ruby Harris*)

[ri]ght: British soldiers on exercise on the Adam Bridge, 1944. (*[R]uby Harris*)

Group photograph of British contingent at STS 43 taken in the Parterre Garden in 1944.
(*Reproduced by permission of English Heritage. NMR*)
Second row: from right, Cpl Bill Harris, Cpl Peter Howe, Sgt Alan Watts, Capt A.H.
McGowan, Adjutant and Quartermaster, Lt-Col A.H. Kennedy, MC, of the Gordon
Highlanders, CGMS Spicer, Cpl Cottiss, -?-, -?-. *Third row*: Driver Alfred S. Fensome is third
from left, with Driver Lionel Henman to his left; Pte, then Cpl, Shepherd is on the far right
(wearing the upside-down long-service stripes on the lower part of the sleeve, introduced
in the latter part of the war). *Fourth row*: Pte Horace Sidell is third from right; Pte Phillips
second from right; Pte Shearing is third from left.

Station 43's British contingent. Group photograph taken from the public road outside the
Lion Gate entrance to Audley End, 15 May 1944. Capt McGowan is seated on the far left
with Lt-Col Kennedy behind him. (*Reproduced by permission of English Heritage. NMR*)

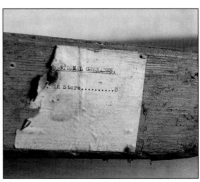

Left: Anteroom below Butler's Pantry, armoury for weapons used in SOE training. (© *English Heritage. NMR*)

Above: Evidence of requisition. Grenade rack in anteroom below Butler's Pantry. (© *English Heritage. NMR*)

Left: The Orderly Room. View from the Nursery windows on the second floor. (© *English Heritage. NMR*)

Below: SOE Tailors. View from the North Turret Room. (© *English Heritage. NMR*)

Poles disembarking at the front entrance to Audley End House. Peter Howe is standing on the far right. (*Polish Underground Movement (1939–1945) Study Trust, London*)

Maj Józef Hartman, Commandant of STS 43, in parachutist garb, with Thompson sub-machine gun and Sorbo rubber helmet. (*Polish Underground Movement (1939–1945) Study Trust, London*)

The British and Polish Commandants. Lt-Col Roper-Caldbeck and Maj Hartman outside the front entrance of Audley End House. Capt Lipiński, who died at Audley End House, is standing behind. (*Polish Underground Movement (1939–1945) Study Trust, London*)

ove: Training Instructors at STS 43. Left to right: Lt
Mieczysław Różański, Capt Maksymilian Kruczała, Lt
Eugeniusz Janczyszyn, Jerzy Zubrzycki, Lt Aleksander
Hatowicz, Maj Józef Hartman, Capt Adam Mackus
, Lt Antoni Pospieszalski, Stefan Piotrowski. (*Polish
Underground Movement (1939–1945) Study Trust,
London*)

ght: Józef Hartman, Antoni Pospieszalski and Jan
Kazimierski walking in the Parterre Garden. Antoni
Pospieszalski thought that Kazimierski was one of the
st Poles to parachute into Poland.

low: Tiptofts Manor, Sewards End. (*Author*)

Left: Polish Instructor, Lt Alexander Ihnatowicz, 'Ataman'. Photograph given 'To E.W. Ha▮ with compliments, on the 5th October 1943'. (*Ruby Harris*) *Right*: 'The Prof'. Capt Anto▮ Pospieszalski (Tony Currie), alias 'Łuk'.

Left: Capt Alfons Maćkowiak (Alan Mack), 'Alma', in June 1944. (*Ruby Harris*)
Right: Private Kazimierz Bilewicz on a motorcycle in the stables yard. Note the Polish Whi▮ Eagle hat badge. Driver Henman is behind. (*Ruby Harris*)

Valentine Tank exploding in the Elysium Garden, Audley End. (*Polish Underground Movement (1939–1945) Study Trust, London*)

Left: Tackling Alan Mack's rope crossing in the West Park. (*Polish Underground Movement (1939–1945) Study Trust, London*)

Below: No Problem. (*Polish Underground Movement (1939–1945) Study Trust, London*)

Above: 'Ungentlemanly Warfare'. Combat Training by the assault course in the Elysium Garden. Antoni Pospieszalski (Tony Currie) is in the background. (*Polish Underground Movement (193 1945) Study Trust, London*)

Left: S-Phone training in the East Park, Audley End. (*Polish Underground Movement (193 1945) Study Trust, London*)

Left: Unpacking Colt pistols. (*Polish Underground Moveme (1939–1945) Study Trust, London*)

Left: Lts Fijałka and Rybka pose during a sabotage exercise. (*Polish Underground Movement (1939–1945) Study Trust, London*) Right: 'The Briefing Room.' Second Floor, Audley End House. (*© English Heritage. NMR*)

Stanisław Stefan Kuczkowski, alias 'Ułany', 'Bułanek', and 'Florian', at STS 43. The central picture is the Virgin Mary, and the two photographs either side are of the Saints' (*see* p. 81). (*Polish Underground Movement (1939–1945) Study Trust, London*)

A lecture thought to b[e] at Chicheley Hall, Buck[s] (*Polish Underground Movement (1939–1945) Study Trust, London*)

'Faces of Concentration'. Students under instruction during the Briefing course. Note the red and white armband of the *AK*, worn by the *Cichociemni* trainee, second from right in the front row. (*Polish Underground Movement (1939–1945) Study Trust, London*)

Forging documents, S[?] 43. (*Polish Undergroun[d] Movement (1939–1945) Study Trust, London*) .

General Sikorski, the Commander-in-Chief of Polish Forces, with Major Hartman and *Cichociemni* students at Station 43, 8 August 1942. (*Polish Underground Movement 1939–1945) Study Trust, London*)

Sikorski's successor, Commander-in-Chief Gen Kazimierz Sosnkowski, talks to *Cichociemni* students at STS 43. (*Polish Underground Movement 1939–1945) Study Trust, London*)

President of Poland, Władysław Raczkiewicz, and Gen Tadeusz Klimecki, Chief of Staff at the Polish HQ in London, arrive at Audley End, greeted by Lt-Col Roper-Caldbeck and Maj Hartman. (*Polish Underground Movement 1939–1945) Study Trust, London*)

Left: Maj Hartman with Capt M. Utnik, Lt J. Podoski and Gen T. Klimecki outside the front of Audley End House. (*Polish Underground Movement (1939–1945) Study Trust, London*)

Below: Festive dinner in the Great Hall in the presence of the President of Poland, Władysław Raczkiewicz. His portrait hangs just above him, opposite the Polish White Eagle and a portrait of Prime Minister Władysław Sikorski on the other side. (*Polish Underground Movement (1939–1945) Study Trust, London*)

Armstrong Whitworth Whitley, the 'Flying Coffin'. (*Jonathan Falconer*)

Halifax bomber, Italy. (*Polish Underground Movement (1939–1945) Study Trust, London*)

Group photograph of a football team at Audley End House in 1944. Bill Harris is seated on the far left in the front row; Horace Sidell is second from right in the same row. Cpl Cottiss standing on the far right in the back row, with Pte Shepherd in the centre. (*Reproduced by permission of English Heritage. NMR*)

A football match in the West Park in 1944. The 200-year-old yew and box 'cloud hedge' is on the left of the photograph. The tall flagpole on the roof of the house has since been removed. (*Reproduced by permission of English Heritage. NMR*)

iatkówka. Volleyball in the Parterre Garden. (*Polish Underground Movement (1939–1945) Study Trust, London*)

A piggy-back race under starter's orders. Bill Harris is on the far right. (*Polish Underground Movement (1939–1945) Study Trust, London*)

Funeral of Lt Lemme. Capt Alfons Maćkowiak (far left) and Capt Antoni Pospieszalski (second from right). (*Polish Underground Movement (1939–1945) Study Trust, London*)

Funeral procession for Capt (post. Major) Jan Lipiński passing the chapel in Saffron Walden Cemetery. *From left to right*: Cpl Cottiss carrying the wreath; Pte Spiers; Cpl 'Jock' (?); Pte Gillett; Pte Shepherd; Pte Hampson; Pte White; Pte Wallbank; Pte Headland; Pte Scott; Pte Barnes; Pte Mudie; Pte Blackmur; Pte Hohnson; Pte Goodwin; Pte Pluckrose; Pte Trusswell; Pte Hagens; Pte Sidell; and the last man in the cortège is CGMS Spicer. (*Reproduced by permission of English Heritage. NMR*)

...-Gun Salute at the Funeral of ... Lemme, 27 October 1943. *Left to right*: ...M Kelly; Pte Pettitt; Pte Trusswell; Cpl ...ttiss; Cpl Howe; Pte Shepherd.

Graves of Maj Lipiński and Capt Lemme in Saffron Walden Cemetery. (*Author*)

Capt Antoni Nosek, alias 'Kajtuś'. (*Polish Underground Movement (1939–1945) Study Trust, London*)

Capt Elżbieta Zawacka, alias 'Zo' and 'Zelma'. (*Polish Underground Movement (1939–1945) Study Trust, London*)

Below: Wanda Skwirut, alias 'Wanda', in Poland during the war.

Right: The German *Kennkarte* issued to Wanda Skwirut.

Above: Val Sandes with Tony Currie and Alan Mack in May 1998.

Right: Front cover of the Polish Home Army Association Presentation Book, *SOE Polish Section in Audley End House 1942–1944*, showing the *cichociemni* badge, given to the House in 1998.

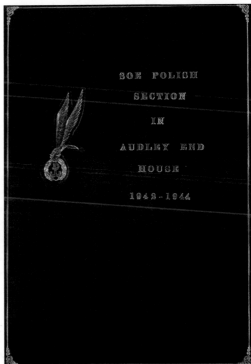

SOE POLISH
SECTION
IN
AUDLEY END
HOUSE
1942-1944

The Polish SOE memorial urn, showing the *Cichociemni* 'Silent and Unseen' emblem, in the West Park on the old Jacobean Mount Garden at Audley End House. (© *English Heritage. NMR*)

The memorial urn in the West Park. (© *English Heritage. NMR*)

towards the Elysium Garden, made from thick tree branches with a deep water trench in the middle. Collapsed culverts have been blamed for marked undulations in this area in recent years, but perhaps SOE and Alan Mack were responsible for certain amendments to Capability Brown's schemes. A precarious crossing of two lengths of rope was strung high up between two large plane trees near the Stables Bridge for candidates to cross the river. Mack states that he would have liked to have made it higher if it had been possible. He was happy for trainees to adopt any style to get over the river, as long as they got over. Some trainees did not make it to the other side and fell waist deep into the shallow water and cloying mud. Trainees also had to construct pontoons to cross the river. Mack constantly impressed upon the soldiers that being fit could save their lives. Being in peak condition had certainly saved Mack's life back in Poland. Bill Harris helped Mack instruct the Poles, Mack stating that Harris was a dynamic man and very good at wrestling and close-quarter fighting. Harris was also responsible for keeping the British soldiers in good fitness.

Harris and Mack became PE teachers after the war. Mack was at many schools, including Westminster College, Oxford, where he taught athletics for twenty-five years. Unsurprisingly, one school recommendation report stated that Mack never had any problems with discipline. Val Sandes (seen in the photograph with Mack and Currie) was taught by Alan Mack at Bishop's Stortford's Secondary Girls' School in the 1960s. She said that he was very fit and a stickler for long cross-country runs. Miss Smitham, the headmistress, said that he had 'the enthusiasm of a maestro'. Currie said that he was not surprised by this, as he recalled (with humour) a gruelling 3-mile run that Mack had sent him on on a hot summer day. In a testimonial of his record at Hadham Hall School, Hertfordshire, in 1967, the headmaster stated: 'In my thirty years' experience in schools, I have never come across such an outstanding teacher of physical education and games as Captain Mack, nor one so dedicated to physical fitness.' Harris was also highly thought of as a teacher, Ruby stating that he was very kind to his pupils.

One of the best runners on his course, Bronisław Wawrzkowicz, recalls regular 7-mile cross-country runs with sandwiches for sustenance. Fitness training was gruelling, but Mack states that after ten days the men showed signs of improving their fitness.

Wrestling was part of the training in close combat, or 'silent killing'. The primary aim of this course was to learn the quickest, most effective way of killing an enemy when firearms were not available or when silence was paramount. The course also trained an agent in self-defence and how to capture and secure an enemy. An instructor had to instil a level of brutality in students, and it was stressed that quick responses would keep them alive. Consequently, a range of unarmed combat was taught: boxing, kicking, knee blows, wrist and throat holds, knife fighting, the silent killing of guards and sentries, strangulation with rope and spinal dislocation. Another source, who did not wish to be named, revealed that domestic cats were put into one of the stable bays. A trainee had to enter the stables in pitch darkness to strangle one of the cats in preparation for the noise and struggle when having to undertake 'the real thing'.

Mack also taught small-arms firing with Ihnatowicz. Students also had to be able to fire the weapons they had been taught to use while tackling the assault courses and rope swings. Weapons training at Inverlochy Castle under Stacey and Strawiński, mentioned earlier, reveals the diversity in arms that students were trained in. It was an obvious importance to familiarise agents in German pistols, rifles and machine-guns, as captured weapons were often used in fighting and air-dropped supplies could not always be relied upon. Training at Station 43 involved firing practice with paper roundel targets, dummies and 'gallows' dummy targets, firing at various ranges and firing at night. Agents were trained to fire Sten guns, Colt pistols, Thompson machine-guns and German Schmeissers. It was also important to know how to keep weapons in good condition.

Mack visited many other special training schools over the

period he was based at Station 43 for specialist instruction. Trainees at Station 43 went to Warnham Court for extensive firing practice, as such exercises at Audley End may have been unsatisfactory from a safety point of view. However, Jędrzej Tucholski states that the War Office had an experimental station in up-to-date weapons (probably The Frythe), demonstrating them in exhibitions combined with shooting practice that took place once a quarter at Audley End.[60] Driver Fensome drove the Poles at Audley End to Chicheley Hall to undertake pistol shooting exercises. A long corridor was used, where a system of ropes and pulleys raised wooden effigies that the Poles had to shoot quickly. Again, some of the Poles rounded up all the household cats in the area to incorporate in the exercise, as the cats were more 'unpredictable in their movements'. Mr Fensome drove Roper-Caldbeck to the Hall as soon as the colonel found out, Roper-Caldbeck maintaining that this 'was very wrong'.

Photographs at the SPP reveal various types of instruction taking place, including using flame throwers, pistol shooting in thick woodland, mine-laying and anti-tank instruction using a captured German tank. Other photographs show Poles in civilian attire, in jumpsuits used for parachuting, and an instructor's inspection of wirelesses and the full kit contained within each agent's briefcase.

British Army and the FANY drivers took the Poles to other SOE establishments for firing and other instruction. Having previously worked as an ambulance driver with the Polish Army in Fife in 1942, Margaret Wilson of the FANY was detached to work with SOE. She remembers driving Major Egdell from Briggens to Audley End House. She was only at the house for the duration of the four-day exercise and knew nothing about the nature of the course. Like many FANY women, she went on to Gaynes Hall, where she drove the agents to Tempsford airfield.

Although not based at the house, Jessica Aldis visited the school while the Poles were there. Aldis was assistant to Colonel Perkins, head of the Polish Section, and later went on to service in Italy. She was in charge of all the Polish FANYs. As an SOE secretary to Colonel Perkins, Ensign (later Lieutenant) Vera Long visited Station 43 on one or two occasions, as she states, 'and hid among the bushes when the Poles were blowing things up!'

Indeed, training in explosives and demolition was a major part of the course. Explosions were an everyday occurrence at Station 43. Even in the house small explosions were common. Bronisław Wawrzkowicz states: 'You couldn't even lift the seat of a toilet without a small charge being set off.' Wawrzkowicz played a trick on an instructor by placing a small charge under his bed. The next morning the officer pointed a finger at the trainee and said, 'I know it's you, Wawrzkowicz.'

Wawrzkowicz was sent on a long cross-country run for a misdemeanour regarding a detonator. Told to attach a 10-inch pencil detonator fuse to a small explosive device, he used an 18-inch length, with the subsequent large explosion resulting in the trainee putting on his running shoes. Time pencils, or pencil detonators, were thin copper tubes. When the top was crushed between finger and thumb, acid was released that set off a charge. Students were also taught to pinch the end of detonators with their teeth.

The 1830s carriage building opposite the stables was used as a garage and for instructional purposes: for practice in the use of arms; and for bomb-making.[61] Captain Mack states that the stables were off limits to many soldiers, as they contained over 20 tons of explosives. It is strange to think that this building, built before Audley End House itself, fulfilled such a role when once it had contained royal racehorses. Local residents recall windows in Saffron Walden being blown out when a nearby ammunition, gas and fuel dump in Chesterford Park exploded. A soldier watched the explosion from outside the stables at Audley End. He saw shells exploding and cart-wheeling in the air and then was promptly blown onto his back by another very large explosion. Having windows blown out was a familiar experience for many people during the war, one, perhaps apocryphal, London resident stating, 'And to think, I'd just cleaned those windows.'

Bronisław Wawrzkowicz was taught to blow the doors from

safes, blow up trees to hamper vehicular advance on roads, simulate the blowing-up of trains and lay mines. The bridges in the grounds at Audley End were used for simulating mine-laying. Second Lieutenants Fijałka and Rybka dressed as women (see photograph) during a 'simulated sabotage action in an English Society' exercise.[62]

A British Valentine tank for training in the use of anti-tank weapons was situated in the Elysium Garden. No doubt the eighteenth-century Italian designer of the gardens, which once contained a statue of Flora and orange trees, magnolias and rhododendrons, would find it a very unappealing addition. The present Lord Braybrooke, JP, writes: 'My parents and I did not appear on the scene [Audley End] until 1943 when I was eleven years old, and I remember how exciting it was to see Lancaster [Halifax] bomber fuselages and the odd tank or two in the grounds which were blown up on a fairly regular basis.' According to Alfred Fensome, the tank was meant to be in the grounds at Audley End only for a short period of time, as it was in transit to go to Catterick Camp. However, the tank was not locked and secured properly. This resulted in the theft of its electrics and motor, which Fensome thought was carried out by civilians. He stated that these thefts immobilised the tank and that was the reason why it stayed in the grounds for so long. Wawrzkowicz blew the turret off it using plastic detonators and hand-grenades. Again, he was reprimanded for using too much explosive. Wawrzkowicz states that all the noise over his stay at Station 43 affected his hearing in later years.

Alfred Fensome taught the Poles to drive motor cars and lorries and to ride motorcycles. He said that the British were initially surprised that the majority of the Poles could not ride bicycles, but then quickly understood that bicycles were often an expensive commodity in Poland and unfamiliar to the majority of the trainees. Archive photographs show soldiers riding bicycles *en masse* on the front lawn. Training in the use of motorbikes was given in the stables yard.

Station 43 had 15-cwt lorries, a few motorcycles and

bicycles, a small van and an old blue Austin motorcar in which Fensome taught Watts to drive. Staff cars and a charabanc were sometimes employed, and occasionally they used 3-cwt lorries, mainly for driving lessons. The lorries invariably had no windscreens, which Fensome described as 'a bit naughty in the winter, but preferred as having glass meant there was a danger from a shattering windshield'.

Mr Howe said that the fuselage of a Halifax bomber arrived in a transport and was erected beyond the stables for training purposes. It was thought to have been put to a good height for learning to jump out of an aircraft and how to land.[63] One other unknown visitor to the house maintained that there were wire parachute 'fans' attached to the roof of the house itself. Mr Fensome stated that the Poles did not even go to these lengths to jump from the top of the house. He says that two men would hold a parachute open as far as they could and then the jumper would launch himself off the roof with nothing to break his fall. Antoni Nosek and Tony Currie state that no such activities took place, as the house was not high enough, and if they did occur, they were the schemes of foolhardy individuals, not part of the curriculum.

As Station 43 served mainly as the last place of training, the fuselage could have served to refamiliarise agents with the interior of the aircraft and jumping procedures. Mock-apertures for teaching exit drill from aircraft were in place at Ringway. Group Captain Newnham stated: 'The sight of other men disappearing through the hole is an unpleasant one and the prospect of scraping one's face on the side is not encouraging.'[64] A disparate view to the theory that the aircraft shell was used for exit drill is that most of the candidates came from the parachute brigade and would have been very familiar with procedures and would not have needed reminding. Other trainees would have recently undertaken the parachute course before arriving at Station 43. In his research, Jeff Bines found documentation from 1943 proposing that a fuselage be sent to STS 43 for training in the use of 'Rebecca' communication. There is no documentation to reveal that the proposal went ahead, but perhaps gives official credence in part to its existence at the house.

From 1942 onwards, an aircraft fitted with 'Rebecca' could enable flight crews to home in on an agent or a 'reception committee' employing a 'Eureka' radio signal from a short aerial on the ground. In the same year, S-phone was developed by SOE boffins. A lighter model than 'Eureka', it enabled efficient communication between the aircrew and the people on the ground. Photographs taken on the high ground in the East Park, beyond the Temple of Concord, show Polish soldiers learning to use S-Phone communication. It was obviously important for some of the *Cichociemni* to have the knowledge that would prepare them to receive other parachutists landing in the field in Poland. A silhouette of an aircraft, thought to be a Hudson, was employed as part of the exercise. Other group photographs show RAF personnel in the grounds.

Tony Currie maintains that he does not recall either a fuselage or a tank in the grounds. However, Currie did not see inside the stables until after the war – certain areas that did not relate to an instructor's speciality were out of bounds. Another explanation for such discrepancies is that training at Station 43 was often in fixed six-week periods, with different training employed at different times. Ted Pretty thought that Ronny Powell, the head gardener in the late 1940s, removed part of a fuselage from the Elysium Garden. The stables yard does seem a conspicuous place to have had such a structure when the milk delivery was dropped nearby. However, Mr Howe said 'beyond' the stables, referring to a more secluded position for the fuselage. Roger Kirkpatrick commented that apparatus in the grounds could well have been accessed by already established paths in the early stages of the war, to avoid beating well-worn tracks that could be seen from the air. By chance, extra scrutiny applied to a photograph of the assault course in the grounds, found at the SPP, shows an RAF roundel and the dark outline of a fuselage hidden among the yew trees. The aircraft shell appears to show the aerofoil section with the wing having been removed.

There were serious accidents and fatalities during the training. Driver Lionel Henman (behind Private Bilewicz in the photograph taken in the stables yard) was walking back from Stumps Cross, a notoriously dangerous crossroads, one night while on exercise with the Poles, when a Pole blew his hand apart with a home-made bomb. They drove him to Addenbrooks but could not save his hand. Mr Fensome saw the man again after he returned to Station 43 and he appeared not to be particularly bothered about the severity of the injury.

While Warrant Officer Gabriel Zając was in charge of an exercise in the local area, a student broke into the stables to make a similar device. The man put a charge into a vice and screwed the detonator in too tightly. The detonator promptly exploded, causing serious injury to his stomach. Fensome said nobody knew what he was doing, as he should not have been in there. Ruby Harris said that her husband spoke about the awful injuries the Pole sustained. Bill Harris and Private Horace Sidell took it in turns to look after him in the Guard Room. Bill remembered with horror how dark and cold it was in the Guard Room and trying to stem the blood.

Perhaps underplaying it, Fensome maintained that the Poles could be 'over-boisterous' at times. Tony Currie stated that fuses were made shorter and shorter, one instructor often surprising the students at Station 43 by fitting fuses to devices so that they exploded almost instantaneously.

One ludicrous rumour was that a Pole committed suicide by drowning himself face down in a fire bucket. One British soldier maintains that a Pole died after playing football and a rigorous bout of drinking, but this is also unsubstantiated.

Another incident took place on the way back from the soldiers' regular trip to use baths in Cambridge. The soldiers took the opportunity to have a few drinks in town before they returned to Station 43 and often paid the driver in kind. On the way home a British soldier fell out of the back of the truck and was found dead in a ditch the following day.

On another occasion Fensome was driving half a dozen agents to the airfield to embark on their flight to Poland. He turned right at Stumps Cross and moved along a track towards Newmarket airfield when he heard an explosion in the back of the truck. A Polish agent had badly injured his leg when a bomb that he was carrying in his pocket had exploded. Fensome remembered the blood in the snow and how the Pole had lost his pistol. The Poles were fond of making various small explosive devices, but, as these incidents testify, small charges were often temperamental and highly dangerous.

There are three graves of Polish servicemen in Saffron Walden cemetery. Major Jan Lipiński died on 12 April 1944, aged 48, from a suspected heart attack; the second, Captain J. Lemme, instructor in combat fighting, German language and conspiracy, died on 27 October 1943, aged 25; the third is a Polish serviceman who died after the war. Peter Howe described the demise of Lemme: 'Lieutenant Lemme was on an exercise [part of the Underground Warfare course] in the fog, and on a motorbike. He ran into a parked lorry and died later in the Guard Room [set up in the Bucket Hall]. He was blond and Aryan-looking, a big man. Everyone was very upset, as he had been very nice and well liked. The bike was repaired and no one had any qualms about using it.'[65]

Alan Mack was close friends with Lemme, and they were on the same map-reading exercise. It was actually about ten o'clock in the morning when the accident happened and the fog was incredibly thick. Mack and Lemme were both on motorcycles and tasked with delivering a package to a point on a map in the middle of a wood. Taking different routes, Mack turned left out of Lion Gate and Lemme turned right, where he later encountered the stationary civilian vehicle near Littlebury. Lemme died, despite efforts to resuscitate him, and later received a Protestant funeral. Mack stated that Lemme would have been ideal for work in Poland.

THE BRIEFING COURSE

Having successfully completed the Underground Warfare course, a candidate had to undertake the Briefing course, his final polishing stage of training. This involved being informed

STATION 43

of the conditions in Poland at the time, and concocting individual cover stories, or 'legends'. The Briefing course lasted a month to six weeks, and Tucholski reveals that 606 agents completed the course.[66] The course was given to all parachutists, including the political couriers.

Briefing was initially taught by Captain Jan Górski, who was replaced by Captain Jan Lipiński when Górski parachuted into Poland. When Captain Lipiński died, he was posthumously promoted to major and replaced by Captain Czesław Stronczak, an ex-police intelligence officer who until then had been responsible for working out 'legends'. Wejtko and Wieroński followed.

Room 8 was one of the principal rooms used by SOE, and was probably the main room used for the Briefing course, where candidates were lectured under photographs of 'the Saints'. Located on the second floor of the north wing, it contains fragments of posted foolscap notices. The only discernible text is 'dzień' and '*dni*' and 'do', with times, for example, '7.30 do 8.30'. *Dzień* is Polish for 'day', and *dni* is the plural 'days'.

After the war, Stronczak donated an album to the Polish Underground Movement (1939–1945) Study Trust (SPP), containing photographs of students deep in concentration in Room 8, surrounded by detailed maps and under supervision.

Opposite the Briefing room, Room 16, currently a book store and archive, was revealed by Dee Alston, one of the English Heritage historic contents cleaners, to be the administration room in which Stanisław Stefan Raczkowski appears (see photograph). The nails that held the pictures are still in place and the wallpaper is recognisable from the photograph. Obviously the protective screen over the fireplace has been removed. The picture in the centre of the photograph is a gold-coloured icon depicting 'The Mother of Christ Patron Saint of Parachutists', made by false documents expert, Albin Bratek, and later given to the Catholic church in Folkland, Scotland.

Many of the candidates were noted as 'experienced' on their training reports, not only for their military background, but from the fact that SOE drew most agents from Poles who had already experienced living and fighting under occupation at the beginning of the war. However, the consistent problem for those instructing the Briefing course was keeping up to date with quickly changing events in Europe, from enemy propaganda to local conditions. SOE relied on intelligence sources in the field, and assessed Nazi propaganda. Every aspect of rural and provincial life had to be known, as witness the famous scenario of the agent who caused suspicion by walking into a French café and ordering *café noir*. Milk had been unavailable for months and everyone naturally just ordered *café*.

Agents had to be familiar with the bureaucracy, structure, uniforms and equipment of political, military and civil organisations. The *RSHA* – and, within it, the *Geheime Staatspolizei* (Gestapo) – was a complex organisation that worked on many levels, including the *Schutzstaffeln* (*SS*) and the *Abwehr*. Each of these branches included different sections. Station 43 certainly had German uniforms, and candidates would have seen all manner of enemy weapons and equipment. Bronisław Wawrzkowicz states that, for the trainees to become accustomed to the preponderance of German soldiers in Poland, there were soldiers dressed in German uniforms in every corridor throughout the house, and it was not uncommon to be addressed fiercely in German by a Gestapo officer.

Although training was refined and changed, correspondence outlining the structure of the early courses at Inverlochy gives one an idea of the scope of the lectures that were undertaken. Emphasis from the onset was placed on instructing candidates on the organisation of the German Army and civil administration in occupied Polish territory. Trainee agents had to know the organisation of executive police organisations and the specification of their different branches: *Schutzpolizei*; *Kriminalpolizei*; Gestapo; *Gendarmerie*. The lectures were illustrated wherever possible by synoptic tables giving pictures of uniforms and armament.[67]

Enemy uniforms were worn in the mock-interrogation exercises that could be sprung upon the candidates at any time of the day or night. These were not always taken seriously by the students, to the consternation of the instructors, who had also risen from their beds at some unearthly hour. However, resistance to interrogation, from simple enquiries on the street to persistent questioning under torture, was a vital part of the training. Candidates were taught methods of interrogation, including the Gestapo's use of 'stool pigeons' and microphones. The course also instructed candidates how to make contact with couriers who would meet them at drop zones designated by the *AK*, so that they could take them to their units or safe houses. Agents also became proficient in using cipher codes and invisible inks.

The second part of the Briefing course was to give individuals a 'legend'. This was to be their alias identity and concocted background in Europe, an intricate compilation of logical lies that fitted with their assumed identity or 'mask'. Lieutenant Eugeniusz Janczyszyn expertly taught the agents their cover stories, which had to be known inside out. Agents also had to have prepared alibis for every seemingly harmless activity, including a cover reason for each journey taken within occupied Europe.

There also had to be minimum training in the trade that agents were supposed to have according to their 'legends', often drawn from their civilian life. All students were in the Regular Army, but it is easy to imagine how some of the Poles' pre-war civilian employment could have been exploited for a particular area of expertise or their 'cover story' when back in Poland. Candidates in 1944 included an engineer who specialised in petrol engines and an engineer from the High Technical School in Warsaw; other civilian jobs represented were railway employee, railway stationmaster's assistant, locksmith, driver, university student, actor, qualified mason, shopkeeper's assistant, farmer, lawyer, motorcar mechanic, clerk, book-keeper, police officer, mining engineer, mechanical engineer, chemist, technician, commercial assistant, civil engineer, civil servant, teacher, electrical engineer, decorative painter and typist.[68]

Many of the candidates spoke Russian, and some were bilingual, with the oldest Pole speaking four languages. Other candidates spoke English, German, Czech, Ukrainian, French or Italian.

Candidates had to be ready at all times, as they never knew when they would be expected to make the jump into occupied Poland or other countries. Antoni Nosek states: 'I was to forget I was Antoni Nosek, and had now become Antoni Niechrzyński, a car mechanic employed by a garage in Chmielna Street, Warsaw. When suddenly woken up during the night, I had to reply, "I am Antoni Niechrzyński." Here I also received new German identification papers, *Kennkarte* and *Arbeitskarte.*'[69] The latter was a work permit that showed where a citizen was employed. Printed like a banknote, the *Kennkarte* was very difficult to forge.

Second Lieutenant Alfred Wiśniewski was in charge of making false documents at Station 43, aided by Albin Bratek and Mieczysław Różański. Other documents and money for all country sections were still being prepared at Briggens. When documents were needed, Wiśniewski set up his office on the first floor, where the only other rooms used were the sleeping quarters for commanding officers (see photograph). The paper was 'aged' by fading it under lamps and taping it to the windows in the lower gallery. It is probable that the forgery section at Briggens did not know that documents were being prepared by the Poles at Station 43.

At the end of the course all those who were ready to work behind enemy lines took the oath customary to the *AK* in Poland before they began their service. The *AK* Oath of Allegiance was as follows:

Before Almighty God and the Holy Virgin Mary, Queen of Poland, I take in my hands this Holy Cross, the sign of Suffering and Salvation, and swear loyalty to my Country, the Polish Republic, to unyieldingly guard her honour and to fight for her liberation from slavery with all my strength – and onto death. I shall remain unwaveringly obedient to the President of the Polish Republic, to the Commander-in-Chief and his appointed Commander of the *Armia Krajowa*, and I shall keep the secrets entrusted to me irrespective of whatever may befall.[70]

Few students had the opportunity of serving, even if they had successfully completed the courses. This was not always due to a severe selection procedure. Only a certain number of flights could be fitted into the relatively short winter season, and by the summer of 1944 the tide of the war had changed. Only five students from the list of seventy in 1944 saw active service. Forty-eight-year-old Wacław Kobyliński, a lieutenant-colonel in the Polish Infantry, completed his SOE training on 25 March 1944. Described as being experienced, energetic and physically tough, he jumped on 16/17 October in the same year, being given the name 'Dziad'.[71] Jan Benedykt Różycki, known as 'Busik', and 'Rola', jumped with Kobliński. A 43-year-old civil engineer, Różycki served as a lieutenant in the cavalry and spoke four languages. He was described by Hartman as energetic, strong-willed and physically tough. He was a combatant in the War of Independence during 1918–21. At the outbreak of the Second World War he was a commander of the Frontier Defence Infantry Regiment, then the 10th Battalion Motorised Infantry and lastly commander of the Company of Engineers. After being interned in Hungary, he served with the First Division of Grenadiers and was interned again in Switzerland until September 1942. Travelling from France, Spain, Portugal and then to Gibraltar, he arrived in Britain to serve in a regular unit and then in sabotage with the SOE.

Agents Sroczyński, Uklański and Matysko jumped into Poland together on 26/27 December 1944. Known as 'Kompresor', Zdzisław Sroczyński jumped having completed his training on 25 March.[72] Described as experienced and physically tough, 38-year-old Major Sroczyński was commended as very good at the use of explosives and demolitions. Forty-eight-year-old Witold Uklański, candidate 57 on the training reports, also jumped just after Christmas Day.[73] Known as 'Herold', Uklański trained with SOE, having previously been a captain in the Polish cavalry. A fierce-looking man, he fought in Poland's struggle for independence between 1917 and 1921. He was interned by the Red Army in 1939 and joined the Polish Army in 1941. Strangely, his training report reveals that the instructors regarded his physical training and irregular warfare work as unsatisfactory, but his expertise in explosives and demolitions as very good. Hartman's remarks conclude that he was experienced, not enterprising, but physically tough. The youngest of the five who jumped was 32-year-old Jan Matysko. He completed his training on 30 June 1944. His detailed character report reveals him to be 'reliable, trustworthy, self-confident, nervous, a bit talkative, conscientious, endeavours to control himself, receptive intelligence, chaotic way of thinking'. The report concludes that he was recommended as a wireless operator, but had a 'delayed reaction and unable to make a quick decision'. Matysko, alias 'Oskard', jumped on 26/27 December 1944.[74]

The weather severely curtailed flights in October and December 1944 and there does not appear to have been a flight from RAF Tempsford on 16/17 October or 26/27 December.[75] Subsequently, the operations almost certainly were from the new stations in Italy (see pp. 117–18).

The seventy SOE reports in 1944 were the last to be completed at Station 43. Bronisław Wawrzkowicz was one of the final candidates. At the time of his impending mission to Poland he was sent to London to a holding school in Harrow. He fully expected to be parachuted into Poland. The fillings in Wawrzkowicz's teeth had already been changed at Station 43 by a Polish dentist to the correct mixture used in Poland. While waiting at a railway station he got the news that the mission had been cancelled and that he should return to his unit in Scotland, the 14th Lancers. An enduring memory from this time in London was the flying bombs that were dropping into the city. Wawrzkowicz thoroughly enjoyed his six months at the SOE training school. Despite the endurance of the course, life at the SOE training school was obviously a luxury compared to the conditions he had endured in Siberia.

SECURITY AND RELAXATION

There are a few disparities regarding how the Poles and the British mixed, both militarily and socially. Peter Howe maintained that there was little contact between the Polish and British soldiers, insisting that communication was channelled only through particular people, particularly Count Stanisław Grocholski. At the fall of France Grocholski was evacuated to Britain, where he was appointed SOE liaison officer in the Sixth Bureau. Although trained himself, he was never parachuted into occupied Poland, as it was considered that his great height made him far too conspicuous for a secret mission. Instead he worked closely with the British military establishment. Peter Howe remembered him at Audley End as being the main interpreter between the British and Poles, Hartman speaking very little English. Grocholski died in Belgium in February 2002.

Alan Watts also maintained that the golden rule was that English was never spoken to the Poles. He says that the only British soldier, apart from the CO, who had direct contact with the Poles was Sergeant-Major Dobbs (seated back row, fourth from right in the photograph of British staff transferred from Briggens). However, Ian Hook, Keeper of the Essex Regiment Museum, states: 'Our SOE connection is an unnamed company quartermaster-sergeant who kitted out agents to be dropped or landed by aircraft covertly operating out of Bedfordshire airfields.' This could refer to Captain McGowan, who took care of quartermaster issues. Despite stating that there was minimal contact between the soldiers, Howe went on to state that some of the Polish officers had English batmen.

Alfred Fensome clarifies the issue. He described himself as having been a 'driver and confidant' to the Poles, and the general set-up between the Poles and the British was that 'we were close as pals but separate in our intentions'. There appears to be a clear dividing line. Tony Currie said that there were defined elements of separation between the soldiers. Banter between the Poles and British obviously did take place at Audley End. The British often shouted '*bardzo dobrze!*' to the Poles, which meant that everything was okay or 'very good', and it was not uncommon for the Poles and the British to rib each other.

The British drivers spent quite a lot of time in the yard outside the stables where most of the vehicles were kept. Fensome recalled Driver Henman talking in the yard and mentioning Warrant Officer Gabriel Zając's name in conversation. On hearing his name, Gabriel, locksmith and driving specialist, ran out of the stables and exclaimed, 'Who is using my name in vain?' Both Fensome and Henman were impressed with his excellent use of English, but more impressive was Zając's excellent coffee, which he always had on the go. Alfred Fensome got to know Gabriel very well, giving him many lifts into Saffron Walden. Corporal Cottiss also struck up a friendship with Private Kazimierz Bilewicz, who was in charge of the workshops and motorcycles. Susan Bilewicz states, 'Dad was born in Lvov in 1917. He joined the army and when Poland was defeated he was rounded up and taken to Siberia for two years. Once freed from there we believe he escorted German POW's to Scotland then joined the SOE. Dad didn't talk too much about the horrors of his war but in general this is what we understand happened to him.' Kazimierz Bilewicz died in February 2001 aged 83.

Bill Harris also built up friendships with the Polish officers. Captain Alan Mack and Lieutenant Aleksander Ihnatowicz gave Harris photographs of themselves. Ihnatowicz wrote on the back of his photograph, 'To E.W. Harris with compliments, on the 5th October 1943.'

It is inevitable that the British soldiers, who were at the Audley End before SOE arrived and who were still there after they had gone, would get an overall impression of the training courses that the Poles had undertaken and the nature of the work they were about to embark on, but they never spoke about it, and sixty years later some ex-servicemen that I talked to were still reluctant to talk about anything connected to SOE. The Poles, on the other hand, are more loquacious.

In the written correspondence between Peter Howe and an English Heritage curator in the 1980s, it is clear that Howe was very concerned that he was giving English Heritage information that he should not have known in the first place. There are obvious discrepancies between what happened at Station 43 and the official line.

As the British contingency was guarding the house and grounds, it would certainly have had a lot less restriction than some of the reports suggest. Bill Harris talked of Station 43 having a private line to Number Ten and the headquarters of SOE in Baker Street. It is understandable that some recollections veer towards the official conduct expected rather than what actually occurred. Yarns and anecdotes, rather than SOE, come to the forefront of recollection, because it was constantly impressed upon them at the time not to talk about what was going on. Hartman and Roper-Caldbeck were jointly responsible for the security of the establishment and discipline of soldiers therein, under an SOE directive.[76] Nearly every day it was impressed upon the British soldiers not to say anything to anyone regarding anything they saw or heard respecting SOE. Walter Leney said that, even as Chief Clerk, he was not allowed to file top secret papers. Fensome described a 'security man' in civilian clothes who visited the house, telling the British to keep quiet. He always felt that he was being watched, 'spied-out', as he had it. When he was driving the agents out to the airfields, it was impossible not to overhear things that were said in the back of the trucks, but nothing was repeated.

Although the British used rooms in the house for sleeping, eating and storage of rifles and supplies, an example given by Fensome revealed a very strict code of conduct in operation. The British were allowed to walk only along the corridors in the house and to enter only the rooms allocated to them. On one occasion a British soldier broke the rules. He was walking along a corridor, and, seeing the person he wanted to speak to through a door that was ajar, he knocked and then opened the door fully to engage him in conversation. An officer promptly shouted at him, physically pushed him out of the room and slammed the door shut. The soldier was then put on a charge for a breach of conduct.

As for security in the grounds, a local girl who had been accustomed to ride her horse in the immediate peripheries of the estate around the house before the war got a shock when she did so during the war and found herself surrounded by dozens of armed Polish soldiers demanding to know what she was doing. However, when asked about security imposed on the instructors, Currie said that the ease with which they could enter and leave the grounds to go into Saffron Walden was brought back to him after the war when he visited Station 43 for the first time in peacetime. He was surprised when he was stopped at the ticket boxes!

Not all the instructors remained at Audley End. A few of the Polish officers married local women and lived off site. Peter Howe said that a Sergeant-Instructor 'Z' (Gabriel Zając) married an Irish nurse from Saffron Walden hospital, and he was almost sure that he attended that wedding.[77] There are several photographs at the SPP, thought to be of the wedding party outside the front entrance to Audley End House. Each photograph shows a different Polish soldier holding the bride's bouquet.

Bronisław Wawrzkowicz states that candidates for *Cichociemni* work never knew the names of instructors or fellow trainees, but did know that the commander of the school was the famous Hartman; his presence could not be missed. As stated, various parts of the house and grounds were out of bounds, as the officers were restricted to the areas where they undertook instruction. This mirrored the *AK*'s security. An individual under duress could divulge only his or her narrow contribution to the training programme and staff. Tony Currie said that the area between the river and the public road was also out of bounds to many men at Station 43, and amazingly he did not see many areas of the gardens, including the stables, until after the war. A guard was placed at the end of Abbey Lane and a police presence was occasionally seen outside Lion Gate. The British soldiers undertook vigilant periods of guard duty and patrols in the grounds. Alan Mack says that the site was completely safe against any prying eyes.

As for the external security of Station 43 and its secret status in Essex as a whole during the war, Regular Army regional commanders were informed of the location of SOE establishments in their area: 'It has been decided by the War Office that static formation such as Commands and Commanders of Areas shall be informed of the existence and location of "Special Training Schools" in their areas . . . The troops at these schools are undergoing training in irregular warfare and in consequence the distribution of information concerning these schools is secret and must be kept on as high a level as possible.'[78] However, relations had to be established with the local police, no doubt as an aid to understanding reports from civilians about strange activities in the countryside, and for arranging help with training exercises. So 'the Headquarters of Formations, Districts and Areas are informed of the secret character of these schools, so that unnecessary visits and enquiries by local security or other military personnel are avoided'.[79] Polish trainees at Station 43 did not stand out from the British soldiers in attire. They wore British Army uniforms with the Polish White Eagle hat badges and 'Poland' flash at the top of the left arm.

Food and relaxation are important to every soldier. As Alfred Fensome mused, 'every British soldier runs on tea'. He thought that there were often up to 100 Poles at the house at one time. He remembers seeing them all sitting together in the Great Hall at Christmas with all the decorations up. Sue Ryder describes Christmas with the Poles at STS 17, Brickendonbury:

Christmas at the ops station was unforgettable. The bods [agents] took over the station, including the kitchen, and managed (despite rationing) to prepare part of their traditional Christmas Eve supper, including *barszcz* (beetroot soup) and fish. Meat is not eaten by Polish Catholics on Christmas Eve; for them it is the day of abstinence. The Poles observed *wigilia* (vigil). Hay was laid on the table to represent the manger, and, after the first star appeared, we handed each other a wafer (*opłatek*) blessed by the priest.[80]

She goes on to state that for many of those present this was their last Christmas on earth.

STATION 43

By the time Major Hartman arrived at Audley End House, every sort of food that had to be rationed in Britain had been, with the exception of sweets, which were restricted in June 1942, and bread, which was rationed after the war in July 1946. The Ministry of Food encouraged the public to preserve fruit and vegetables for the winter months and suggested recipes for meagre rations. A Ministry advertisement in the *Strand Magazine* in December 1943 boasted the versatility of the dreaded dried egg, 'Eggs, five days a week – more than in peacetime!'

The public were allowed one packet of dried eggs per ration book every four weeks, so the profusion of duck eggs on the Audley End Estate must have been greatly appreciated. Supplements to Army rations were always welcome, and the River Cam that runs through the extent of the West Park provided a plentiful supply. The Poles fished the Cam for pike and carp, and when they caught them, kept them alive in the disused Victorian fountain in the Parterre Garden so that they could pick one for dinner at their leisure. When the spigot mortar was first produced, the Poles had one and were keen to test it. They set off the mortar, also known as the Blacker Bombard, near the main entrance to the house. The anti-tank shell promptly exploded in the river, killing two large pike, which were eaten that night.

The British also took advantage of the Essex larder. Being brought up in the country, Bill Harris would often take the work punt out with Captain McGowan to collect duck eggs, which would be fried for dinner. Despite the added benefits of training in a countryside that could provide extras to the table, the Poles were provided with substantial rations. Private Horace Sidell, who died in early 2003 aged 83, stated: 'We and they [the Poles] had the very best of food which I presumed was to build up their stamina.' Fensome agreed, but said that none of the British begrudged them that because they knew the nature of the work they were training for and respected their dedication and bravery. As a trainee, Bronisław Wawrzkowicz said he enjoyed the very best rations, including American cigarettes and bully beef.

The milk delivery for the soldiers was dropped outside the stables very early in the morning. Jeff Bines has extensively researched the Polish Section of SOE. In his article on Audley End published in the *Newport News* he states: 'Sylvia Felix, née Thurston, was a girl of sixteen when she travelled by van from Elms Farm, Stansted, to deliver the dozen or so bottles that was taken every two days. She and her companion were always met by an officer and paid in cash. She thought it was simply another army camp but says it was "creepy during the early morning, especially in the winter".'

The Poles were allowed to install a wrought-iron bread oven into the Old Kitchen on the ground floor, changing the historical fabric of the house by the partial bricking-up of one of the three arches above the extensive kitchen range. Soldiers would queue for their food, using the original serving hatch.

As Driver Fensome's billet was upstairs in the rooms above the kitchen, he knew when the kettle was on the boil. He also knew that the tea was kept in a large wooden box under a bench, and used to make illicit cups for himself. Once, he heard someone approaching. He raced back to his billet having spilt boiling water on the stone paving, leaving the officer looking at the steam coming up from the floor.

Servicemen could also purchase chocolate and biscuits from Corporal Cottiss in the Old Kitchen. Cottiss had been a police constable before serving in the Essex Regiment and was at Station 43 for two years. After that he served in the War Office in London. His release leave certificate in 1946 describes his military conduct as exemplary. Cottiss also died in 2003. Walter Leney states, 'We had our own little canteen in the house and a contraption called, I think, a soda fountain. This operated with a gas canister and various flavoured fruit tablets. One had to be careful that the glass, gas tablets and water did not explode and make a frightful mess!' Leney, now 84, visited Audley End House in 2004. When he reached the top of the many stairs to where the Orderley Room was located, he stopped and said, 'I didn't think there was so many stairs, but of course I used to take the stairs three at a time in 1941!'

STATION 43

The present-day restaurant, to the left of the main entrance to the house, was used as a recreation room containing comfortable chairs. The Dining Parlour was used as a billiards room. Mrs Pickering states that a Polish officer visiting the house after the war said that they had made a makeshift drinks bar in one of the rooms. Mr Fensome said that the Poles used the billiards room during the day, but the British servicemen were then allowed to use it between the hours of ten o'clock in the evening until midnight. One unnamed ex-*Cichociemni* returning to Audley End House in recent years said that a dance evening was held, with a local band being brought in for the occasion.

The Polish staff and instructors mixed socially with the British off duty in Saffron Walden. The Forces Club was situated above a shop in King's Street, a five-minute walk away from Audley End. The room, which spread above two shops, was set up as a Toc H Club, an organisation founded by Revd Philip Thomas Byard 'Tubby' Clayton in the First World War. Toc H derives from Talbot House in Poperinge, a soldiers' club behind the lines in Flanders. In the army the signallers' code of the time for the letters 'TH' was 'Toc H'. The Toc H members were often disabled or ex-servicemen acting as Home Defence. They would light a candle to promote peace in the world. This small light gave rise to the disparaging term, 'dim as a Toc H lamp'. The Forces Club was open to both Poles and British at the same time. It was common for them to sit together to write letters to families at home. Many of the Poles did not know if the loved ones that they had left behind in Poland were still alive. Tony Currie knew Saffron Walden well, regularly visiting a café in the town. However, he felt awkward when questioned by the locals, as he could not tell anyone what his duties were and why he was living at Audley End House. Unlike the instructors, the trainees, according to Bronisław Wawrzkowicz, were not allowed into Saffron Walden at all during their six-month course. Antoni Nosek also states that he did not see much of the countryside outside the grounds of the house.

As a boy, Roy Rodwell lived locally and saw many Poles in

uniform walking around Saffron Walden. He also came into contact a couple of times with Lieutenant-Colonel Kennedy. He remembers talking to him once when they heard a shot coming from the direction of Audley End House. Kennedy paused, raised a finger in expectancy of another to follow, and then exclaimed, 'Ah, he must have got it that time', as another shot, followed by a large explosion, was heard. Rodwell thought that Kennedy liked to collect military badges, and, incredibly, remembers him mentioning Frogmore Hall.

Saffron Walden town hall had dances three times a week and the Rose and Crown pub, by convention, was used by officers, with other ranks meeting at the Cross Keys. Intemperance seems to play a large role in the soldiers' recollections. It was well known that one British soldier went out with a married woman in Saffron Walden. Mr Howe once had to go into town and help him and his girlfriend. 'They were both very drunk,' Mr Howe recalled, 'and she was very ill'. The soldier used to ring from Saffron Walden for someone from the orderly room to come and fetch him; one night he had fallen out of a truck into a ditch. Howe, late one night, cycled into a recumbent cow near the Abbey Lane gate, describing it as a 'chastening experience for both of us, and a sobering one for me'. He goes on to state: 'I recall several Brits, I included, in full uniform, returning from a day's leave in London, took an unscheduled ducking when we overloaded the big work punt, by the road bridge, and it slowly but inexorably sank beneath the waves. The punt was mainly used when clearing weed from the river – especially the "back of beyond" on the far side of the road bridge.'[81]

The soldiers often had to go off site to have baths because of the scant washing facilities in the house, and a 'liberty truck' took them into Cambridge to the public baths and if they were lucky a quick pint in a public house.

Many of the Poles and the British shared a love of football. Second Lieutenant Kazimierz Zdaniewicz, although only 'passing through', spending a short six weeks' 'hurried training' at the house, remembers the football matches, and playing on the left wing (see photographs). A tennis court was located behind the large eighteenth-century cedar tree in the Parterre Garden, and photographs show soldiers playing volleyball, with a net strung up near the English Parterre. Other archive photographs appear to reveal a Sports Day in the West Park. There are pained expressions and laughter on the faces of a large group of soldiers who seem to be taking part in a 'slow bicycle race' on the front lawn. Sack races, wheelbarrow races and various athletic events were also photographed. Chalked lines are clearly marked out on the lawn and two large marquees are visible in front of the Mount Garden. Bizarrely, some of the women present, presumably FANYs, are dressed in Japanese kimonos, complete with fans. Another photograph shows a laughing Polish officer in full uniform, waist deep in the Parterre fountain.

Audley End remained an SOE training station until special operations were discontinued at the end of December 1944, operations having been transferred to newly liberated southern Italy, which provided shorter, but not always safer, routes to Poland. When Alfred Fensome left Station 43 for Germany after D-Day he said that the Poles were still in Essex, although the house was 'beginning to lose clarification'.

Polish instructors moved to the advanced HQ near the Adriatic coast at Monopoli, near Bari, and a training school at Ostuni. SOE utilised Bari and Brindisi airfields for shorter flights into Poland, the latter being adapted for larger aircraft. The HQ at Monopoli was known as Force 139, codename 'Punch', and was the administrative unit that organised operations in Central Europe under Lieutenant-Colonel Henry Threlfall. 'Punch' was the prefix used in telegrams covering Poland, Czechoslovakia and Hungary. It was from here that the Poles sent their agents to support the Warsaw Uprising in the summer of 1944, and it was also the jumping-off point for Operation Freston. At the end of 1943 Colonel Okulicki started to operate a training centre called 'Base 10' ME 46 'Impudent'. Later, as a brigadier-general, Okulicki became Commander-in-Chief of the *AK*. The training centre was located in the unfinished buildings of a sanatorium between Bari and Brindisi. The training, although shortened (there were no extra courses), had a similar character to that at STS 43. Force 399 was located at Bari and concentrated on flights to Yugoslavia.

The future possibility of using southern Europe for Polish operations had been considered back in 1942. Shortly before his death, and unbeknown to SOE, Sikorski had instructed General Anders to start to recruit Polish personnel for these bases.[82]

Tony Currie, Aleksander Ihnatowicz, Terry Roper-Caldbeck, Stanisław Stefan Raczkowski and other faces that had become familiar in the sleepy streets of Saffron Walden were moving on to the warmer climes of Italy. FANY personnel also embarked for service in Italy. Visitor to Station 43, Vera Long, was also posted to 'Punch'.

After his work as an SOE instructor, briefly at STS 43, Major John Oughton was posted to Europe for active SOE service, spending twenty-two months abroad. He was assigned for twelve months to 'Massingham', SOE's command in Algiers, run by Sir Douglas Dodds-Parker, responsible for the liberation of occupied Corsica and concerned with infiltration in southern France. Dodds-Parker described Oughton as 'an excellent officer and colleague in those heroic years'.[83] When a student had completed training and became operational, his personal history of training particulars was passed on to Oughton. He went on to Sicily, Italy and France. Reticent about his SOE work up until his death, Oughton was tasked with finding a safe beach and guarding King George VI while he swam in the waters off Algiers. In France in 1944, Major Oughton was seconded to the American Seventh Army, chasing the German forces up the Rhône valley, following the route Napoleon had taken to Paris. Shortly after the D-Day landings in northern France, the Allies were also landing in southern France, Oughton being the first British officer into Marseilles. At the end of the war Oughton had to follow up what had happened to agents in Europe, and was present at the unveiling of the SOE plaque at Beaulieu.

For other instructors, leaving Station 43 marked the end of their work with SOE. Captain Mack was kept on at Station 43 as an instructor, but left when he was required for Operation Market Garden in September 1944. He was captured and interned (for the third time), this time in Oflag IXA Spangenberg until liberation by the American Army on 4 May 1945. Mack states, 'After my registration with the British Red Cross, the Germans discovered that I was born in Berlin and a regular officer of the Polish Army. They took me away from the POW unit and tried to persuade me to collaborate with them. Of course I rejected such a degrading suggestion!' Lieutenant Aleksander Ihnatowicz also found himself in another country, parachuting into Italy in 1944.

Many dignitaries had visited Audley End House during its existence as a training school. Major Nosek states: 'We often had important visitors here. The most frequent was General Sikorski, Commander-in-Chief of the Polish Forces and Prime Minister. Our President Raczkiewicz used to visit us as well.'[84] Driver Fensome drove the commanders at Station 43 to SOE Headquarters in Baker Street on many occasions, especially when the station had visits from men in high places. Fensome maintained that he also drove some British officers at night to a house in Aspley Guise near Milton Keynes, where Rudolf Hess had been brought from Scotland. Other premises in Aspley Guise were used by the broadcasting research units of the Political Warfare Executive, who created propaganda programmes to broadcast to Germany and other occupied countries, including news transmissions intended for Polish agents in Poland and Germany.

General Sosnkowski, who succeeded Sikorski as Commander-in-Chief of Polish Forces, also visited Station 43, as Nosek remembers: 'He talked about Russian relationships with the Home Army. He predicted a persecution and he was quite right.'

FOUR

Special Duties Squadrons

THE TEMPSFORD TAXI SERVICE

In 1940, with resistance groups forming in Europe to fight the German occupation, two Special Duties (SD) Squadrons were formed in the RAF to offer support by dropping personnel and supplies. Supplies included weapons, money and transmitters dropped in hardy metal containers or by parachute. Throughout the war No. 138 and No. 161 Squadrons dropped agents and supplies to support clandestine operations. Before the birth of these squadrons, early operations flew from Stapleford Tawney in Essex, Stradishall in Suffolk and North Weald, where No. 419 Special Duties Flight was formed. The site of Stradishall airfield now incorporates HM Highpoint Prison and an MOD training area. Captain W.G. Cole, DFC, AE, was stationed at Stradishall and recalls Whitleys and Lysanders arriving in 1940. He states: 'The Whitleys and Lysanders were engaged solely in dropping agents throughout Europe. I was a sergeant pilot flying Wellingtons and one occasion had the privilege of dropping an agent in France, in the vicinity of Bordeaux.'

Flights to Poland and Czechoslovakia were the longest and most dangerous. Assisting the resistance in Poland meant a journey of 2,000 miles both ways over enemy territory in a single night between dusk and dawn; such operations were possible only in the course of long winter nights. The aircrews consisted of British, Polish, Canadians, Australians, New Zealanders and South Africans. Flight distances were often beyond the range of the normal Whitleys and Halifaxes, which were all that could be provided until American Liberators became available. The Consolidated Liberator III had four engines and a range of 2,500 miles at 220 mph, where the twin-engined Armstrong Whitworth Whitley V had a range of 1,940 miles at 210 mph. The Whitley was designed from the onset for bomber operations at night, but was overshadowed by rapid advance in aircraft design. Production of the aeroplane ceased in 1943. Losses to crews and agents were high and Whitleys were very unpopular. Group Captain Maurice Newnham, commander of Ringway Parachute School, describes them as 'difficult to get into, difficult to get out of, frightfully uncomfortable and horribly dangerous'.[1] Small wonder that the aeroplanes were known as 'coffins'.

The first flight to Poland was on 15 February 1941, when three Polish agents were dropped by a Whitley approximately 80 miles from the Polish border, destined for the Cracow (Kraków) region. It was reported that the flight had been extremely hazardous. All three couriers reached their reception point, with one man returning to London in 1942 via Lisbon.

Special Duty flights began at Newmarket Heath in the summer of 1941. In a flat Fenland landscape and not far away from Audley End House, No. 138 Squadron utilised part of the Rowley Mile racecourse for its special operations. As with many airfields used during the Second World War, scant evidence of the airfield's existence remains. RAF Snailwell on the eastern peripheries of Newmarket was home to various squadrons, including No. 309 Polish Squadron. The Polish Air Force colours were secretly made by women in Poland and smuggled to England, and were received at Snailwell during a special parade held by the squadron on 1 July 1943.[2]

Geoffrey Matthews writes about the presence of the RAF in the sleepy Cambridgeshire town in 'Nocturne', reflecting how local residents would be innocent of the airfield's secret activities:

> Smoke from the municipal dump blows sleepily over
> Newmarket; racehorses on the heath are ridden down

STATION 43

To breathy paddocks, and the last lights are all covered.
Evening in Air Force blue leans at the end of the town.

A special operation to Poland at the beginning of November 1941 exemplified the vicious weather conditions that crazed operations. The Polish crew picked up their Halifax from Newmarket and took off from Linton-on-Ouse with three agents, including Lieutenant J. Piwnik ('Ponury'), who became a Polish field commander in the *AK* and sadly was killed in action in 1944. Ponury's exploits are dealt with in the next chapter. Freddie Clark states: 'Near the Polish border the hydraulic fluid froze and the undercarriage lowered. East of Poznań they found the reception committee waiting and parachuted onto it the three agents, six containers and two packages. The lowered undercarriage and flaps would not retract due to the hydraulic problems, this coupled with a strong headwind found them over Denmark at 04.15 hours, left with only 1½ hours of fuel.'[3] Successfully crash-landing in Sweden, the crew were interned and later returned to England.

Many flights had to be cancelled owing to bad weather, with aircraft having to abort to other airfields. Some flights experienced such bad winter conditions that there were many losses of aeroplanes and crews. In winter, freezing conditions were a major problem, with ice forming on wings and propellers.

In December 1941, No. 138 Squadron returned to RAF Stradishall. Mrs Pickering's husband served in No. 138 as a bomb aimer on SD flights. She states that when her husband asked what their Whitleys were carrying on one particular mission from Stradishall, the reply was the euphemistic 'Christmas puddings and blankets'. Mr Pickering also instructed and flew operations at Ringway in the early part of the war.

No. 161 Squadron was based at Newmarket in early 1942, but shortly set up shop at RAF Tempsford, 50 miles from London. An off-shoot from No. 138 Squadron, No. 161 provided valuable assistance to SOE and SIS.[4] No. 138 Squadron moved to Tempsford in March 1942 and remained there for three years, the rate of sorties increasing dramatically. Freddie

Clark describes the airfield: 'Tempsford was built on a swamp and was reported to be the foggiest and the boggiest airfield in Bomber Command. If your wheels wandered off the taxi-track they sunk up to their axles in mud.'[5] Tempsford was in a relatively isolated location, and to confuse enemy reconnaissance it was made to look as if it was disused. Odette Sansom and Peter Churchill flew from the airfield in what became known as the 'Tempsford taxi service'. Special operations ranged from the Arctic to Africa, comprising flights to nineteen countries. The insignia of the squadron at Tempsford was a released shackle with the motto 'Liberati'.[6]

By the time the *Cichociemni* training courses were up and running at Station 43 at the beginning of May 1942, operations to Poland, Czechoslovakia and Norway had ceased for the summer months because of the insufficient hours of darkness. At the beginning of October flights resumed, and there were several sorties to Poland dropping agents and equipment. Operation 'Wrench' in 1942 was a bombing raid destined for the Gestapo headquarters in Warsaw. Straight bombing raids were sometimes called 'standard load operations', and SD operations where agents were to be dropped were 'body operations'. Although this flight was standard load, it has a particular significance for me. Over Warsaw the captain on the Wrench mission decided that his bombing runs were more likely to cause damage to his fellow countrymen than to the Gestapo, so he chose an alternative target, the German airfield at Okęcie, Warsaw. Having been attacked by two Me 110 fighters off the Danish coast, the crew ditched within sight of the English coast and were rescued by the Sheringham lifeboat – *The Forester's Centenary*.[7] The crew included my grandfather, Henry. The Royal National Lifeboat Institution (RNLI) has a written report detailing the rescue. All six airmen were rescued, given hot baths, dry clothes and food, including a special issue of bacon. When they had got to the lifeboat station, Tempsford rang the boathouse to ask for the names of the crew.

Fifteen minutes later another question came through from [Tempsford], and the pilot officer had to be disturbed in his hot bath to answer it. In two hours and fifty-one minutes from the first call, the lifeboat had been launched; the airmen had been rescued, bathed, dressed, fed and returned to their station; the lifeboat had been out a second time to save the aeroplane, and was ready for another service.[8]

A total of 29 men, 74 packages and 119 containers were dropped in twenty-six operations to Poland in March 1943, including two non-moon operations, eight of which were missions to drop supplies and personnel, the remainder supply-only missions and one where the aircraft was lost.[9] No. 138 Squadron had six flights to Poland on 13/14 March, all of which were successful. Here are two examples of reports of operations in March. Operation 'Brick' dropped four men and six containers: 'In spite of the fact that the third man hesitated before jumping this operation was accomplished on 13 March and was 100% successful.'[10] Operation 'Attic' successfully dropped three men and six containers: 'The aircraft was in the target area for 25 minutes before the reception lights went on. This was probably due to the fact that a train was passing on the railway and the lights of the car were picked up on a road to the east. When these had disappeared the reception lights came on and the operation was a success.'[11] Major-General Klimecki wrote to Major-General Gubbins on 12 April to express his thanks to SOE for the flights to Poland in the 1942/3 season, which in Gubbins's opinion 'was the greatest reward which could ever be expected'.[12]

Twenty-three flights to Poland took place in September 1943. By this time it had become preferable for Polish agents to be flown by their own countrymen (on 9 and 10 September six sorties to Poland were completed using Polish crews), and three Polish crews were operating within No. 138 Squadron.[13] General Sikorski had thought that Polish airmen had the most right to fly over Poland. He maintained that an all-Polish affair using Liberators was the only suitable outfit for SOE Polish operations.[14] The lengths of these flights were almost beyond the compass of the Halifaxes, and the American four-engined bomber was increasingly favoured. However, the Air Ministry in 1943 expressed the view (in relation to the Polish demand) that there was no great advantage to the Liberator: the range and speed were similar to the Halifax; parachuting from Liberators had not been perfected and trials would have to be undertaken; and use of Liberators caused difficulties of maintenance and spares.[15]

In October 1943 No. 1586 Special Duties (SD) Flight was formed, an all-Polish flight comprising three American Liberators and three Halifaxes. This was known as the 'Co-operation with Home' Squadron. SOE also utilised Liberators at the USAAF airbase at Harrington.

On 21 February 1944 two supplementary stations were set up to relieve the demand for flights at Tempsford. These were at Mepal and Tuddenham. In total No. 138 Squadron flew well over 2,500 SD flights from Tempsford. A total of nearly 29,000 containers, over 1,100 agents and 10,000 packages were delivered to the field between April 1942 and the beginning of May 1945.[16]

Special operations to Poland were discontinued at the end of December 1944, operations having been transferred to southern Italy. The shortest route to Poland from Britain meant flying over Berlin, with its fierce anti-aircraft fire and night-fighters. Subsequently, operations moved to Tunis, and then Brindisi. Before the move there were many more flights to Poland, with No. 138 Squadron often running multiple operations in the same night. Although more successful, the new flights from southern Italy were still fraught with danger, as weather conditions were prone to be poor, especially over the Tatra Mountains.

ON THE BRINK OF UNCERTAINTY

Once training at Station 43 had been successfully completed and allegiances to the *AK* had been sworn, the Polish agents waited for the call to engage in active operations, often remaining in Essex, or at one of the Polish holding stations. This was a time of flux for the *Cichociemni*, when they had no idea of when they would be called upon.

The army drivers at Station 43 always drove the Polish agents to the airfields under a cloak of darkness. When Fensome took them to Newmarket Heath, he had to stop at an agreed location before the airfield. At this point a second driver took over to double the security. It appears that the close proximity of Debden airfield and Little Walden airfield (completed in 1943) to Station 43 was not exploited for SD flights.

Antoni Nosek states:

In early autumn, right through the winter and early spring on a moonlit night, an army lorry with tarpaulins down would arrive. Six men would come out in special jumpsuits worn over civilian suits, and with full equipment (which included a heavy money belt, two Colt pistols, ammunition, special knife, a poison tablet and some personal things). The men would quietly get into the lorry and would then be taken to Tempsford Aerodrome.[17]

Sue Ryder takes up the situation at the airfield on arrival:

The Bods [agents] were driven down to the airfield along the familiar roads of Hertfordshire, Cambridgeshire or Suffolk. The aircraft originally took off from a runway converted from one of the race courses at Newmarket, but later on they flew from Stradishall and Tempsford airfields. Each nationality had its own changing hut near the airfield and, for security reasons, was kept apart from the others. The FANYs also prepared sandwiches and flasks for the flight – sometimes an agent's last meal was from one of these 'hayboxes'.[18]

In the 'dressing huts' the agents were searched for any tell-tale objects that might have been overlooked: a tailored cigarette that had been manufactured in Britain; a good-luck note; labels on clothing. Sue Ryder states that the Polish agents displayed a marked sense of humour and cheerfulness in the tense hours before their mission.

RAF liaison officers were an integral part of the smooth running of SD operations. They provided a channel of information between the RAF and SOE and also between other airfields. Those liaison officers at Tempsford lived at Gaynes Hall, which they looked upon as their home. The officers were responsible for making sure the correct loads were put on each aircraft, so that the reception committee on the ground received what they were supposed to (packages were often identified by a number, and so their contents had to be checked).[19] These stores were packed by SOE at the aforementioned stations. Early stages saw the containers packed *ad hoc*, but later operations had supplies jointly packed by the Sixth Bureau and SOE and simplified into two standard sets – one designed for partisan activities and consisting of mainly arms, ammunition, grenades and a small amount of explosives, and the other for sabotage groups, which consisted mainly of explosives, time pencils and detonators. The content of these sets altered from time to time depending on the requirements of the *AK*. Special packages – for example, propaganda tracts – were packaged by the Poles and dispatched to the airfield. Considerable patience was required by the equipment officer of SOE regarding last-minute changes and changing Polish demands. The *AK* had squirrelled away weapons after the 1939 hostilities, and captured German arms by disarming soldiers and raiding arms warehouses. However, the demands from the Poles to SOE for more weapons were unrelenting. Tension existed between the Poles wanting an increased supply of weapons to use for their uprising and SOE's vision of a solely 'sabotage and diversionary campaign'. Drops were substantial but minimal for the Polish cravings.

Liaison officers gave the aircrews details concerning the drop zone, dropping heights, speed, signal letters and 'Rebecca', 'Eureka' and 'S-phone'.[20] To brief the crews successfully a liaison officer had to mix well with the crews to gain their confidence. 'It reflects greatly to the Liaison Officer's credit that the morale of the agents was so high when they went into their aircraft, as during dressing an agent can lose all his courage unless well handled.'[21] The final briefing of the agents at Station 43 or a holding station was undertaken by the Sixth Bureau, with SOE taking no part in the work. 'Indeed once the men left the holding stations they were completely lost to us, since they were invariably allotted new pseudonyms, unknown to us, before dispatch on operations.'[22]

Gibraltar Farm Barn to the east of Tempsford airfield was built to look like a normal farm building. Wooden slats were placed over a solid brick interior. This simple, innocuous barn was where the agents were supplied with the equipment they needed to survive on enemy soil. Today, there are trees planted outside the barn in thanks by Czechs, Norwegians and Poles. One plaque reads: 'Oak tree presented on behalf of the Polish resistance, 1988'. On 9 November 1943 Tempsford airfield was honoured by a visit from Their Majesties the King and Queen, who undertook a thorough inspection of the airfield, showing particular interest in the equipment of the agents being dispatched: 'e.g. "striptease clothing", methods of jumping, arms, rations &c &c'.[23] Gibraltar Farm Barn can be approached along a footpath, its dusty interior filled with wreaths. On a cold, winter day, walking alone along the track, banked on one side by hawthorn, elder and rosehip, one has a feeling of trepidation as the barn comes into view, standing out in the flat fields.

Flight Lieutenant Thomas C. Stevens spent five months at Tempsford, from March to August 1942. He was temporarily assigned to No. 138 Squadron while waiting to go on a radar course at Hooton Park, a large mansion in the Wirral, and also a gunnery course at Mona on Anglesey (where Stevens remembers pilots flying under the Menai Bridge until the RAF installed a steel curtain). As he had already passed his wireless training, it was thought that a stint at an operational unit would be good experience.

This bottleneck within the training system led Stevens, then Aircraftsman Second Class (AC2), to serve as an additional body on three SD flights under the supervision of senior crew members. Despite the short period he was at the airfield, he reveals how Tempsford was very different from other airfields in its security: Stevens said that he never saw the dispatch barn. No cameras were allowed on site, and entry in and out of the airfield was strictly controlled – one could not just wander down to the local pub. As at Station 43, it was impressed upon the RAF personnel never to say anything about the activities at Tempsford. Also, his logbook entries do not include the Tempsford missions, as no SD entries were allowed.

Stevens was acquainted with the farmer's house on the periphery of the airfield. The house was situated near the dispersal hangars and where the aircraft were hidden under trees. The farmer's wife dished out cocoa and 'dripping toast', which was far better than anything that could be got in the NAAFI, and very welcome, as Tempsford was invariably a horribly wet place. Even the squadron commander could be found there eating toast by a blazing fire.

Stevens says that Tempsford personnel were roughly split into thirds between the British, Czech and Polish crews. Although the Czechs and Poles had separate crews, the ground crews were formed of British personnel. One of the men who stood out to Stevens was Flying Officer, later Squadron Leader, Count Anderle, DFC, the longest-serving Czech pilot in No. 138 Squadron. Before his Halifax disappeared, among his missions he flew *NKVD* agents into Germany and Czechs into their homeland to re-establish links with the *AK* in 1942. Stevens said he owned a large white Alsatian dog, and wore a striking Air Force blue cloak with a silk lining. Stevens flew with Anderle on one occasion. Walking along the runway to the large bomber, he said to Stevens that he liked to fly a Halifax like a Spitfire. Stevens said this was not an exaggeration, recalling coming into land from a sharp turn.

Stevens recalls the procedure for take-off on an SD flight. The crew would have the Halifax on the runway all primed, with the engines fully running and ready to go with the crew in their positions. The operations were timed to the minute. A vehicle, usually a van, would arrive, often with curtained windows so that one could not see inside. The agents then got into the aircraft and quickly sat down in the back of the bomber, and the navigator would strap them in. The navigator was usually given the task of getting the agents ready for the flight and instructing them to leave the aircraft when over the drop zone. Later in the war the RAF created a 'dispatcher' role, or 'chucker-out'.

Once the weather conditions were confirmed as suitable, then there was no going back. If the weather was bad, British flight crews would be relieved at the reprieve from going on a mission. However, Stevens remembers the Poles arguing with Flying Control that they wanted to go despite the weather. On one such occasion a captain was persuaded to take off anyhow. Mr Stevens states that the ideal weather conditions for an SD operation were a full moon or the nights either side. The idea was to fly out quickly across the Channel at zero feet, the moonlight allowing the pilot to keep the aeroplane as low as possible. If successful, they would avoid detection from the first band of enemy radar. If the radar was pointing down, the aeroplane would be blotted out by the 'return off the water'. If not detected by the Germans, the Halifax would be able to roam relatively freely. George Iranek-Osmecki states: 'The flights took place when atmospheric conditions were favourable along the proposed line of flight, and in Poland as well. The *AK* would report, "Radiogram 159-KKP. Visibility good, no cloud. 770-15° Centigrade. Wind NE." And if the weather was favourable at the base, too, the engines were warmed up and off we went.'[24]

Similar to SOE training instructors, individual crew members knew only information relevant to their job in hand. Too much information was dangerous when under stress in enemy hands. For instance, only the navigator knew which country an SD flight was bound for or what the agents sitting in the cramped and dark interiors of the rear section of the aircraft looked like. Crew members were not privy to the operational codes given to their missions and were instructed not to engage the agents in conversation. Despite the close proximity to fellow emissaries and crew, it could be a lonely time for an agent. Major Nosek states:

There [at Tempsford] a four engine Halifax bomber waited for them. They climbed up and sat quietly on the floor. It was not long before they were in the air flying into the unknown. They realised that suddenly they were cut off from the security of the British Isles, from the comfort of Audley End House, and now exposed to powerful German security forces such as the Gestapo. They sat quietly on the floor for they could not speak to each other over the noise of the four engine bomber. Their heads were full of thoughts as they quietly accepted, 'whatever will be, will be'.[25]

Major Nosek describes the flight into occupied Europe:

The flight was long, six or seven hours, sometimes they heard strong anti-aircraft fire, but it did not bother them, because they were concentrating on adjusting themselves to this new role. They were possessed by a strong desire to do well and to accomplish everything that was expected of them, but more importantly, not to disappoint SOE, Audley End House training staff, General Sikorski and the army staff. They were ready to undertake any action, even if there was little chance of survival. When they were in prison, or Gestapo torture chambers, their thoughts went back to Audley End House, the place of birth. Pleasant memories gave them strength and the will to survive. That is why Audley End House is such a dear place for us.[26]

Very little conversation could be had in the aeroplanes because of the noise of the engines. All that was left was to wait for the signal to jump: the green light.

FIVE

On Dangerous Ground

THE GREEN LIGHT

When nearing the dropping zone, the captain of the aircraft told the agents to get ready and the wireless operator assisted the navigator in opening the hatch. Thomas Stevens says it was always dim in the aeroplane, but he remembers that on one occasion the green jump light lit up the very young face of a girl with blond hair. With the green light on, agents would fall through the hatch and parachute into uncertainty.

Antoni Nosek, codenamed 'Kajtuś', took off in a Halifax from Brindisi and parachuted into Poland on 4 May 1944, aged 27 years. He was carrying all the accoutrements of an agent, including two pistols and a large money belt strapped around his waist. He states that the noise inside the bomber was deafening and the agents sipped a little brandy that they had been given in small flasks. Once the red light came on, the agents got prepared as quickly as possible. Rubber parachute helmets were adjusted, and when the green light flashed they went through the hole in the bottom of the Halifax as quickly as possible to minimise a wide distribution of drops across the countryside. Once the agents were out, the aircraft circled again to drop containers. A poignant point for Nosek was watching the dark outline of the bomber get smaller as it circled away and headed for home.

At the beginning of the war when there were few, if any, radio links with SOE command, many agents had to be dropped 'blind' without reception committees waiting for them. These men and women attempted to link disparate and uncoordinated pockets of resistance. Mr Stevens states that some agents were still jumping from up to 10,000 feet without reception committees in the latter part of the war. When resistance networks began to formulate and wireless connection was established between resistance forces like the *AK* and SOE back in Britain, agents would hopefully be quickly picked up by a waiting party. They would have heard the aircraft's engines and then exchanged light codes by the use of torches. Natural features were used to enable flight crews to pinpoint where the waiting allies were, and the valley of the Vistula was a favourite location.

As discussed, bad weather and unforeseen circumstances did not make this a simple operation, and agents occasionally dropped miles from the prearranged coordinates, or the mission had to be aborted. Curfews were in place in Europe, and it was sometimes difficult for the *AK* to meet the agents, so they often had to fall back on training they had learnt in Scotland until contact was made. Some of the Polish agents had flown on aborted missions over half-a-dozen times.

Presumably because of ever-changing political and military circumstances in Poland, agents often required six to eight weeks of acclimatisation before they could safely move about the country. However, 'No case ever arose where a man was arrested during the critical period immediately after landing. This record can be partly attributed to the training organisation here and partly to the excellent reception methods in the field.'[1] Reception committees were arranged in two groups for any given moon period, and stood by alternately for four-day periods during the moon.

Reception committees were warned to get ready by a system of musical signals put out by the BBC. Dummy signals were put in to deceive German intelligence, who were trying to make sense of coded signals within traditional Polish folk music. Very short notice was required if an operation had to be aborted through bad weather. During the April moon of 1944, the peak period, ninety-three reception committees stood by and safely received stores from sixty-four aircraft. In May the same year, this rose to seventy-five successful operations.[2]

Despite the obvious dangers of the police and armies, Poland's topography aided safe reception. Kampinos Forest, now Kampinos National Park, south of the Vistula river, is very close to Warsaw and begins close to the boundaries of the city. It stretches 25 miles to the west and at its widest point stretches 12 miles north to south, an obvious place for resistance. Palmiry cemetery, within the forest, contains the graves of hundreds of partisans executed by the Nazis. There are large expanses of forest and marshes where *AK* groups were based where reception committees could be organised.

Once on the ground, wireless communication was of utmost importance. It is clear how much importance the Poles placed on training and developing wireless links. This was vital, not only in maintaining links from Warsaw to the Sixth Bureau, but for wireless operators in the field and the reception committees. The Polish long-range radio sets were designed at Letchworth and Stanmore. In 1943 the Poles used the BP-3 and AP-4 sets, and in 1944 the updated BP-5. The sets were very well designed and of high-quality performance. The technical superiority of the Poles in wireless development was beyond question. The input of SOE to the work being carried out at Stanmore was in the practical capacity of finding the premises and obtaining tools and in the provision of all parts and components.

All signals were sent using Morse code, and ciphers were used to disguise messages. Wireless operators like Jan Matysko from Station 43 faced almost certain death if they were caught with their set, and risked their lives every time they transmitted messages. As the losses among the wireless operators were high, the Poles had difficulty in maintaining their numbers in the field. Jan Matysko, alias 'Oskard', parachuted into Poland in later December 1944. He survived the war and died in Bydgoszcz in Poland in 1970.[3]

Wireless operators needed to be proficient and quick in sending messages in Morse code, and had to practise their W/T skills regularly during and after training to maintain a level of expertise that was paramount to survival in Nazi-occupied Europe. Training was carried out at Station 43 and in specific establishments, including Polmont Wireless Training Centre under the direction of Lieutenant-Colonel Bernacki. Again, SOE assisted in setting up the school and did some of the administration work there.

W/T liaison from England to the *AK* was always through Polish command, and the Poles took overall control of staffing and organisation of their W/T stations, and obtained frequencies for their own exclusive use. Organisation in the field was exceptional, and there was often triangular communication between area commanders, Warsaw GHQ and large reception committees. The Hippopotam reception committee in the Zamość region was known to acknowledge safe receipt of equipment and agents before the aircraft had returned to base.[4] During 1944 and 1945 up to 103 stations established communication, either with Britain or with the forward bases in Italy. Maintaining this large-scale communication network in Poland was exceptionally difficult when German intelligence was so dedicated to destroying it: 'The Germans were well aware they were sitting on an inferno of Underground activity. They went to extraordinary lengths in order to discover and eliminate Polish Underground W/T stations, and it is said that at one stage of the war they even employed street fiddlers with receiving sets concealed in their instruments, to detect and identify Polish transmitting stations in Warsaw.'[5] In the end the Polish stations were forced to relocate to rural areas, and remained under the protection of large numbers of troops while transmitting.

During the months before D-Day a homogeneous censorship was installed on all wireless transmissions from Britain, and all SOE national sections had to filter communication through the British for outgoing censorship. But the Poles were insistent that they wanted to maintain their own independence and security. Finally they took their Polish protests to the door of the Prime Minister, and it was eventually agreed that the Poles could retain their own ciphers, but SOE kept the right to censor all messages prior to the Poles' encryption.

After D-Day, SOE relaxed the strict wireless censorship ('John has a long moustache' was one of the coded signals used by the French Resistance to mobilise their forces once the Allies were landing on the Normandy beaches). However, they carried on with their censorship until the Uprising, when Soviet–Polish political strain made the British government intervene again. This time, however, only censorship after encryption of Polish messages was undertaken. This was insufficient for the Allied concern about maintaining relations with the Soviet Union. Consequently, pre-censorship was reinstated at the end of 1944 until the end of the war.

After a landing, hopefully without injury and with supply containers nearby, the initial concern for the parachutist and the reception committee was whether he or she had been seen from the ground and whether the enemy was nearby. Some of the hundreds of reception points in Poland were as short a distance as 2 miles from large German garrisons – from the serenity of an English country house in Essex on one day to the dangers of occupied Poland on the next. Peter Howe said that, from what the British soldiers at Audley End House heard, many of the Poles who were parachuted back into Poland did not last long, either killed in action, murdered or imprisoned by the Gestapo and the *NKVD*. They were also under threat from the local police; a very small proportion of the population who were hostile to their cause; and different resistance groups with different politics and affiliations. Capture often meant execution or being sent to a concentration camp. The book does not delve into detail of what some of the agents obviously went through at the hands of the Nazis, the Soviet secret police and the Polish security services. The depravity of torture and the concentration camps during the Second World War needs no description: their abject cruelty to human life is deservedly well known and documented. The head of the SS, Heinrich Himmler, was reported to state: '[Agents] should certainly die, but not before torture, indignity and an interrogation have drained from them the last shred of evidence which would lead to the arrest of others.'

As described in earlier chapters, despite these dangers there were never shortages of volunteers for *Cichociemni* work. The greatest danger to parachutists was at the moment of touchdown and during the journey to a point of contact. Tucholski states that agent 'Lewica' in 1943 sent a telegraph to Britain detailing the enemy's strategy for eliminating the threat of the parachutist. The German Army organised a net of police and motorised patrols, rapid sections of police, between four and six per region. As well as this, orders were given to the civilian population in the villages: never to put up a stranger for the night, under the threat of death; never to breach the curfew regulations, civilians being shot without looking at identification documents; no movement of motorised vehicles between six at night and four in the morning; any strangers in the vicinity or traces of activity on the land to be immediately reported; everyone to report to the German authorities if they were staying at a property not their own; and an order to the police to be especially vigilant. There were frequent restrictions on free movement and travel between towns and villages, house-to-house searches, identification checks. Any doubtful cases led to immediate arrest, a posting to a concentration camp or being shot on the spot.[6]

Many men trained by SOE who fell into the hands of the *NKVD* or Gestapo were executed or held prisoner for a long period of time. Some thought that the threat had been born in England within the walls of Audley End House itself. Alan Watts stated that statistically it was likely that German infiltrators were put through the SOE training course.[7] This was remarked on by another British soldier, but it is almost certain that German intelligence did not physically infiltrate Station 43, and most people spoken to on the matter dismiss this notion out of hand. Antoni Nosek thought that most men arriving at the house were from military units in Scotland, so any strangers would automatically be under suspicion. However, it is clear that the German Intelligence Service knew about Station 43. While being interrogated after capture in Warsaw, a *Cichociemni* agent was shown a photograph of

Audley End House by a Gestapo official and asked if he knew the place. He replied that he had no idea where it was. It is probable that the photograph was taken from the pre-war Baedeker guide. Although not naming the agent, Józef Garliński mentions this account in *Poland, SOE and the Allies*.[8]

As most of the Poles were dropped into Poland wearing civilian clothes, a discrepancy exists as to whether the *Cichociemni* were considered 'agents' or 'soldiers', and definitions blur, especially as each *Cichociemni* had an alias. It is worthwhile readdressing the issue in terms of uniform. For the purpose of this book, 'agent' and 'emissary' have been used (to differentiate between Regular Army personnel – for instance, those fighting under Anders – and those in a secret army – for example, the *AK*). *Cichociemni* parachuted into Europe in civilian attire, despite virtually all of them being army officers. The *AK* was organised on a strictly military basis and was a branch of the Regular Army. However, its members had to be hidden if they were to survive, carrying on a clandestine war rather than 'out in the open'. There were other 'civilian' sections of the army, for instance, the couriers, who worked in civilian clothes. Some even worked as soldiers in the German Army, feeding out information. Before *Cichociemni* parachutists were attached to an *AK* group, they stood a chance of avoiding capture if they were in the clothes of the civilian population. The job of supplying these was given to skilled Polish tailors like Julian Czarnecki at Station 43.

The *AK* was created out of necessity, and as such its members had to blend in with the local population and topography if they were to move around in an environment teeming with German soldiers and intelligence services, especially in the cities. They obviously avoided all distinguishing items of clothing or badges that could indicate they were part of the Underground Army. When clandestine warfare against the occupiers began, partisan detachments of the *AK* had already been fighting *en masse* using pre-war battledress from the Polish Army and also captured German uniforms that had been doctored to remove German badges. Some fought in no more than civilian clothes with differentiating badges. Certain *AK* detachments, however, operating in areas covered by Allied airdrops, wore British battledress.[9]

General homogeny in uniforms was eventually favoured for military and propaganda reasons – revealing to the population that there was a united front in resistance rather than bands of fragmented detachments. Consequently, in 1942 an order was issued that the red and white armband was to be worn by those going into battle and pre-war Polish Army distinctions were to be shown.

The *AK* also had to distinguish itself from other insurgent groups once the Uprising had begun. A red and white armband was worn on the sleeve and reflected the colours of the Polish flag. The Polish eagle badge was very important, and with great historical significance, nationally acknowledged, for the crowned white eagle was the emblem for the Republic of Poland. It was worn on different parts of the uniform in different units.

Having landed safely, Kajtuś was taken by a girl courier to Warsaw, where he was placed with a family in a block of flats for 'acclimatising' to life in occupied Poland. During this period he crossed the street in the centre of Warsaw, only to be told to halt by a Gestapo official. As his papers (made in Audley End House) were scrutinised, he expected the German to state, 'Made in England!', and was relieved when they let him go. During the German occupation of Poland all citizens had to have a *Kennkarte* on their person at all times, and papers were often checked. There were four types of *Kennkarte*, in different colours based on the Germans' desire for racial categorisation. Germans living in Poland who had been born in Germany were known as *Reichsdeutschen* and given one type of identity card; Germans who could prove that they had third-generation German ancestry received a different *Kennkarte* as *Volksdeutschen*. The non-Germans were obviously seen as lesser citizens and received separate identity cards: those non-Germans who could prove absence of Jewish ancestry were termed *Nichtdeutschen*; and the *Juden* were of Jewish or partly Jewish ancestry. In addition to a separate

Kennkarte, they were required to wear a yellow armband bearing the Star of David.

The type of *Kennkarte* one possessed determined different curfew hours, where one lived and the number of food coupons one received. Jews found in the 'Aryan District' of Warsaw were subject to execution, as it was forbidden for them to leave the Ghetto. Consequently, forgers at Briggens and Station 43 had a difficult task ahead of them and relied on intelligence in Poland to determine any changes in procedure or documentation if false *Kennkarten* were required. After a jump, documents on the person were scrupulously controlled and checked by the reception delegate of *Komenda Główna*. Tucholski reveals a telegram sent by General 'Bór' Komorowski: 'if the photograph (with left ear exposed) and personal details are sent in advance it allows us to achieve better results. Photographs on characteristically English paper attract attention.'[10]

The curfew meant that Nosek played bridge in the flat to pass the time. His bridge partner was the managing director of a civil engineering and building contracting company. Without questioning, he offered Nosek a job in his company. A short time afterwards Nosek was arrested by the Gestapo in Cracow on the way to an Underground meeting and taken to the notorious Monteluppi prison. His genuine papers were checked, and after the Gestapo had contacted the managing director, they released him. However, so few people were released from Monteluppi that Nosek had trouble convincing friends in the Underground that he had not done a deal with the Nazis. Nosek remained active with the *AK*, but was arrested by the Soviets in 1945. He remained a prisoner for six weeks before he was eventually released. He received the *Krzyż Walecznych* medal (Cross of Valour, for valour and courage in battle) four times, and settled in Britain at the end of the war.

Jan Piwnik, alias 'Ponury' (which translates as 'Grim' or 'Gloomy'), was perhaps one of the most famous Underground fighters in Poland during the war. Along with two agents from Britain and a dozen agents already in Poland, SOE-trained

Ponury undertook a daring and successful raid on Pińsk prison on 18 January 1943. M.R.D. Foot describes the raid:

> Four of them – one dressed as an NCO in the SS – drove up to the main gate, talked the warder into letting them in, shot him, forced the inner gate, and met their comrades, who had come in by ladder over the back wall. Between them they found and killed the commandant, took the keys of the men's wing off his body, released over forty prisoners, and got away unscathed; taking with them another parachutist, Paczkowski ('Wania') and his two companions, whose rescue was the object of the raid.[11]

Sabotage action towards areas in the Eastern Front in Poland was codenamed *Wachlarz* and aimed at destroying the Third Reich's industrial power and infiltrating its lines at the rear of its front, and also stopping any possible Soviet incursions into the Polish border. *Wachlarz*, or 'Fan', command posts were assigned to SOE-trained *Cichociemni* and worked from August 1941 to March 1943. 'Fan' operatives also organised operations outside Poland's borders. 'Fan' commander Ponury operated in the Świętokrzyskie Mountains in the summer of 1943 and had 300 soldiers. They had to avoid German dragnet operations, and consequently moved around constantly.[12]

Agents from Audley End were being trained to fight with these groups, known as 'Ponury's Partisans'. Waldemar Szwiec, alias 'Robot', was born in Chicago in 1915, is almost certainly the Polish soldier pictured on a motorbike outside the stables at Audley End. He flew from Tempsford on Operation 'Hammer' at the beginning of October 1942, along with three other men, having completed training at Station 43 in August 1942. As for most *Cichociemni*, his journey before eventually arriving at an SOE training school had been a difficult one. He fought in an artillery battery in 1939 in Poland in the defence of Warsaw and was imprisoned by the Germans. He escaped to Hungary, France and Gibraltar, and from October 1940 was in Britain. He eventually became a commander with *AK* Group No. 2 from

June 1943, part of Ponury's network. 'Robot' was killed while fighting the Germans on the night of 13/14 October 1943 in Wielka Wieś (Great Village).[13]

Second Lieutenant Michał Fijałka, alias 'Kawa' (coffee), 'Wieśniak' (peasant) and 'Sokół' (falcon), was born in 1915 in the local district of Brzozów in south-eastern Poland (see photograph). He served in the Fifth Parachute Battalion in Hungary and with a tank division in France before arriving in Great Britain and serving in the First Battalion of Engineers. He retrained in sabotage with the SOE, completed his training at Station 43 and took the *AK* oath on 7 September 1942. Parachuting into Poland on 1/2 October 1942, Fijałka was assigned to the *Wachlarz* network as an officer of the second section. He then served with the third section for the mission to Pińsk Prison. From March 1943 he fought with the *AK* in the region of Wołomin. He became a deputy commander organising groups of partisans and was wounded, but recovered to become the commander of the 'Sokół' Battalion and then commander of the First Battalion of the Tank Division. For a distinguished period serving his country during the war he received the Virtuti Militari V Class, the *Krzyż Walecznych* three times, the Gold Cross of Merit with Swords and the Silver Cross of Merit with Swords. He died on 20 September 1983 in Lublin.[14]

D-DAY AND THE BUILD-UP TO THE UPRISING

Reports in English concerning *Cichociemni* work with the *AK* in Poland are often brief. No doubt personnel files and memoirs exist in archives in Poland, and others reside (written in Polish) at the SPP, London. Consequently, this chapter deals with the work undertaken in the field by a small fraction of individual Poles, mostly those who had passed through STS 43. During the war, often only incomplete reports of sabotage and achievements filtered through to Baker Street. 'Otherwise there is little to report but large Polish projects and occasional reports of sabotage; the claims for 1941 and 1942 included 2,600 locomotives damaged, 75 trains derailed, 8 bridges destroyed, some 700 Germans killed. There was substance behind this – the Poles were certainly fighting – but no evidence for details will ever be available.'[15]

There is a danger in looking at the Underground offensive in Poland throughout the war in terms of percentages, losses and gains, and comparing achievements with other SOE country sections. This seems inappropriate when one looks at individual sacrifices and the general Allied stance to discourage premature risings in Poland in favour of one large offensive, initially planned to coincide with D-Day. When the rising eventually occurred, it had its potential impetus crushed before it could begin.

One of the Soviet Union's grievances against Poland was provocative. In 1943 the Soviet Command thought that the Polish Government 'was tending to discourage active resistance in Poland'.[16] The British Government explained that the general policy in other Allied governments was to implement an organised large-scale resistance. However, they were concerned that Stalin should receive documented proof of overt action by the Poles. Soviet Foreign Minister Molotov's reply was acerbic and directed at the Polish Secret Broadcasting Station, Świt. Molotov stated that Świt's 'attitude to USSR had sometimes been no less hostile than Goebbels's own'.[17] Henceforth, Sikorski ordered that Świt's broadcasts concentrated on anti-German propaganda. This is just one example of the political wrangles between the Polish and Soviet governments. The Foreign Office, SHAEF (Supreme Headquarters of the Allied Expeditionary Force) and SOE were all too aware of the disaffection between Poland and the USSR, a distrust that ran like a seam of iron ore through their histories.

The Poles *were* certainly in a state of preparedness to rise and were doing all they could to maintain readiness to assist with D-Day operations in the West. However, general cooperation with Soviet strategy in the East was unlikely. A report dated 26 May 1944 revealed that the *AK* comprised around 6,500 platoons, each platoon consisting of up to fifty members at full strength subsumed within the Polish landscape. The total potential strength was estimated at between 250,000 and 300,000 men, 40 per cent of whom were armed.[18] Men, women and children of all ages were active in the Resistance. Older men and women, not fit to fight, engaged in industrial sabotage; school boys and girls participated in minor sabotage and in the distribution of the Underground press.[19]

An interesting piece of intelligence reveals the activities in the Warsaw District in the previous year, in February and March 1943. 'Sixty-nine German casualties were reported, mostly from Warsaw city, which were ascribed to the Polish Underground Army and the Communists and in addition an unspecified number of Polish collaborators had been murdered.' The economic situation in Poland had deteriorated steadily and agricultural produce was difficult to find owing to 'bandits' 'who set fire to and plundered food stores, dairies and barns and raided livestock . . . the bulk of the population's food was purchased through the black-market'.[20] Other reports for August activity in Poland state that 'the execution of particularly objectionable Germans and of Polish traitors continued . . . two SOE students were killed in a clash with the Gestapo . . . two special groups of saboteurs destroyed projecting apparatus and German propaganda films in four Warsaw cinemas . . . eleven Gestapo agents were executed in the Silesian and Cracow coal basins during August'.[21]

Soviet infiltration into the city by parachute was also mentioned as being frequent. These men were dropped to undertake sabotage, arson and attacks on transport. To avoid reprisals, the Poles very seldom took part in their activities. However, Stalin stated that the general inaction of the Poles was anti-Communist and wanted his *NKVD* agents to speed-up an uprising.

The Soviets were often as much of a threat to the lives of the *Cichociemni* as the Germans. The main charge made by the *NKVD* against the *Cichociemni* was that the Polish Underground had been planning armed action against it, even though the Red

Army had invaded Poland and shared out its territory with Hitler in 1939. It is conceivable that British politicians, including Foreign Secretary Anthony Eden, underestimated the threat posed by the Soviet Union. Moreover, it was played down because the Soviets were vitally important in crushing a German victory. One cannot escape the irony that No. 138 Squadron at Tempsford was engaged in dropping *NKVD* agents into Europe and that these agents could be flown by Polish aircrews. Under the general operational code 'Pickaxe', agents were dispatched from the USSR to Britain, and then, having been trained by SOE, were dispatched on operations in Europe. Freddie Clark details the parachuting of three *NKVD* agents into France. Flown on their mission by Flying Officer L.M. Anderle, the agents in question had arrived in Scotland by a Soviet ship and were given parachute training at Ringway.[22] A Polish pilot was assigned to drop into Czechoslovakia two *NKVD* agents who had originally arrived on the same ship. The mission was aborted.[23] Four Soviet agents were dropped into Austria in Operation 'Sodawater' on 25 February 1943.[24] This operation was also flown by a Polish crew. Two months later, to the day, Stalin broke off all relations with the Polish Government in London.

While sabotage activities continued, there were growing concerns for a coordinated effort before D-Day by SOE sabotage in Hungary, Czechoslovakia and Poland, in which *Cichociemni* leaders would be at the forefront. The aim was to prevent the movement of German reinforcements from the Russian Front by intensified sabotage, particularly on the railways in Central Europe. Plans were also drawn up in anticipation of the unlikely event of a voluntary German withdrawal from Hungary, Czechoslovakia and Poland. Resistance groups were to be instructed to take the maximum toll of the enemy.[25] However, there was a marked awareness that any Underground action could have severe reprisals. The frustrating disparity of immediate action weighed against severe reprisals by the Germans was felt in the earliest days of the organisation of the Polish secret army,

In dealing with all classes of Polish organisations . . . all activity must, for the present, remain 'insatiable'. We have discussed, at some length, with both the Polish VI Bureau and the Kot organisation, the possibility of some specific acts of sabotage. It has been made quite clear that the price of blowing up a bridge, for instance, which will take no more than two or three days to repair, is inevitably anything between 50 and 1,000 men's lives as the Germans resort to wholesale arrest and execution as a deterrent measure.

As a result of this the Poles, for the present, will not undertake any activities which can be attributed to them, though the programme of petty sabotage continues unabated.[26]

The coordination and timing of combined action were vital. Discussions were held throughout 1943 between the Foreign Office, SHAEF, the Polish Government and SOE, including Generals Gubbins and Sosnkowski, on the subject of an eventual Polish offensive for Operation 'Overlord'. Decisive action came in the form of Operation 'Tempest'. Tempest began in February 1944 with AK action against the retreating Germans and sabotage concentrating on lines of communication. Once the Red Army had begun its push, the operation was instigated, involving pitched battles of the amalgamated Infantry Division of the AK and columns of German divisions. It was agreed that cooperation would be set up with the Red Army, but this temporary alliance was quickly aborted by Stalin.

Major-General Stanisław Tatar, 'Tabor', the Director of Military Operations (DMO) of the AK, was brought out of Poland by Dakota in April 1944 and provided SOE with details of the structure of AK appertaining to cohesive Allied action. He revealed that the AK was divided into two parts: the one, 'conspiratorial', concentrating on the general insurrection, against the Germans; the other focused on continuing operations against the Germans. This second part was itself divided into two parts: the partisan army, and forces devoted entirely to sabotage, diversion and anti-reprisal.[27] Highly organised, the AK ordered that no opportunist killings should take place. There was a definite order from the high command of the *AK* against the liquidation of any Germans. 'Only those Germans are eliminated whose death will cause the greatest impression on the enemy, most inconvenience and the greatest tactical discomfiture.'[28] The document goes on to reveal that the *AK* cut German communications in south-east Poland on both lines running east–west from Cracow through Przemyśl and from Bielsko to Lwów, and also the line from Łódź to Lwów, on 6 and 9 April 1944 under Operation 'Jula', severing German communications for 33 to 48 hours. Between 0150 hours and 0230 hours on 6 April the *AK* destroyed an important railway bridge near the village of Tryńcza, which resulted in three partisans being wounded in a fight with a guard on the bridge; track lines and a culvert were blown under a freight train, stopping trains from both directions.[29] This revealed that the *AK* could carry out orders that were given to it by a commander-in-chief (Sosnkowski) from Britain, and the operation be seen as a test of efficiency. Further disruption to the Germans was planned: 'Nevertheless, if General Sosnkowski orders an interruption of traffic along any given route, it has already been proved that the Secret Army will do their utmost to put his orders into effect regardless of losses.'[30]

As the invasion of Europe approached, further sabotage of railway lines was organised by Sosnkowski through special messages transmitted by the BBC in liaison with SHAEF from its headquarters in Southwick Park, Hampshire. There could be no doubt that the *AK* was highly effective and the largest, most organised secret army in Europe – an army primed and ready for instruction. This is not to say that the general consensus among the Poles in London was an uprising against the Germans. There was the opinion that action against the Germans would hinder defence against Russian action.

Allied correspondence continued in a tentative vein regarding Soviet involvement in Poland. A report was issued by the Combined Staff planners for the Polish Secret Army to receive equipment. A letter written on 15 September 1943, marked 'Most Secret', reveals:

The rejection of this plan is based primarily upon the unfavourable effect upon our relations with Russia or any large-scale equipment by the Polish Secret Army . . . it is for consideration whether we should not point out to the Poles the extent to which their present relations with Russia have contributed to the rejection of this plan. This might prove a contributory factor in persuading the Poles to come to some agreement with the Russians, which would simplify many of our problems.[31]

A directive to SOE for operations in Central Europe, unavailable as retained under Section 3(4) of the Public Records Act 1958, came with the covering note dated 21 October 1943, 'You will no doubt inform the Polish authorities of such portions of this document as you see fit.'[32]

By 1944 it was clear to SOE that the *AK* was suffering daily losses in maintaining a high degree of preparedness for D-Day in order that the now tried-and-tested attacks on communications could be carried out at the drop of a hat. Consequently, this level of readiness was cancelled and replaced by seven days' notice, and, under codes already set in place, the Poles were told to 'stand down'.[33]

The overall plan now was to interrupt all the principal east–west rail communications in Poland in eight sections. However, SHAEF appeared keen to state that Polish sabotage would not have a marked effect in aiding Overlord. Five days after D-Day, Major General H.R. Bull wrote a letter marked 'Top Secret' to Special Forces Headquarters. Once again, the conclusion was that such action would not have any appreciable effect on the German war effort and the continual small-scale sabotage was equally ineffectual regarding Overlord. Bull made the familiar conclusion that the Polish resistance at the time of D-Day was judged as a non-starter and was predicted to have little effect on German reinforcement lines to counter the invasion.

Despite these views, it was requested that Poles be told that 'their plan is receiving the favourable consideration of SHAEF.

In the meantime, detailed planning may continue between SOE and the Poles.'[34] It appears that the Combined Chiefs of Staff generally requested the Polish Underground to confine itself to sabotage and diversion. However, the political crisis intensified as the advance of the Red Army approached areas containing a Polish population, the worry being that the *AK* would be overrun by the advance without having initiated an attack against the Germans.

Allied High Command concluded that, despite Soviet–Polish political concerns, the *AK* should be used to aid the Red Army campaign, once its main offensive had been launched, as the Polish force was thought by some to be too divorced from operations in Western Europe. Major-General Bull thought that it was doubtful whether the Red Army and *AK* would act in concert, so that any coordination was set to be under the orders of the British Chiefs of Staff.[35] Also, back in May, it was agreed that 'The Chiefs of Staff further decided that no increased assistance was to be given to the Poles, thus ruling out the possibility of arming them for a general rising. They recommended that the timing of a general rising should be left to the Poles . . .'.[36]

However, when the rising began, the Allies in the West knew that they had to support it with supplies, in accordance with general support given to as many resistance groups in Europe as possible.

Soviet–Polish relations came to a dreadful point when the Uprising, or Battle of Warsaw, finally began on 1 August 1944. The Allies made efforts to supply Warsaw from Brindisi in Italy, and suffered terrible losses. Between 13 and 16 September, seventy-nine planes were sent, fifteen were lost and most of the rest were damaged. Fifteen out of sixteen Polish Halifax crews flying out of Italy had been shot down.[37] During the latter part of Bronisław Wawrzkowicz's time at Station 43, the stables were being used to pack containers to aid the ill-fated rising.

After pressure to allow the use of Soviet-controlled airfields, the Americans sent over 100 bombers, but little of what they carried reached the besieged *AK*. The flights were then stopped to avoid any more losses. The Germans and renegade Red Army soldiers proceeded to raze Warsaw to the ground, despite a tardy attack by the Soviet forces east of the Vistula. The Germans bombed the city from the air unchallenged, and then began house-to-house murdering and burning. They poured poison gas down manholes into the sewers where the Poles were trying to evade the Germans.

Surrender after sixty-three days of bitter fighting came at the beginning of October, with Warsaw almost completely destroyed and 200,000 civilians dead. Without the support of the Soviets the *AK* could not achieve its great victory, and the event fractured the *AK*'s resistance in Poland. The Uprising ended in the defeat of the *AK* and complete political collapse of the Government-in-Exile. One Polish woman living in this country told me that her parents had been active members of the *AK*. Her mother had been a fully trained nurse at the age of 16. Her mother's entire family was killed in the bombing. She was the only one to survive, as she was taking part in the fighting and hiding in the sewers at the time. The Red Army looked on as Warsaw was wiped out, *tabula rasa*.

When the Soviet leaders and *NKVD* ranks caught up with the advance into Poland, *Cichociemni* soldiers were arrested and never seen again. The threat the Soviets posed to the Polish agent appears also to have been affected by whereabouts in occupied Poland the agent was, territory being a major issue between Stalin and the Polish Government-in-Exile. M.R.D. Foot states, 'A few other parachutists, trained by SOE and dropped by the RAF, found their way into north-eastern Poland – lands far behind the lines the Germans held on the eastern front in an area that was regarded in Moscow as Soviet territory, because it lay east of the German–Russian border fixed by the treaty of friendship of 28 September 1939.'[38] There were threats in Poland from Polish security forces as well. Close friend of Antoni Nosek, Mieczysław Szczepański, 'Dębina', was killed by Polish security under Soviet Communist influence in Lublin Prison in September 1945.

SOE-trained *Cichociemni* from STS 43 were already well

established in Poland in 1944, and SOE stepped up its missions to Poland in the days preceding the Uprising. Bogusław Ryszard Wolniak was flown into Poland in July 1944. He joined the *AK*'s central headquarters and was taken prisoner by the Germans, but survived the war.[39] One can make out the blurred north wing of Audley End House behind him in the small photograph that accompanies all listed agents in Jędrzej Tucholski's *Cichociemni*. Wolniak was one of four passengers on the Dakota transport aircraft that took off from Brindisi to Poland on Operation Wildhorn III, detailed earlier, to retrieve the secrets of the V-2 rocket. Rather than the agents parachuting from the aircraft, the Dakota landed near the Vistula. Wolniak and three other agents left for their designated missions, to be replaced by five new passengers, complete with parts of the V-2 and the smuggled reports.

Cichociemni were in the forefront of the fierce fighting in Warsaw itself, and the last agents parachuting into Poland did so after the Uprising had begun. Station 43 instructor Stanisław Stefan Raczkowski (seen in a photograph taken inside Audley End House) parachuted into Poland on 8 April 1944. He was an officer with the *AK* in the mountainous region of Kielce, south of Warsaw. He was killed in a confrontation with the Germans in Suchedniowo on 29 July 1944 while travelling to take command of II Battalion.[40]

Tadeusz Starzyński, the German Affairs specialist at Audley End, also jumped on 8 September 1944, at the age of 41. He was tasked with joining Department '997' Counter-Espionage and Security, at the central command of the *AK*. He became deputy chief of the section. He died in Warsaw in 1970.[41]

At 42 years old, Adam Piotr Mackus, Conspiracy and Tactics expert, and commander of Station 43's Underground Warfare course, jumped on 22 November 1944, in Operation 'Kazik I', a special operation for the Sixth Bureau. He survived the war, emigrating to Britain in 1946.[42] Mackus parachuted at 6,000 feet from a Liberator with supplies and five other agents, but one of the packages fouled the landing skid beneath the tail and was still there when the aircraft safely landed.[43]

Jan Benedykt Różycki took the *AK* oath on 12 September 1944 and parachuted into Poland on 16/17 October 1944. He was assigned to the Piotrków region as a commander.[44] Zdzisław Sroczyński, alias 'Kompressor', jumped with Jan Matysko into Poland in late December. Sroczyński was dropped to work with the Komenda Główna, the General Command of *AK*, and was a temporary cadet officer instructor of I Battalion.[45] Sharing a fate of many parachutists, Wacław Kobyliński was unable to serve with the *AK* in view of an injury he sustained to his leg on jumping. After the war he lived in the USA.[46]

There is still debate regarding how much SOE and the Western Allies could help the Poles in their struggle to free their homeland of the German occupation throughout the war, as well as how much they all knew about the timing of the Uprising and their conformity to Stalin's wishes. SOE, the War Office, British politicians and the American Government often pulled in different directions, sometimes in vituperative exchanges. Indeed, it must be stressed that the information above concerning the build-up to the Uprising and D-Day predominantly comes from the angle of fragmented SOE communiqués. The only feasible way to supply the *AK* with personnel and supplies was by air, and this created many losses to aircrews and agents, particularly acute during the Uprising. Poland was a major user of SOE's resources, but this had to remain justified as long as Poland was occupied. Air support was intrinsic to the success of a rising, and SOE was all for it. Approval had also been sought to fly the Polish Parachute Brigade and a large quantity of supplies to Poland, utilising 120 aircraft, but this obviously did not come to fruition.[47]

Operation 'Bardsea' was another let-down for the Poles. SOE monopolised many agents from different national sections to work in France as part of Overlord. Bardsea was set to use Polish agents drawn from Monica. Bardsea troops were highly skilled and intensively trained paratroopers for use in operations just behind the bridgeheads on D-Day, mirroring the established three-man 'Jedburgh' teams already in place in France. The

Bardsea teams were then meant to work in close contact with the Special Air Service (SAS). The centre of Bardsea operations in May 1943 was Inchmery House, and then Erlestoke Park in Wiltshire. The Bardsea team totalled 120 French-speaking Poles undertaking continuous training, which kept them at the peak of fitness and expertise. They utilised different holding stations, including Warnham Court, where Leo Marks visited them. Many sources feel that these élite troops were not utilised to their full potential. Leo Marks puts it in stronger terms, to say the least, blaming the ineffectuality on internal fighting within the Polish authorities, calling it a complete waste of a 'magnificent bunch'.[48] Their frustration must have been felt when they were denied the chance to assist in D-Day or in the Uprising in Warsaw, as it was thought to be logistically impossible. The strength of the Bardsea teams was never really put to the test, and when the invasion happened at a rapid rate the Polish teams never really got off the ground.

The schisms and disaffection between the different resistance units in Poland have already been touched upon. The *AL* and the *NSZ* were in constant conflict, as they effectively embodied the extreme left and extreme right of the Polish nation. At the time of the Uprising the *NSZ*, *AL* and *AK* were by no means a homogeneous army. The *NSZ* and *AL* were being blamed for provoking German repression by their strategy of immediate insurrection and assassination rather than a build-up to an effective onslaught against the occupiers. As discussed, it was vitally important to assess what was actually happening in an occupied country before a mission was undertaken, and agents had to memorise a wealth of information when they took the Briefing course.

British liaison with the *émigré* governments was not always a smooth process, as Field Marshal Lord Wilson of Libya maintains in the conclusion to the aforementioned Gubbins lecture: 'We appear to forget that their [*émigré* government] information fails in many cases to be objective, and you may get distinct political bias in that information which may lead you into pitfalls.'[49]

The truth about what was going on in Poland was often concealed by a cloak of Nazi and Soviet 'agitprop' and Polish–Soviet friction. It was also difficult to maintain contact with the *AK* in Warsaw, especially after 1 August 1944. With this in mind, Operation Freston was conceived by SOE in 1944 to assess the situation in Poland at the time of the Warsaw Uprising.

Polish missions generally consisted of six agents, but for Freston it was a multinational team of five: Lieutenant-Colonel Duane T. 'Marko' Hudson, also known as Bill, a South African who led the raid having formerly undertaken the sabotaging of shipping in Belgrade; Major P.R.C. Solly-Flood from Yugoslavia, Major P. Kemp from Albania, Sergeant-Major D. Galbraith and a familiar face from Station 43, Tony Currie, 'The Prof', 32-year-old radio-communications expert Antoni Nikodem Pospieszalski, who could interpret. Kemp later wrote about his SOE experiences in *No Colours or Crest* and *The Thorns of Memory*.

At the time when Audley End House's importance as a training centre was winding down, Currie, along with other colleagues, including Lieutenant-Colonel Roper-Caldbeck, was sent to southern Italy (Roper-Caldbeck also served as the commanding officer at SOE's purpose-built Camp X in Canada).

The Freston agents flew from Bari in a Liberator, on their fourth attempt owing to bad weather, and landed near Cracow on 26/27 December 1944. They were eventually interned by the Soviets in the middle of January after narrowly avoiding contact with the Germans. For the interested, Jeff Bines has written comprehensively on Freston in his book *Operation Freston: The British Military Mission to Poland, 1944*. Bines states, 'Many attempts were made by the exiled Polish Government to persuade Churchill to send a team, and eventually he agreed.' He goes on to say:

On the 12th January 1945, the Soviets launched an offensive which drove the Germans some distance back into Poland. On the 18th of that month London issued instructions for the British Mission to make their way to the nearest Soviet command. This they did and were promptly thrown into Częstochowa prison. They remained interned until the final day of the Yalta Conference on 12th February, finally making it back to Britain via Moscow, Baku (on the Caspian Sea) and the Near East.[50]

It marked SOE's last, albeit unsuccessful, work for Poland. Bines states that Currie considered himself lucky to be dropped into Poland wearing a British Army uniform. Most SOE operatives during Overlord were also in uniform. However, in some cases this did not prevent the Germans executing captured parties.

COURIERS

Couriers undertook an oath similar to the *Cichociemni*'s and were subject to the Underground *Delegatura* authority, a political body headed by a delegate appointed by London.[51] This highlights the difference between the *Cichociemni* and the couriers, as Tucholski explains: the difference between the 'kittens' (couriers) and *Cichociemni* were as follows: both groups were volunteers, but the *Cichociemni* had to swear the oath that was compulsory for soldiers of the *AK*, on whose behalf they were to fight. Kittens were given the name after the name of the Minister of Internal Affairs Stanisław Kot (cat). For security in telegrams and in Underground parlance, couriers were termed as 'burger' or 'politic' and *Cichociemni* as 'birds' or 'birdies'.[52] Some of the couriers completed full sabotage training, and after completing their political missions applied for transfer to the Underground Army.

Couriers worked within Warsaw itself, between Warsaw and other towns, from Poland to other countries and finally, from Poland to the Government-in-Exile in England. The Courier Communication Department contained another section dealing with international communications. This was concerned with keeping in contact with authorities in exile. Postal and courier routes went from Warsaw to London via nearly the whole of Europe, including Hungary, Italy, Switzerland, Germany, France, Spain, Sweden and Turkey; and also North Africa.[53] The Poles were keen to establish lines of overland communication with Poland, often by courier, in the Balkans and in other countries, including Greece. A plan to create a safe passage between Romania and Istanbul was curtailed when a Polish woman who supplied documents was suspected of having worked with the Russians (Soviets).[54] SOE also employed the Swiss diplomatic bag to allow Polish mail to travel between Bucharest and Istanbul.

Couriers were an important part of maintaining a flow of intelligence for the *AK* and Government-in-Exile. Thirty-four SOE-trained couriers were dropped into Poland by parachute. Second Lieutenant Kazimierz Zdaniewicz, 85 years old in 2003, was born in Kołomyja in eastern Poland, which is now in Ukraine. During the war he was in Anders's Army, and found himself working on radar in Baghdad. Military Command found out that Zdaniewicz could speak fluent Russian and so set him aside for special work. He was sent by the military to England and arrived at Station 43 in March 1943 at the age of 25. He spent six weeks of intensive training ready for his role as a political courier. He recalls brushing up his Russian language skills, wireless training, a little PT. The course naturally culminated in forming a legend for himself under the alias Vasyl Tkachuk.

Having completed his training, he was destined for work in the USSR. He was taken directly from Station 43 in a lorry driven by an army driver to Marsworth airfield in Buckinghamshire, where a Dakota transport aeroplane was waiting. He flew to Gibraltar, Alexandria and Cairo, and eventually arrived in Tehran after three days.

Zdaniewicz's journey took time and was treacherous. He travelled by train from Tehran to Meshed in Persia (Iran); on to Mary in Turkmenistan near the Köpetdag Mountains; to Charcdz, then eventually to the Russian border. Crossing borders was particularly tricky. He was told at one border to be careful about stepping on mines at border sections where there were gaps in the barbed wire. Adhering to this advice, he made it safely into Russia. Working as a courier, he carried important documents to and from the Polish Embassy. All diplomatic post was opened by the *NKVD*, so a courier was chosen rather than a diplomat, as diplomats were always stopped. After one illicit delivery, he was told to wait at the Embassy to take a package back to his contacts. To this day he has no idea what information was contained in the packages.

The second time he worked as a courier he was caught by the *NKVD*, who asked him who he was. He replied that he was in the Polish Army. They replied, 'What Polish Army?', and, knowing what answer they wanted, he replied 'Berling's Army', and they let him go on his way. General Zygmunt Berling's Army was formed in the Soviet Union. It originally comprised Poles who had been forcibly subsumed into the army when they were caught after the Germans had been defeated at Stalingrad. It was under Soviet control, unlike Anders's Army, which managed to break free from Stalin's shackles.

In September 1942 Zdaniewicz was stopped a second time by the *NKVD* and was arrested when they found his pistol. He was sentenced to fifteen years' hard labour in work camps and collective farms in Russia, where he was to be given a meagre portion of bread and onions per day.

He was sent by rail to Turkestan and from here by boat along the Amu-Darya to undertake forced labour. Zdaniewicz said he was one of the hundred people who survived out of 600 labourers. The dead were placed on the ice, so that by spring the corpses would sink under the water. If one got sick, the food ration was stopped and the ill would 'be sent to hospital', which was a euphemism for execution by a bullet in the head. He still suffers as a result of getting severe frostbite in his legs. Amazingly he escaped on 15 December 1943 and made it back to the Middle East. He has lived in Cambridge, England, for the last fifty-six years.

Sue Ryder shared a room at Brickendonbury with Polish courier Elżbieta Zawacka, alias 'Zo' and 'Zelma'. Trained by SOE at Station 43, she was the only woman to parachute back into

Poland. The work she undertook in occupied Europe, often in terrible adversity, is documented in Ryder's autobiography, *Child of my Love*. Zawacka jumped into Poland, aged 34, on 9 September 1943.[55] However, she had been operating in Poland before this and worked as an instructor of the Polish Women's Military Training Organisation before the war. She later escaped to England only to parachute back into her homeland. She describes taking a suitcase of dollars from Berlin to Silesia in 1942, having to jump from a moving train at night to avoid the Gestapo. Her sister was interrogated and a colleague arrested and beheaded in Katowice in the same year.[56] Under arduous conditions she and other couriers carried information intended for the Polish Commander-in-Chief in London. The information they carried was incredible in its diversity and included intelligence concerning U-boats in the Baltic, German troop movements, V-1 jets and V-2 rockets, Auschwitz, photographs for forged documents, escape routes, German industry, munitions factories, sabotage, information and plans of enemy aircraft and armour, the Jewish ghettos, cooperation with the Resistance in Hungary and Germany, extermination of Poles and Jews, particularly in the parts annexed by the Reich.[57]

Not all agents used an SD flight to get them directly into the country they were to operate in. Owing to problems in acquisition of aircraft and operating them on the peripheries of their maximum range, Czech and Polish couriers often had to travel long distances to keep in contact with their networks, taking overland routes through France, Germany and Austria. 'Sometimes members of the Unseen and Silent in Poland were sent back to Britain as couriers of the *AK* Commander-in-Chief. In this way they made the journey from London to Warsaw and then back again. The journey from Warsaw to London lasted a few weeks, or a few months, sometimes even a year, depending on the courier's luck.'[58]

Wanda Skwirut illustrates the remarkable work achieved by couriers. She also 'received' agents from STS 43, and eventually visited the house after the war. With the help of her son, Jerzy

Grochowski, who lives near Stansted, Essex, her story unfolds. Born in 1923, Wanda was an active member of the Polish Underground from 1941 onwards, and first joined the ZWZ, AK's precursor, as a courier. Although she was 18, she was a tiny slip of a girl, with hair down to her waist that she wore plaited in two long strands. She was very thin and very young looking, passing for a 14-year-old. This was advantageous, as she was able to pass through German checkpoints unsuspected of any nefarious activities. The ease with which she could move around Poland was exploited by the ZWZ and later the AK to the point where she became a fully paid regular soldier with rank and privileges. She became a liaison officer as well as a local courier, all the while maintaining the notional employment as a clerk.

During the early years of the war she carried oral messages and small packages, but by 1943 was taken into *Orbis*, the radio communications section of the AK's General Headquarters, which had been set up by the Polish High Command, to pass information and orders between Poland and London. Led by Captain Alexander Jedlinski, alias 'Franek', and located in the Forest of Kampinos, *Orbis* was a highly secret organisation whose achievements were not released into the public domain until the later 1980s.

Now a staff sergeant, Wanda was soon tasked with carrying documents that would invite immediate arrest and the ensuing consequences of Gestapo interrogation and death. She was also being used to meet and guide agents parachuting into Poland from England. In 1943 she met and fell in love with a *Cichociemni* captain who had been at Station 43 – she made a blouse from his SOE parachute. They were on the verge of becoming engaged when he was killed by the Germans.

After receiving one 'unseen and silent' parachutist in Kampinos Forest, Wanda and her party had to flee as the Germans were very close. In an effort to escape in the forest she took off her shoes so that she could run quickly. However, she caught her foot in between the large roots of a tree and fractured her ankle. She did not cry out, as to have done so would have meant death. Helped by the *Cichociemni* soldier, she managed to hobble to safety. She later said that afterwards her work was, for several months, much easier, as hobbling about on crutches and wearing a plaster cast seemed to put her above suspicion.

Cichociemni personnel and containers were brought to collection points, where couriers took them to their required destinations. Wanda distributed radio sets and ciphers to outlying stations around Warsaw. The sets and cipher books were contained in ordinary-looking suitcases, having been 'distressed' by SOE and dropped with the agents. Months before the Warsaw Uprising, Wanda had to distribute five suitcases.

One suitcase contained a complete transceiver, a Colt .45 automatic pistol with a loaded magazine and a pack of 200 cigarettes, weighing a total of 20lb – a lot to carry for a 'tiny girl' to carry about. On one occasion when she was taking the case to the centre of Warsaw by train, a man in the compartment she had just entered took her case so that he could help her by putting it on the rack above the seats. He immediately went very white, realising that it weighed far more than any clothes would. Very slowly and carefully he placed the case on the rack and sat down. When the train stopped at the next station, the man got up and left the carriage. Wanda thought about getting off the train and finding an alternative route into Warsaw, fearing the man was calling the Germans. Just as she was making these plans the man returned, carrying a single red rose in his hand, which he gravely presented to her. He told her that she was a brave girl and that if she was going into Warsaw then she should alight at the second station before the central terminus, as the Germans had set up a check and control point at the penultimate stop.

Wanda had many narrow escapes like this one. Railway workers hid her in the coal tender of a steam locomotive. The train was carrying part of a *Waffen SS* Panzer division across Poland, and she travelled in safety at the Germans' expense. On another occasion she found herself travelling in a carriage reserved for Germans. She had successfully delivered a radio set and its operator, who had just parachuted in from England, and was on the return journey from Cracow to

Warsaw. Inside the lining of her coat were several envelopes containing dispatches and reports. It was an extremely cold day in February and she stood perishing on a platform waiting for a train. Suddenly a large German soldier approached her and in excellent Polish told her that she could travel with them in their carriage as she looked dead with cold. The German carriages were all first class and heated. The soldier appeared surprised when she readily agreed. She sat with a whole crowd of German soldiers all the way from Cracow to Warsaw, a distance of nearly 140 miles. The Germans gave her bread and real coffee, the first she had drunk for over a year. They deposited her at Warsaw, where she made her way back to her unit in Kampinos Forest. The soldiers had protected her, as the Gestapo never checked the *Nur für Deutsche* carriages.

Wanda escaped another time from almost certain capture. Caught in an ambush, Wanda felt a German Army soldier catch hold of her pigtails, and shout to the others that he must get a car to take the girl away. A car arrived and the soldier drove Wanda away at speed, and amazingly to her freedom; the German soldier had been a *Cichociemni* agent in German uniform.

On 3 August 1944 Wanda passed unseen through the German lines that encircled Warsaw, carrying quartz tuning crystals and three situation reports from commanders outside the siege ring. She was tasked with swapping her crystals for some that were already in Warsaw, as there had been a mix-up. One set was bound for Warsaw to use in radio contact with England and the other set was to be kept back for use in Kampinos. Unfortunately the crystals that a courier had taken to Warsaw were the wrong set and Wanda volunteered to exchange them. In a short but treacherous journey, Wanda set off and walked down the road towards the centre of Warsaw, a distance of about 10 miles. At first the road was empty, but as she neared the orbital railway that surrounded the city she saw the German roadblocks. Putting on the tears, she approached the roadblock, where she was stopped by a German *Feldpolizei* corporal, who asked her where she was going. She replied that she had been at her aunt's but was going back to 'her mummy and daddy'. The corporal told her to be careful as there were 'bandits' everywhere and it was dangerous to be out in the open, but let her pass. Wanda decided to get off the main road and use the side streets, which took many hours of dodging enemy patrols and the odd burst of machine-gun fire. At one point she saw a house in which there were still some people staying, and she asked them the way to Wola, where the GHQ was supposed to be situated. They warned her that the Germans had started air raids and that it would be safer for her to stay until the danger had passed. When she was about to move again two hours later, her attention was drawn to a commotion in the garden, where she saw some men with the familiar red and white armbands of the *AK*, the people she wanted to contact. When their suspicion had passed, they escorted her under fire to the GHQ, where she delivered her dispatches and crystals. She had been on the road for almost ten hours and was under immense strain. Exhausted, finding a spare bed in the room where the runners and liaison officers slept, she fell into a deep sleep. She awoke suddenly to a tap on the shoulder. She looked up to see a tall, slim man of about 50 years old. He said, 'Thank you for what you have done. You're a very brave girl and will get something for this.' Wanda, still tired, replied: 'It is not the time for such nonsense. This is not what we are working for.' He smiled and ruffled her hair with his hand. He told her that she had to go back that night as they had the quartz crystals ready. They had information that the Germans were preparing to attack, and the Kampinos drop zones were immensely important. The *AK* had to contact England, only possible with the crystals that she had to take. She was later asked if she knew who the person was who had praised her efforts. Replying that she did not, she was informed that it was the Commander-in-Chief of the *AK*, General Tadeusz Komorowski. Komorowski, commonly known as 'Bór' (Forest) and 'Lawina', was appointed Sosnkowski's successor in winter 1944 (Bór was held captive at the time, and so the duties of C-in-C were divided between four parties, including the President of Poland).

The journey back to the forest was worse for Wanda. Leading two cipher clerks who were needed at Kampinos, she crawled across railway lines and escaped through Ukrainian, *Waffen SS* and Cossack lines. The Germans used the Cossacks as internal security troops, and they were very unpopular, to say the least. She was shot at by snipers but delivered the crystals and messages to Kampinos Forest just as dawn was breaking on 4 August.

'Franek' was waiting for her. For her bravery, Wanda received the *Krzysż Walecznych*, the Cross of Valour. She was the first woman to be awarded the cross in the Warsaw Uprising. The medal reads, '*Na Polu Chwały*', or 'On the field of glory', and is the equivalent of the British Military Cross. In England after the war, Wanda was also awarded the Partisan Cross '*Za Polskę, wolność i lud. Partyzantom 1939–1945* (For Poland, freedom and people. To the Parisans 1939–1945)', and the medal awarded to survivors of the Uprising.

Because of the nature of the work she undertook with the *AK*, dealing with documents detrimental to both armies, she was under sentence of death from the Soviets and the Germans. However, she evaded capture, but had to escape from Poland towards the end of the war, after the collapse of the Uprising. She managed to escape to the American lines and eventually settled in Huddersfield, England. When she visited Audley End House, some of the large tree roots in the grounds reminded her of Kampinos. Wanda died in November 2001. Veteran members of the *AK* buried her ashes in Warsaw Cemetery with full honours.

SIX

Audley End and the Post-War Years

Before the end of the war, Henry Seymour Neville began to consider the problem of Audley End's future. He consulted the National Trust's representative, James Lees-Milne, who recorded in his diary a visit to Audley End in June 1944 in the company of Lord and Lady Braybrooke. After some difficulty they gained entry to the house and had 'an excellent picnic luncheon'[1] at one of the garden temples. Lees-Milne kept a detailed war diary, revealing sometimes humorous insights into requisition. Visiting Tattershall Castle in Lincolnshire in 1942, he found the rooms filled with stacks of fossils: 'The whole place reeks of mothballs.'[2] When he visited Stoke Ferry Hall in Norfolk in 1944, he commented, 'The soldiery have just left – therefore the condition is deplorable.'[3]

SOE left Audley End House in 1944, as the centre of command was being set up in Italy. The wartime title of 'Station 43' was no more. However, Audley End House was not de-requisitioned until 1945, when the war was over. Despite minor damage to an exterior wall near the Bull Lodge (far more damage to this entrance has been caused by large delivery lorries in recent years than by military vehicles in the 1940s), and a broken stained-glass window from the chapel, which had been stored in a box in the stables, the house had suffered less damage from its wartime role than many other country houses. Other houses did not get off so lightly. 'At Greystoke Castle in Cumberland, Polish soldiers, as well as running an illicit still in an old lime kiln, did so much damage to the late-eighteenth-century Gothick wing that it had to be demolished after the war.'[4]

AUDLEY END AND THE POST-WAR YEARS

Many houses were pulled down owing to fire damage during the war, sometimes caused by the Army lighting open fires in formerly dormant hearths. Egginton Hall in Derbyshire was demolished in 1954 after the military had wrecked the interior. Interior damage was caused not so much by abject vandalism but in an attempt to make the place habitable, in particular by heating the premises.[5] When asked about their memories of Audley End House during the war, nearly every soldier said something on the lines of 'morale was excellent, but it was very cold'. However, although an open fire was lit in the orderly room (Nursery), Audley End did have serviceable boilers that were constantly stoked by the British soldiers – in some properties wooden fittings were taken down to use as fuel. The interior of Audley End during the war was not luxurious by any stretch of the imagination. The owners had stored valuable possessions and done their utmost to persuade the Office of Works to cover any panelling. It is small wonder that servicemen returning to Audley End hardly recognised the cold barracks where they had slept on mattresses on bare floorboards.

Ted Pretty said that ministry inspectors destroyed a lot of evidence from occupation by SOE in the 1950s and 1960s, particularly wall notices that were deemed irrelevant to conservation of the rooms. When he had first worked at the house in the early 1950s, all of the protecting boards that had been put up in the rooms had been taken away by the Army. Unable to touch the historic fabric within the house, the Army also had to fix wooden battens across the ceilings for the electric lighting. Evidence of this could be seen in the Coal Gallery that runs between the north and south wings on the second floor. Audley End had no electricity before the Army arrived, so perhaps this was a small return for the years of forced occupancy.

When the River Cam was drained, many spent, and 1,000 live, .303 cartridges, Sten-gun ammunition and other ordnance were found in the mud near the timber camp-shedding by the Stables Bridge, although a present contractor's advice for me to 'have a good poke about with a stick in the mud by the Stables Bridge' was not taken up.

STATION 43

The munitions were found in 1976, and the grenades were verbally reported by one source as being German stick-grenades. Ted Pretty describes finding the ordnance. He was overseeing the repairing of the 'cutwaters' that divide the flow of water under the Stables Bridge. The sluice gates had been opened and the level of the River Cam lowered to 9 inches so that the work could be undertaken. Digging down by one of the bridge's pillars, a labourer pulled from the mud a cylindrical object and washed it in the shallow water. Tossing the object up to one of the gardeners watching the work from the bridge, the labourer said, 'What do you think this is?' Ted said that by the time the device had landed on the bridge, not one gardener or Department of the Environment worker was in sight. The object turned out to be a dummy anti-tank rocket. Colchester Barracks were informed of the cache and took the ordnance away. When the Ice House was opened in the 1960s, large coils of barbed wire were found 6 feet down into the 25-foot-deep interior, and two milk crates full of Molotov cocktails were sitting at the bottom. These could have been put there by the Home Guard when the country was under the threat of invasion.

The nails that held the pictures and maps are still in place in some of the rooms. However, Ted states that there was no evidence of any damage to the walls, timber and architraves caused by SOE, which left the building exactly as it had found it. As an aside, the Coal Gallery got its name from the large coal bunkers in the room. Ostensibly it would seem strange to locate the bunkers on the top floor. However, it was thought that it was less work for the maids to carry the coal downstairs to the fires in the main rooms. Loading the bunkers, however, took time, with pulleys raising baskets in through a false mullion in the exterior wall.

Ted Pretty has proved a valuable source of information, having worked at Audley End for many years. On a dull and rainy day in the winter of 2000, I found pencilled graffiti on the walls in Room 38 on the south wing that read: 'Sargent Snudge was Statin tengent', 'Servile Rech' and 'Subie Rech'. I thought that 'Sergeant Snudge' had to be a post-war graffito. However, knowing that SOE had utilised rooms on the south wing of the second floor, I looked a little too deeply into the text. I thought that 'Statin' could be a corruption of 'Stettin', or Szczecin, a town in Poland on the west bank of the Oder estuary, and 'Servile Rech' was something to do with the Third Reich. After he had stopped laughing, Ted gave me the actual source, which was a builder who had worked in the house after the war. 'Servile Rech' meant 'servile wretch', a misspelling: the builder was talking about himself and the drudging work he thought he was undertaking!

The family's difficult decision not to resume living in the house meant an uncertain future for Audley End House. William Addison states that maintenance costs were at such a level that only the very wealthy could afford upkeep of such a house.[6] Occupying only a few rooms would have been detrimental to the rest of the house, as it would most certainly have fallen into decay. The prospect of incurring death duties inevitably played a large part in the decision to gift the house to the nation through an agreement with the Treasury.

Initial attempts by the Earl of Wilton to purchase the house came to nothing, but Lees-Milne eventually negotiated its purchase, and in 1948 Audley End was bought for the nation for £30,000 through the National Land Fund. It was put into the care of the Ministry of Public Buildings and Works, the Department of the Environment from 1974, the Historic Monuments Commission and English Heritage since 1984. Lord Braybrooke states: 'When I was sixteen my father tried to sell it. The Chancellor of the Exchequer, Hugh Dalton, came to see us. The future of the house was settled over lunch, when a deal was brokered that the family could keep the contents of the house and be paid £30,000 for the property.'

After the acquisition of Audley End, the land east of the line from Icehouse Lodge and the land north to the stream remained as arable farmland. The kitchen garden began to decline (photographs taken during the war show that the Parterre Garden had been kept in good condition, with beds planted up and the lawns cut short). However, the Victorian vinery was restored in 1996, using over 50 per cent of original materials. Catherine Ruck described the garden as being divided into four quadrants. In 1948, it was let to commercial nursery growers.

Apart from the wider historical perspective, the period of wartime occupation by the British and Poles and its aftermath can be seen as a significant turning point in the history of Audley End and its estate. However, the aftermath of war saw more dramatic events unfold for the Poles.

SEVEN

The Hope of the Polish Nation

In the latter part of the war Alfred Fensome was sent to Germany, and his journey through Europe was to lead full circle back to his Polish friends from Station 43. Held up in the Isle of Wight for four days, he sailed for Europe after D-Day, with his division's orders being to follow up the Allied advance into Germany. He says that they often found themselves in front of the leading infantry divisions. As part of a special unit of army drivers forging into Germany, they were told to get into the town halls, any place of previous German command, and collect paperwork. Fensome worked with a Glaswegian safe-breaker in Berlin. Taken out of prison, put into the Army and immediately made a sergeant, the thief was employed to open safes to retrieve any paperwork. Fensome stated: 'He never marched on parades, the only marching he did was when he went to pick up his pay.'

Under armed guard they took the documentation to Ostend, Belgium, so that it could be shipped back to England in a steam yacht. There were often three tons of paperwork in the back of the lorries. Part of this paper trail led to the Nuremberg Trials. It often took them many days to travel short distances back to the coast, because of the blown-up bridges.

Fensome described having to enter Belsen concentration camp on several occasions at the end of the war, dropping off various British officers. He says that he was asked to look for Polish SOE agents that he had known at Station 43, and he discovered that some agents were indeed in the camp. Most tragically of all he says that it was a matter of the Poles recognising him because they had changed so much that he could hardly recognise them. He got information from the *Cichociemni* agents regarding the conditions within Belsen, being told that they were tortured and forced out in all weathers in wire cages. The British authorities wanted them out quickly because they had been tortured and had suffered so much. Fensome saw the Allies using flame throwers to clear the temporary buildings, and bulldozing the buildings and bodies into pits.

The overall contribution of the Polish people was of utmost importance in securing an Allied victory. The Poles revealed the secrets of the V-1 pulse jet and V-2 rocket; their Underground intelligence pinpointed many key industrial and military sites for destruction; they defended their beloved Warsaw to the last; they fought in every theatre of war; and they were integral to the unravelling of the 'Enigma' code.

After the Uprising, fierce political wrangles ensued between Stanisław Mikołajczyk and Winston Churchill. The complicit agreement made by Roosevelt, Churchill and Stalin regarding moving Poland's borders was out in the open, and Stalin rigidly refused flexibility regarding his territorial plans for Poland. Mikołajczyk resigned.

Political machinations in the British War Cabinet played their part in the fate of Poland from the onset. In 1941, the British Government knew that it could not admit to Poland that it had known of Stalin's inflexibility regarding territory gained in 1939. Mikołajczyk's resignation effectively dissolved the political viability of the exiled government in London, and a new government was formed, with Edward Osóbka-Morawski as prime minister and Władysław Gomułka as Communist Party leader.

Only ostensibly 'independent' again, Poland, with the consent of its Western Allies, and as a result of the Big Three Yalta Conference in February 1945, was left under the control of Soviet Communism. At Yalta in the Crimea, Churchill and Roosevelt conceded lands in the east of Poland to Stalin and reclaimed lands back from Germany. Count Grocholski, former staff member at Station 43, was the Secretary-General of the Federation of Poles in Britain in the 1950s. As his unpublished obituary reveals, by all means at his disposal and at every opportunity, he denounced the post-Yalta division of Europe, what he called 'the tragic nonsense of Yalta', which, he believed, could not last for ever.

After Yalta, in July 1945, the territorial demarcation was rubber-stamped by Stalin at Potsdam, where the former German territories lying east of the Rivers Oder and Neisse came under Polish sovereignty. Poland's frontier with the USSR was shifted westwards, and with it the beginnings of Poland becoming a people's democracy on the Soviet model. The Government-in-Exile had rejected the agreement. In March 1945 sixteen Polish leaders of the resistance, including Leopold Okulicki, commander of the *AK*, who had gone to Moscow under written guarantee of their safety to discuss the formation of a post-war all-party government, disappeared, never to be heard of again.[1] One of the hollow charges made by Stalin was Polish collaboration with the Germans.

An advocate of Poland's independence, Mikołajczyk returned to Poland to welcoming crowds and a position as deputy prime minister of the Provisional Government. The majority of the Poles were against the Soviet Leviathan in their country, and Mikołajczyk's presence in non-Communist politics caused defection away from party membership. Mikołajczyk was accused of complicity and contact with the renegade resistance groups. Poles in the east of the country began migrating away from this now Soviet sector, and the country began coming to terms with its incredible losses. Many towns had been completely levelled, the war destroying in seconds what centuries had built. In 1945 the regeneration of Warsaw began, faithfully replicating many of the historical buildings destroyed. On another level, citizens of Warsaw built shelters by hand and shovel.

The end of the war left the majority of the Poles feeling that they had been betrayed by the Allies. Demoralised and utterly deflated, many of the Poles remained in Britain. If servicemen returned to Poland they ran the risk that they would be tried as war criminals for fighting against the Red Army at the beginning of the war. Many of the Poles were fiercely anti-Communist; Stalin was responsible for the deaths of their friends, families and colleagues and they were not prepared to live under his tutelage. The Polish Government-in-Exile remained in London until 1990 in order to oppose the Communist rule.

After the war, remnants of the AK fought on against Soviet-backed Communist forces and the new regime. However, the clampdown by the *NKVD* and the new Polish security forces, the *Urząd Bezpieczeństwa* (*UB*), put the surviving *AK* into hiding. The *UB* hunted out former *AK* members and *Cichociemni*, murdering those on a list of 'troublesome Poles', as the *NKVD* had done when the Soviets had invaded Poland with Hitler in 1941. Over 30,000 Poles died in less than two years. When British soldiers were being given their 'de-mob' suits, the Poles were fighting on in the face of a cruel oppressor who sought to accuse them of collaboration with the Germans when they had fought so hard against them in six years of Nazi occupation. One cannot help but see the Allies as capitulating to Stalin.

One *AK* member who carried on fighting was Witold Uklański. After a stay at Audley End House, he parachuted into Poland in 1944 and became a commander in the Cracow region. Tucholski states that Uklański was arrested in Poland on 27 November 1945 and sentenced to death for activities with *Wolność i Niezawisłość*, or Freedom and Independence (*WiN*),[2] but the sentence was later changed to life imprisonment. Tony Currie explains more about *WiN*:

> I know *WiN* rather as the abbreviation of *Wolność i Niepodległość*, *Niepodległość* being a more commonly used word for independence. *WiN* was the unofficial continuation of the *AK*, which was disbanded by General Okulicki in January 1945. However, a great number of *AK* soldiers

decided to continue the fight for independence against the other occupant, the Soviet Union. Since the latter was a formal ally of the Western powers, the political status of *WiN* was naturally ambiguous and enjoyed the support of the most uncompromising elements of Polish public opinion.

There was nothing dishonourable in the activities of *WiN*. Major Uklański, a professional officer, was obviously a patriotic member of *WiN*. Having been dropped into Poland, apparently in the same night as I had been on 26 December 1944, he managed to return to England in the course of 1945. In November of that year he went back to Poland under the assumed name 'Sawicki'. He was immediately arrested and sentenced to death by the Soviet-dominated authorities. Tucholski published his book in the 1980s when Poland was still under Communist rule, and he had to be careful about what he was saying. Some critics charge him with having been too careful, and Tucholski produced a later, less ambiguous, version of the book. Thus, he says that Uklański was sentenced by a court of the '*Rzeczpospolita Polska*' (Republic of Poland). He would not have risked anything if he had said that it was a court of the *Polska Rzeczpospolita Ludowa* (Polish People's Republic), the official name of the Soviet–Communist institution. As you can see, he has unwittingly blackened the name of an honest Pole. Uklański died in prison in 1954.

Approximately 20 per cent of the Polish population perished during the war. However, under Stalin no Polish servicemen were allowed to take part in the victory parade in 1946. No Poles took part in the victory parade in London, either because of the whole diplomatic approach to the USSR by the newly elected Socialist Government or as a protest by the Poles themselves. The RAF protested, and an exception was made for the Polish pilots. However, they were not prepared to march without their compatriots, so no Poles were represented on VE Day (Victory in Europe) in London. This affected over a quarter of a million servicemen in Britain.

The bitter irony is that out of the depths of sorrow at the end of the First World War, when the nation had lost over a million casualties, Poland regained its independence, which had been lost for over 100 years. At the end of the Second World War, when VE celebrations proliferated, Poland was being handed over to Stalin and his brutal regime. It is staggering that more than six million citizens perished in German hands and about two million died in Soviet labour camps and specific places of execution, including at Katyń, where Stalin denied any blame for the deaths of the Polish officers. Between 1939 and 1941 the treatment of Poles by the occupying Soviets was savage and indefensible, but it can be said that Nazi atrocities in the country have been better reported, perhaps because of the imposing threat the Soviet Union posed to the West in post-war Europe, and also the West's alliance with the Soviet Union during the war. Matters of Soviet brutality were far from out in the open.

In the late 1940s embryonic fears were getting bigger in America. These fears were predicting what Stalin's ideological intentions were and the threat he posed. President Truman maintained that he did not recognise Stalin's territorial demands in Poland, wanting Germany to occupy more Polish soil as a buffer zone against the USSR and so squeezing Poland once more. This was devastating, and seen as the West's final betrayal.

In the allegedly corrupt elections of 1947, Mikołajczyk was defeated, and, fearing arrest, went back to Britain. Intransigent resistance against Communism continued in Poland, but the Cold War saw Britain supporting the American wish to control Communism. Threatened, Stalin forced Poland to reject Western aid, and the Polish United Workers' Party was amalgamated with other parties in Poland. The country had become a one-party state and suffered under Stalinism and his plans to collectivise Poland. Members of the *AK* and other veterans who had fought with the Western allies continued to be imprisoned or worse.

THE HOPE OF THE POLISH NATION

Demobilisation and the impossibility of returning to Poland gave rise to Poles settling in many areas of the British Isles. There are Polish churches, clubs and communities throughout the United Kingdom. However, demobilisation did not happen right at the end of the war, and many Polish servicemen were demobbed in 1947 and 1948, especially high-ranking servicemen.

The ex-servicemen had come from many divisions of active service: General Anders's Second Corps, which took Monte Cassino; the Polish Air Force; the Polish Navy; General Maczek's First Division; the Polish Independent Airborne Division; and *Cichociemni*. In 1946 the Polish Ex-Combatants' Association was formed to work for the welfare of those who chose to stay in Britain. Other organisations were formed separate from their own divisions. These included the *Związek Polskich Spadochroniarzy* or Polish Airborne Association (*ZPS*), and the *Koło Cichociemnych Spadochroniarzy Armii Krajowej*, the Polish Home Army Parachutists' Association.

Cichociemni instructors and agents Tony Currie, Antoni Nosek, Alan Mack, Józef Hartman and many others stayed in Britain when they were released from the Army, some remaining close friends. Hartman became godfather to Currie's daughter. Currie tells of the time he had a compulsion to visit his old friend at his house in Hounslow. It was a sad visit. He found the front door to the house open and Hartman having died at his table. Currie speaks with fond memories of Hartman's strong but kind character. In a way he said that he felt glad for Hartman when he died, as he could now be with all the men whom he had felt close to, 'his boys' who had been killed after leaving Audley End House. Tragically, despite his great character and service to Britain during the war, Hartman worked washing dishes in a restaurant. Work was very difficult to find for Poles like Hartman, who did not speak any English, a situation that has to be seen as totally unjust.

Tony Currie went on to work for the BBC after the war and now lives in London. Still fit and very active, Alan Mack, now in his late eighties, and known since his teaching days as Captain Mack, forged his career in teaching after being demobbed in Fife in July 1947. Mack's exploits did not end when the war ended. In 1950 he was proprietor of the Abbot's Manor Hotel, very close to Debden airfield. One evening around midnight a Wellington bomber crashed on the edge of the airfield, 100 yards from Mack's fence and narrowly missing his house. Mack was playing bridge at the time with his gardener and one resident, and they rushed out to see what had happened. As he had parachuted from a Wellington during the war, Mack knew where to get into the aircraft, and managed to free two of the crew from the burning wreck, including the unconscious pilot, who was still strapped into his seat. With the help of the gardener, who cut the belt with his knife, he managed to get the pilot out just in time. The aircraft then exploded after they had escaped to the safety of a ditch.

In August 2003 Bronisław Wawrzkowicz revisited Lwów in what is now Ukraine, the first visit there since he had been arrested by the *NKVD*. He has written about these experiences, under the name Peter Wawrzkowicz, in his book *The Shadow of the Hammer and Sickle*, which is published in the USA. He has also collaborated in *Stalin's Ethnic Cleansing in Eastern Poland: Tales of the Deported 1940–1946*, translated by Bronia Kacperek and Eric Whittle. *The Shadow of the Hammer and Sickle* ends after his safe arrival in Persia, having survived two years of slavery under Stalin. Visiting Poland in 1965, Wawrzkowicz said he was followed all the time by the security forces, and was told, 'We know who you are'. Lieutenant Kazimierz Zdaniewicz had a similar experience when he visited his homeland after the war. Approached by the police, he was told to produce his documents at a police station the next day. Zdaniewicz agreed but left the country straight away.

Courier and Station 43 trainee Elżbieta Zawacka worked as a mathematician, humanist and teacher after the war. She was responsible for the foundation in 1990 of the 'Pomeranian Archive of the Home Army', which is devoted to the history of the Underground resistance in Pomerania, the area between the Odra and Vistula rivers in Poland, and of the Polish Women

War Service and the activities of 'Zagroda' during the war. She still lives in Poland.

The decades before independence saw many protests and deep unrest among industrial workers who defied Soviet threats. There were struggles to dilute the single model of Socialism, and tensions grew between the Catholic Church and the State in the 1950s. There were student riots, shipyard workers' revolts and a revival of Polish nationalism in the 1960s. The strikes of the shipyard workers in Gdańsk in the 1970s gave rise to a new hope. Lech Wałĺsa formed *Solidarność* (Solidarity) in 1980. Solidarity was a trade union that strove for industrial workers to have a control that was non-existent under Communist rule. The government's drive against the union gave rise to martial law in the country, and tanks rumbled along the streets and members of Solidarity were arrested. Martial law finally ended in July 1983, but in October 1984 Father Jerzy Popiełuszko, a pro-Solidarity priest, was abducted and murdered by secret police. The outcry was so great that the policemen were brought to trial in February 1985. In 1990 Lech Wałęsa was elected President of the Republic of Poland.

In the summer of 1983, with martial law still in force in Poland until 22 July, a memorial urn was placed in the West Park at Audley End House on the remains of the Jacobean Mount Garden. Colonel Sir P.A. Wilkinson, senior commander in SOE, unveiled the urn in memory of 108 Polish parachutists who lost their lives (Wilkinson had married Theresa Villiers, stepdaughter of Lord Aldenham, the Poles' landlord at Briggens). Present at the memorial event were the Polish Prime-Minister-in-Exile, Kazimierz Sabbat, and the then British Minister of Defence, Michael Heseltine. Ted Pretty was responsible for erecting the steel circle supporting the Polish flag and Union Jack that was drawn open by Heseltine to reveal the urn. Mr Pretty was understandably relieved when the unveiling was successful.

The inscription on the north face of the urn reads:

STATION 43

Between 1942 and 1944 Polish members of the Special
Operations Executive trained in this house for missions
in their homeland. This memorial commemorates the
achievements of those who parachuted into enemy occupied
Poland and gave their lives for the freedom of this and their
own country. *Dulce et decorum est pro patria mori* (sweet and
beautiful it is to die for one's own country).

Polish (and Dutch) agents suffered an enormous percentage of
losses, not to mention the heavy toll on aircrews risking the long
and dangerous flights. Seventy-three aircraft were lost on Polish
sorties. A total of 527 SOE agents passed through STS 43. Between
1941 and 1945 316 *Cichociemni*, including one woman, Captain
Elżbieta Zawacka, parachuted into Poland, 108 giving their lives.
A total of 485 drops were made into Poland during the war, 192 of
them into Warsaw during the Uprising. The relationship between
Britain's first ally and SOE was a strong one. One cannot doubt
the importance that SOE played in training *Cichociemni* to become
effective regional commanders and in other posts. Likewise, the
Poles forwarded wireless research, ciphers and code-breaking and
revealed the secrets of the V-2.

The anchor-shaped emblem depicted on the other side of
the memorial urn represents three levels of Polish service. The
eagle-wing surround is the badge of the Polish paratrooper; the
wreath at the bottom means that the serviceman had undertaken
a parachute jump; and the PW within stands for *Polska Walczy*,
or 'Poland is Fighting' (see p. 13). The complete badge represents
the Polish *Cichociemni* agent, and was worn on the uniform rather
than on a cap.

In a modern age where the news headlines on 11 November
2002 spoke of memorial services and wreaths being laid at the
Cenotaph, in one breath, and impending war with another
nation, in the next, it is often difficult to shake the reader
and television viewer out of complacency. Perhaps only the
insidious threat of world terrorism against civilians can have
far-reaching effects. The constant exposure in the media of

images of conflict, in both fact and fiction, can desensitise us to the horrors of war. Memorial tributes like the urn in the grounds at Audley End can only hope to help perpetuate the courage both of those who survived and of those who perished. These important tributes throughout the world, from graveyards on the edge of deserts to memorials on small village greens in Britain, often bear individual names of those who lost their lives, but invariably include the unknown, Everyman. War memorials often lift conflicts out of the large-scale historical arena and bring them into the closer perspective of the individual; they make the difference between war as a vast impersonal strategy on a map and war as the experiences of the individual soldier.

Audley End House, STS, Station 43, is an important part of Polish and British wartime history and was an integral part of many people's lives during the war. The Polish and British servicemen were the last residents to live in Audley End before its doors opened to the public. In honour of the Poles, a wreath bearing the *Cichociemni* badge is laid every year at the Remembrance Service in Saffron Walden. In 2003, the wreath was laid by Alan Mack, and despite his age many had to keep up with him in the march from the war memorial to the church.

On 24 May 1998 Major Antoni Nosek visited Audley End with other members of the association for their final reunion at the house. He presented the house with a book entitled *SOE Polish Section in Audley End House 1942–1944*, written by members of the Polish Home Army Association and for eventual show to visitors. In a speech that he made on the day he said: 'Although we had the opportunity to see round the house, now so beautifully refurbished, none of us could recognise the room in which we slept.' He went on to state: 'We say goodbye with tears in our eyes but at the same time we ask Audley End House to forgive us for any damage we might have caused, but I wish to add that we used the explosives very carefully and tried not to blow you up.' Nosek described Major

Hartman as a magnificent man: 'When he received bad news, he planted a rose in his garden for each man killed, with tears in his eyes – he knew and loved each one of us. Finally, the garden was full of roses, because losses were so heavy. The losses continued after the end of the war, as Russian–Polish security forces were hunting us as they considered us Western spies.'

Presenting the book to Marilyn Dalton, the general manager at Audley End, he said, 'We would like to leave a souvenir of our stay here, and I think a suitable souvenir would be a Rubens picture, and that is what we would *like* to leave. But we are a modest people and we leave a modest souvenir, a book, as proof that we were here and loved the place. I hope when my grandchildren, who are here today, come back to Audley End House with their grandchildren, they will explain to them that their great-grandfather left this book on behalf of all freedom fighters who stayed in Audley End House.'

APPENDIX I

Sabotage in Poland, June 1942–January 1943[1]

RAILWAY SABOTAGE

Locomotives damaged	1,268
Railway trucks and coaches damaged	3,318
Railway transports set on fire or damaged	76
Trains derailed	25
Interruptions caused in railway traffic	90
Bridges destroyed	7
Railway telecommunications cut at (points)	22
Railway workshops set on fire	2
Other railway damage (cases)	22

INDUSTRIAL SABOTAGE

Machinery damaged in factories	622
Petrol and lubricants destroyed by fire (tons)	4,605
Factories, workshops set on fire	14
Factory products executed faultily* (tons)	300

In many factories a considerable drop in output and wastage was caused by sabotage.

GUERRILLA ACTIVITIES

These consisted mainly of attacks against German communications. In January 1943, as a result of the forcible evacuations of villages carried out by the Germans in the Lublin area, the Underground organisation carried out extensive operations. The net result was: 8 villages burnt down, 40 Gestapo officials killed and 16 German civilians killed.

In addition to the above, a number of German spies, provocateurs and officials were executed by the Underground organisation.

* Dud explosive shells. As an aside, similar acts of sabotage were attributed to German prisoners of war in Britain when they were assigned work in British factories. A Maquis section in France, desperate for footwear, reeived an airdrop of hundreds of boots, but only for left feet. POWs were blamed for this incredible episode.

APPENDIX II

Confirmed Sabotage/Diversionary Actions of the Związek Walki Zbrojnej (ZWZ) and the Armia Krajowa (AK), I January 1941–30 June 1944I

Action Type	Totals
1. Damaged locomotives	6,930
2. Delayed repairs to locomotives	803
3. Derailed transports	732
4. Transports set on fire	443
5. Damage to railway wagons	19,058
6. Blown up railway bridges	38
7. Disruptions to electricity supplies in Warsaw grid	638
8. Army vehicles damaged or destroyed	4,326
9. Damaged aeroplanes	28
10. Fuel tanks destroyed	1,167
11. Fuel destroyed (tonnes)	4,674
12. Blocked oil wells	5
13. Wagons of wood wool destroyed	150
14. Disruptions of production in factories	7
15. Built-in faults in parts for aircraft engines	4,710
16. Built-in faults into cannon muzzles	203
17. Built-in faults into artillery missiles	92,000
18. Built-in faults into air traffic radio stations	107
19. Built-in faults into condensers	70,000
20. Built-in faults into (electric-industrial) lathes	1,700
21. Damage to important factory machinery	2,872
22. Various acts of sabotage performed	25,145
23. Planned assassinations of Germans	5,733

Intrigue in the Middle East: The Case of Maczinski and Mikiczinski

Traitors and collaborators were rare in a nation devoted to ridding itself of its oppressors. However, the Poles were not immune to questionable loyalties and treachery. For instance, there were disloyal, suspect and compromised Polish agents working in the Middle East in a cell organised by 'Kurcyusz', the Polish Ministry of the Interior representative in Istanbul.[1] The list of suspects and details below exemplify how factual accounts are always more interesting than their fictional counterparts in espionage novels. The emissaries included a courier named Mrs Weber, who made a number of journeys through the Balkans in the full knowledge of the Germans; a compromised Polish wireless operator 'Kowal', who continued to send messages under German control; and Mrs Buczyńska. The accusation against her was that she was selling information to the Germans. Although this was not proved, the evidence weighed against her. SOE could have arrested her in Jerusalem, but chose to wait two months, during which time it was hoped that her stepfather, a notorious German agent, would be enticed from Istanbul to British-occupied territory. The results of this plan are not known, but it was revealed that every single activity undertaken in Kurcyusz's cell was known fully or in part by the Germans, compromising SOE's position in the Middle East.

An SOE interrogation report details the layers of intelligence that SOE built up in order to assess an agent it suspected of corruption. The findings below are taken from this document.[2]

It reveals that a Pole, Ryszard Maczinski, was released from prison in Poland after he had agreed that he would work for the Gestapo. The day after he was freed, he was given his first job, to find a W/T set that was being operated by a Russian. Undertaking this first job successfully, he received payment from the Gestapo for his work. Briefly working at the Chilean Consulate, which he disliked, he was employed as a commercial traveller, taking messages and money to German agents. He was later introduced to a Dr Scholtz, alias Major Heinz Fabian and Krestopejoff. Maczinski gained the trust of the Gestapo by 'persuading' a businessman to work for the Germans. Maczinski was then asked to persuade an agricultural machinery importer in Istanbul to export to the Germans. Using trips to Turkey as cover, Maczinski set up communications with the Polish Consulate (one Polish contact had worked for him in full knowledge of his German connections).

While in Turkey, Scholtz decided that he did not want to go back to his German masters, and returned to Poland. However, on his return, the Germans sent him on another mission to Sofia. Before he left, he told his wife and family and Polish contacts, some of whom knew or guessed he was working with the Gestapo, that he would join the Polish Army. When he arrived in Sofia, he handed over what he had brought, got a Turkish visa and went back to Istanbul to the Polish Consulate.

In the hands of SOE, Maczinski talked about Scholtz, his four assistants and other agents in Europe. He described the family and movements of Fabian: 'Dr S is chairman of "Feld". He drives (in Breslau) a Praga Piccolo black saloon with longitudinal wireless aerial.' He goes on to describe the movements and characteristics of his assistants: 'ARTUR HERMANN. Stein Strasse [street] 14, Breslau. Allots tasks, places where agents live and finds new agents. Meetings of all four [assistants to Fabian] take place at his flat. Guards in mufti [civilian clothes worn by one who usually wears a uniform]. Door opened by maid who has camera under violet-shaped brooch between breasts . . . A. Herm is a heavy drinker, avaricious (takes 33% of all agents' profits and bribes).'

Maczinski also blew the cover of an agent in London

called 'Stolkin'. He was the husband of a female agent, Flora Stolinkinowa, who worked in Europe. Stolkin could be contacted through an advertisement in a London morning paper that read 'Fiancée of Miss Flora has arrived – Margolin dead'. Margolin was the name given to the German agent working at the Chilean Consulate in Warsaw who was reported to be poisoned.

Maczinski detailed a German agent, Paul Gluck, a merchant in Turkey (small ears, bad teeth, tall and close-cropped beard), who knew that Maczinski was meant to be in Sofia. Gluck threatened him on a train going to Adana and was thought to have reported Maczinski to the German authorities. A selection of legends to lost or retained photographs reveals other intriguing characters in the jigsaw: 'Veronica', a dancer and mistress of a clerk in the Japanese Consulate, worker at the Bulgarian Police and the Gestapo; 'Margaretta', a dancer in a trio in Sofia and former mistress of one of the secretaries of the Italian Legation; and 'Bobojewski' (alias 'Boby' and 'Oscar'), a Russian who formerly worked at the Chilean Consulate in Warsaw. Maczinski describes the latter as a very clever and dangerous man, one of the most valuable men in Breslau.

Although no documentation appears to exist regarding the establishment of Maczinski's authenticity, the report on the agent states that SOE's impression of him was favourable. They conclude that it seemed improbable that he should give so many references that could easily be checked upon and still be an enemy agent. 'He sometimes hesitates over answers, but even an honest man could do that . . . all that can be taken as being in his favour could, of course, be skilful acting and be proofs against him, but it seems to me that if the bona fides of his Warsaw and local Polish references is beyond doubt, he must be genuine or mad to give them.'[3]

The Polish authorities were less convinced. They were gravely suspicious of Maczinski owing to three factors: first that Maczinski began his 'career' in the Chilean Consulate in Warsaw; secondly that the man Maczinski said he met at the consulate in Istanbul on his first visit denied all knowledge of him; and finally that Maczinski had mentioned a 'Mikiczinski', who was another suspect agent in 'Kurcyusz's' cell (the names 'Maczinski' and 'Mikiczinski' are probably corruptions from the Polish spelling 'Maczyński' and 'Mikiczyński'). There was a general concern about Poles in the Middle East arriving from German-occupied territory, e.g. by crossing the Bulgarian–Turkish border, and measures were put in place to increase security.

Jeff Bines explains the fate of 'Mikiczinski'. He was originally doing great service to the Poles by smuggling Poles out of Europe and into England by using his position in the Chilean Consulate and access to documents therein. Mikiczinski also successfully smuggled Sikorski's daughter into Britain. There were ingrained suspicions from the Polish Second Bureau that he was using the trust that had been placed in him to smuggle spies into England using similar documentation. The Polish authorities were reluctant to acknowledge suspicions because of important figures arriving safely in Britain. However, the Second Bureau sent operatives to Cairo to kidnap him. They caught him, drugged him and rolled him up in a carpet. In no doubt that he was a German agent, they took him out into the desert and executed him.

Lieutenant-Colonel D. (Denys) Hamson had been assigned the task of kidnapping Mikiczinski back in December 1940. He states that Mikiczinski was wanted 'for having sold to the enemy the Warsaw Underground organisation in 1940'.[4] Hamson was put in touch with three other men in Istanbul. Two were from the Polish Secret Service and the third from the Turkish Military Secret Police. Nobody knew the others' real names. An attempt to kidnap Mikiczinski failed, and Hamson states: 'Unfortunately we had not reckoned on Mikiczinski's immunity to drugs, acquired through excessive drinking of spirits.'[5] A second attempt in January 1941 was successful. After ineffectual drugging, Mikiczinski was manhandled and put in a car bound for the aircraft that was standing by. 'Once in the car, he was handcuffed and at the aerodrome he was again drugged and put into a sack. I am told that in Egypt he eventually divulged all he knew and was disposed of by the Poles.'[6]

Notes

Preface

1. A. Nosek, transcription of a speech made by Major Nosek at 'SOE–Polish Section reunion at Audley End House', 24 May 1998.

Introduction

1. S. Ryder, *Child of my Love: An Autobiography* (London, Colins Harvill, 1986), p. 98.
2. English Heritage (East of England Regional Office, Cambridge), HBMC13 CBMAG (2SP) 386: P. Howe, 'Recollection of Cpl P. Howe, Audley End 1942–44' (1986) (also quoted in D. Church, 'A Tour of Audley End House', in K. Jeffrey (ed.), *Audley End* (English Heritage, 1999), p. 37).

CHAPTER 1. *'Poland is Fighting'*

1. N. Ascherson, *The Struggles for Poland* (London, Michael Joseph Ltd, 1987), p. 6.
2. *Ibid.*, p. 59.
3. M.R.D. Foot, *The Special Operations Executive, 1940–1946* (London, Pimlico, 1999), pp. 270–1.
4. Ascherson, *Struggles*, p. 60.
5. National Archives, HS 8/237, HQ History 1941, Note on the Czech and Polish Organisations, I. Polish Section. (a) The organisation of secret armies, paras 2 and 3.
6. A. Suchcitz, *Poland's Contribution to the Allied Victory in the Second World War* (Sussex, Caldra House Ltd, 1995), p. 14.
7. Ascherson, *Struggles*, pp. 106–7.
8. National Archives, HS 7/277, Polish Affairs in the Balkans

and Middle East, August 1942–August 1943 (Polish–Russian Relations), p. 66.

9. Suchcitz, *Poland's Contribution*, pp. 12, 16.
10. G. Iranek-Osmecki, *The Silent and Unseen* (London, Sheed and Ward, 1954), pp. 161–2.

CHAPTER 2. *Cichociemni*, 'Silent and Unseen'

1. Major-General Sir Colin Gubbins, 'Lecture on Resistance Movements in the War', Wednesday 28 January 1948, *Journal of the Royal United Services Institute*, volume XCIII, no. 570 (May 1948), p. 210.
2. *Ibid.*, p. 211.
3. J. Garliński, *Poland, SOE and the Allies*, 1st edn (London, George Allen and Unwin Ltd, 1969), p. 27 (footnote).
4. National Archives, HS 4/253, STS 43, Student Training Reports.
5. Sir Douglas Dodds-Parker, private correspondence with author, 12 November 2003.
6. J. Tucholski, *Cichociemni* (Warsaw, Instytut Wydawniczy Pax, 1984), p. 63.
7. Iranek-Osmecki, Silent, p. 5.
8. Garliński, *Poland*, p. 62 (footnote).
9. Tucholski, *Cichociemni*, pp. 62–3.
10. Iranek-Osmecki, *Silent*, Preface.
11. Tucholski, *Cichociemni*, p. 75.
12. *Ibid.*, p. 62.
13. *Ibid.*, p. 62.
14. Garliński, *Poland*, p. 28.
15. National Archives, HS 8/237, HQ files, Note on the Czech and Polish Organisations, I. Polish Section. (b) Sabotage Groups, para. 3.
16. Imperial War Museum, Sound Archive 8188/4 (transcription), interview with Fergus Chalmers-Wright, 1984, p. 26.
17. *Ibid.*, p. 35.
18. *Ibid.*, pp. 36, 38.
19. *Ibid.*, pp. 38–9.

NOTES

20. L. Atherton, *SOE in Eastern Europe: An Introduction to the Newly Released Records of the Special Operations Executive in Czechoslovakia, Hungary, Poland and Russia* (London, PRO Publications, 1995), p. 15.
21. National Archives, HS 8/237, Note on the Czech and Polish Organisations, I. Polish Section. (b) Sabotage Groups, para. 4.
22. *Ibid.*, I. Polish Section, para. 6.
23. National Archives, HS 5/576, Operation Bracing, Poles in the German Army, from Major P. Howarth (FORCE 266) 'Cipher Telegram Out' to FORCE 133, 13/6/44, and 184/44, 16/6/44, Captain Mitko to Howarth.
24. National Archives, HS 7/277, The Polish Sixth Bureau in the Middle East, (b) Istanbul: Colonel Suliman, p. 63.
25. Foot, *Special Operations Executive*, p. 271.
26. National Archives, HS 7/183, Polish Section History, 1941–1950, V. Joint work of the VIth Bureau General Staff and Polish Section – SOE, p. 18.
27. National Archives, HS 7/51, Training Section 1940–1945, 2. (a) Polish Section Training, p. 72.
28. Gubbins, 'Resistance Movements', p. 212.
29. Garliński, *Poland*, p. 29.
30. *Ibid.*, p. 29.
31. *Ibid.*, p. 59.
32. Atherton, *SOE in Eastern Europe*, p. 40.
33. National Archives, HS 4/185, SOE training, Poles/Czechs, letter to Brigadier C.E.D. Bridge from Major C.H. Cassels, 13 November 1940.
34. *Ibid.*, Reply letter to Major C.H. Cassels from Brigadier C.E.D. Bridge, 13 November 1940.
35. *Ibid.*, Enclosure to No. 488/III tj., 3/Fighting Practice.
36. Iranek-Osmecki, *Silent*, p. 11.
37. Tucholski, *Cichociemni*, p. 80 (footnote).
38. Iranek-Osmecki, *Silent*, p. 14.
39. M. Newnham, *Prelude to Glory: The Story of the Creation of Britain's Parachute Army* (London, Sampson Low, Marston & Co. Ltd, 1947), p. 203.

40. Iranek-Osmecki, *Silent*, p. 23.

41. Tucholski, *Cichociemni*, p. 70.

42. Newnham, *Prelude to Glory* (photograph caption).

43. *Ibid.*, p. 69.

44. National Archives, HS 8/435, SOE Training Section, 1940–1945, The Headquarters of the Training Section. 1. General, p. 6.

45. National Archives, HS 7/183, Polish Section History, pp. 22–3.

46. National Archives, HS 8/960, Special Training Schools, 1 January 1941–31 December 1943.

47. National Archives, HS 8/435, SOE Training Section, 1940–1945, p. 7.

48. Garliński, *Poland*, p. 60.

49. National Archives, HS 4/185, SOE training, Poles/Czechs, transcription of telephone conversation on 13 September 1940 from Advance HQ of No. 4 Military Mission to No. 4 Military Mission.

50. Tucholski, *Cichociemni*, p. 65.

51. National Archives, HS 4/185, SOE training, Poles/Czechs, outline programme of the Special Course at Inverlochy. Enclosure to No. 488/III tj. 10/Time Distribution to different Topics.

52. *Ibid.*, Programmes of work carried out for the period 7 September 1940–2 October 1940.

53. *Ibid.*, Letter from Chief of Staff.

54. *Ibid.*, Letter from Major D.H. Stacey to Captain Perkins, ref. I/TC/T/2.

55. *Ibid.*, Letter (from Brigadier, G.S.) to M.T.7 – War Office from No. 4 Military Mission, 6 November 1940.

56. Garliński, *Poland*, p. 60.

57. *Ibid.*, p. 61.

58. Tucholski, *Cichociemni*, p. 78.

59. *Ibid.*, p. 79.

60. *Ibid.*, pp. 78–9.

61. National Archives, HS 7/174, Norwegian Section History, 1940–1945, p. 52.

NOTES

62. National Archives, HS 7/183, Polish Section History, pp. 18–19.
63. Tucholski, *Cichociemni*, p. 79.
64. *Ibid.*, p. 79.
65. *Ibid.*, p. 83.
66. Ryder, *Child of my Love*, p. 121.
67. *Ibid.*, pp. 88–9.
68. National Archives, HS 7/183, Polish Section History, p. 19.

CHAPTER 3. *Station 43*

1. M. Sutherill, *The Gardens of Audley End* (English Heritage, 1995), p. 8.
2. *Ibid.*, p. 8.
3. R. Kirkpatrick, *Audley End at War* (Saffron Walden Town Library archive, V4949, 1992), p. 7.
4. *Ibid.*, p. 8.
5. Essex Record Office, C/W 1/2/61, Air Raid Damage Report, Audley End Station.
6. English Heritage, P. Howe, letter, 9 October 1986.
7. J.F. Bowyer, *Air Raid! The Enemy Air Offensive against East Anglia 1939–45* (Wellingborough, Patrick Stephens Ltd, 1986), pp. 71, 103, 123, 318.
8. J.M. Robinson, *The Country House at War* (London, Bodley Head, 1989), p. 14.
9. Kirkpatrick, *Audley End at War*, p. 6.
10. *Ibid.*, p. 6.
11. *Ibid.*, p. 8.
12. M. White, *Saffron Walden's History: A Chronological Compilation* (Saffron Walden, 1991), p. 223.
13. Kirkpatrick, *Audley End at War*, p. 7.
14. National Archives, HS 8/435, SOE Training Section, 1940–1945, 2. Functions of the Training Section. 2 (a).(iii) Administration, p. 7.
15. English Heritage, 'Recollection of Cpl P. Howe'.
16. *Ibid.* (also quoted in Jeffrey (ed.), *Audley End*, p. 37).
17. *Ibid.*, p. 37.

18. *Ibid.*, p. 37.
19. *Ibid.*, p. 37.
20. Jeffrey (ed.), *Audley End*, p. 37.
21. National Archives, HS 8/435, SOE Training Section, 1940–1945, V. Stores, p. 8.
22. *Ibid.*, p. 8.
23. M.R.D. Foot, *SOE in the Low Countries* (London, St Ermin's Press, 2001), p. 252.
24. Kirkpatrick, *Audley End at War*, p. 14.
25. *Ibid.*, p. 13.
26. National Archives, HS 7/159, Dutch Section History, December 1940–December 1941, Section VI. No page ref.
27. *Ibid.*
28. *Ibid.*
29. *Ibid.*
30. *Ibid.*
31. *Ibid.*, Outline of planning for the field in 1942.
32. *Ibid.*, Actual resistance in the field during 1942.
33. Per B. Andersen, 'Interview with Ralf Hollingworth, 27 December 1966', *Berlingske Tidende* (Copenhagen, 1966).
34. *Ibid.*
35. Kirkpatrick, *Audley End at War*, p. 9.
36. *Ibid.*, p. 19.
37. *Ibid.*, p. 19.
38. Garliński. *Poland*, p. 61.
39. *Ibid.*, p. 60.
40. *Ibid.*, p. 62.
41. Iranek-Osmecki, *Silent*, p. 11.
42. National Archives, HS 8/435, SOE Training Section, 1940–1945, (b) Preparation of Syllabus and Training Instructions, p. 8.
43. National Archives, HS 9/1130/1.
44. Tucholski, *Cichociemni*, pp. 87–8.
45. Garliński, *Poland*, p. 56.
46. Iranek-Osmecki, *Silent*, p. 46.
47. Tucholski, *Cichociemni*, pp. 58–60.

NOTES

48. M. Ney-Krwawicz, *The Polish Home Army, 1939–1945* (London, Study Trust (*SPP*), 2001), p. 117.
49. Tucholski, *Cichociemni*, p. 60.
50. *Ibid.*, p. 59.
51. *Ibid.*, p. 60.
52. *Ibid.*, p. 67.
53. *Ibid.*, p. 68.
54. National Archives, HS 4/253, STS 43.
55. Garliński, *Poland*, p. 58.
56. Kirkpatrick, *Audley End at War*, p. 14.
57. English Heritage, 'Recollection of Cpl P. Howe'.
58. Iranek-Osmecki, *Silent*, pp. 11–12.
59. Nosek, speech.
60. Tucholski, *Cichociemni*, p. 67.
61. Jeffrey (ed.), *Audley End*, p. 37.
62. Tucholski, *Cichociemni*, p. 68.
63. English Heritage, 'Recollection of Cpl P. Howe'.
64. Newnham, *Prelude to Glory* (photograph caption).
65. English Heritage, 'Recollection of Cpl P. Howe'.
66. Tucholski, *Cichociemni*, p. 77.
67. National Archives, HS 4/185, SOE training, Poles/ Czechs, letter from Colonel Mitkiewicz to the General Commanding Polish Forces in Scotland.
68. National Archives, HS 4/253, STS 43.
69. Nosek, speech.
70. Ney-Krwawicz, *Polish Home Army*, p. 167.
71. Tucholski, *Cichociemni*, p. 338.
72. *Ibid.*, p. 413.
73. *Ibid.*, p. 428.
74. *Ibid.*, p. 365.
75. F. Clark, *Agents by Moonlight: The Secret History of RAF Tempsford during World War II* (Stroud, Tempus, 1999), pp. 277–86.
76. National Archives, HS 8/435, SOE Training Section, 1940–1945, (vi) Discipline, p. 8.
77. English Heritage, P. Howe, letter.
78. National Archives, HS 8/960, Special Training Schools, 1

January 1941–31 December 1943, Lieutenant-Colonel S.S. Hill-Dillon, Location of Special Training Schools, HF/IB/OM/12, 25/8/41.

79. *Ibid.*
80. Ryder, *Child of my Love*, p. 87.
81. English Heritage, 'Recollection of Cpl P. Howe' (also quoted in Jeffrey (ed.), *Audley End*, p. 37).
82. National Archives, HS 7/277, The Polish Sixth Bureau in the Middle East, 3. Operations to Poland from the Southern Bases, p. 60.
83. Dodds-Parker, private correspondence.
84. Nosek, written correspondence with author.

CHAPTER 4. *Special Duties Squadrons*

1. Newnham, *Prelude to Glory* (photograph caption).
2. J.F. Hamlin, *The Royal Air Force at Newmarket*, 2nd edn (J. Hamlin, 1989), p. 59.
3. Clark, *Agents by Moonlight*, pp. 27–8.
4. National Archives, HS 7/13, SOE History, RAF Station Tempsford, p. 1.
5. Clark, *Agents by Moonlight*, p. 49.
6. '"Scarlet Pimpernels" of the Air. The Secret Out: Tempsford HQ Fed Resistance Movement' *Bedfordshire Times*, 15 June 1945.
7. Clark, *Agents by Moonlight*, p. 72.
8. Author unknown, *The Life-Boat Service and the War: Three and a Half Years* (Royal National Lifeboat Institution), p. 10.
9. National Archives, HS 7/277, The Polish Sixth Bureau in the Middle East, Operations, p. 74.
10. *Ibid.*, p. 75.
11. *Ibid.*, p. 76.
12. *Ibid.*, Congratulations from G.O.C. Polish Secret Army, p. 77.
13. Clark, *Agents by Moonlight*, p. 48.
14. *Ibid.*, pp. 199, 200.
15. National Archives, HS 7/277, Liberators (13), p. 78.
16. National Archives, HS 7/13, SOE History, RAF Station Tempsford, p. 1.

17. Nosek, written correspondence.
18. Ryder, *Child of my Love*, p. 85.
19. National Archives, HS 7/13, SOE History, RAF Station Tempsford, p. 3.
20. *Ibid.*, p. 3.
21. *Ibid.*, p. 3.
22. National Archives, HS 7/183, Polish Section History, p. 18.
23. National Archives, HS 7/13, SOE History, RAF Station Tempsford, p. 2.
24. Iranek-Osmecki, *Silent*, p. 26.
25. Nosek, written correspondence.
26. *Ibid.*

CHAPTER 5. *On Dangerous Ground*

1. National Archives, HS 7/183, Polish Section History, p. 18.
2. *Ibid.*, p. 21.
3. Tucholski, *Cichociemni*, p. 365.
4. National Archives, HS 7/183, Polish Section History, p. 20.
5. *Ibid.*, p. 21.
6. Tucholski, *Cichociemni*, p. 77.
7. English Heritage, 'Recollection of Cpl P. Howe'.
8. Garliński, *Poland*, p. 59 (footnote).
9. Ney-Krwawicz, *Polish Home Army*, p. 143.
10. Tucholski, *Cichociemni*, p. 78.
11. Foot, Special Operations Executive, pp. 267–8.
12. Ney-Krwawicz, Polish Home Army, pp. 40–1.
13. Tucholski, *Cichociemni*, p. 420.
14. *Ibid.*, p. 310.
15. W.J.M. Mackenzie, *The Secret History of SOE: The Special Operations Executive 1940–1945* (London, St Ermin's Press, 2000), p. 314.
16. National Archives, HS 7/277, Liberators, Poland and Russia, p. 87.
17. *Ibid.*, p. 88.
18. National Archives, HS 8/291, OVERLORD, The Role of Polish and Czech Secret Armies, Polish Secret Army,

MUS/891/978. 26/5/44, 4. Organisation of the Secret
Army, para. 2, p. 2.

19. *Ibid.*, Appendix B, Current Operations of Polish Secret
Army, para. 7.

20. National Archives, HS 7/277, Liberators, Internal
Conditions in Poland, Report by the German Governor of
the Warsaw District, pp. 85, 86.

21. *Ibid.*, Other activities during August, p. 87.

22. Clark, *Agents by Moonlight*, p. 47.

23 *Ibid.*, p. 51.

24. *Ibid.*, p. 138.

25. National Archives, HS 8/291, OVERLORD, D-Day plans,
Possible German voluntary withdrawal, (4), p. 2.

26. National Archives, HS 8/237, Note on the Czech and Polish
Organisations, 25/11/41, (b) sabotage groups, p. 3.

27. National Archives, HS 8/291, OVERLORD, Action
coordinated with D-Day, Polish Secret Army, 2.
Organisation, para. 3.

28. *Ibid.*, para 3.

29 *Ibid.*, 3, Planned operations already carried out, paras 6, 7.

30. *Ibid.*, 4, Operations at present planned, para. 8.

31. *Ibid.*, Plans/410/125I, 15/9/43.

32. *Ibid.*, J.P. (43) 356 (Final), 16 October 1943 (Directive to SOE
for Operations in Central Europe).

33. *Ibid.*, HBP/PD/5976 letter 23 May 1944.

34. *Ibid.*, SHAEF/17240/11/Ops(A), 11 June 1944.

35. *Ibid.*, SHAEF/17240/11/Ops(A), 11 June 1944.

36. *Ibid.*, CDS/300, 23 May 1944.

37. Foot, *Special Operations Executive*, p. 275.

38. *Ibid.*, p. 269.

39. Tucholski, *Cichociemni*, p. 437.

40. *Ibid.*, p. 395.

41. *Ibid.*, p. 414.

42. *Ibid.*, p. 360.

43. K.A. Merrick, *Flights of the Forgotten: Special Duties Operations
in the Second World War* (London, Arms and Armour, 1989),
p. 225. (Note that Merrick misspells 'Mackus' as 'Mackers'.)

44. Tucholski, *Cichociemni*, p. 390.
45. *Ibid.*, p. 413.
46. *Ibid.*, p. 338.
47. National Archives, HS 7/277, Liberators, (b) SOE's Views on the Polish D-Day Plans, p. 83.
48. L. Marks, *Between Silk and Cyanide: A Codemaker's War 1941–1945* (London, HarperCollins, 1999), p. 533.
49. Gubbins, 'Resistance Movements', pp. 222–3.
50. J. Bines, 'Secret Training Station 43, SOE', Newport News, winter 1997 (see also J. Bines, *Operation FRESTON: The British Military Mission to Poland, 1944* (Hart-Talbot Printers Ltd, 1999)).
51. Garliński, *Poland*, p. 29.
52. Tucholski, *Cichociemni*, p. 75.
53. Ney-Krwawicz, *Polish Home Army*, p. 107.
54. National Archives, HS 7/277, Liberators, A suspected Soviet agent, p. 57.
55. Tucholski, *Cichociemni*, p. 441.
56. Ryder, *Child of my Love*, pp. 99–116.
57. *Ibid.*, pp. 99–116.
58. Iranek-Osmecki, *Silent*, p. 349.

CHAPTER 6. *Audley End House and the Post-War Years*

1. Jeffrey (ed.), Audley End, p. 37.
2. Robinson, Country House at War, p. 100.
3. *Ibid.*, p. 159.
4. *Ibid.*, p. 167.
5. *Ibid.*, p. 131.
6. W. Addison, Audley End (London, J.M. Dent & Sons Limited, 1953), pp. 223–4.

CHAPTER 7. *The Hope of the Polish Nation*

1. J.H. Waller, *The Unseen War in Europe: Espionage and Conspiracy in the Second World War* (London, I.B. Taurus & Co. Ltd, 1996), p. 384.
2. Tucholski, *Cichociemni*, p. 428.

Appendix I

1. National Archives, HS 7/183, Polish Section History, p. 73.

Appendix II

1. Ney-Krwawicz, *Polish Home Army*, Appendix 6, p. 166.
   Source: Bohdan Kwiatkowski, *Sabotaż i dywersja* (London, Bellona, 1949), vol. 1, p. 21.

Appendix III

1. National Archives, HS 7/277, Liberators, p. 64.
2. National Archives, HS 4/201, Interrogation of agents, Report on an interview with Ryszard Maczinski.
3. *Ibid*.
4. National Archives, HS 8/875, Middle East Security, Repatriation of displaced persons from the Middle East, 1 January 1945–31 December 1946, para. 3.
5. *Ibid*., para. 6.
6. *Ibid*., para. 9.

Notes on the Sources

All attempts at tracing the copyright holder of the following books were unsuccessful: *Audley End* by W. Addison; *Poland, SOE, and the Allies* by J. Garliński (permission kindly given by the author); *The Silent and Unseen* by G. Iranek-Osmecki; *Prelude to Glory: The Story of the Creation of Britain's Parachute Army* by M. Newnham; *Child of my Love: An Autobiography* by Sue Ryder; *Cichociemni* by Jędrzej Tucholski and *Saffron Walden's History: A Chronological Compilation* by M. White. The stanza from 'Return to Base' by William Clarke and the stanza from 'Nocturne' by Geoffrey Matthews appear in *Poems of the Second World War: The Oasis Selection*, published by the Salamander Oasis Trust (1985). Their latest poetry anthology is *In the Voice of War*. The National Archives Registered File 'HS' prefix refers to HS 4, SOE: Eastern Europe, 1938–1949; HS 5, SOE: Balkans, 1938–1972; HS 7, SOE: Histories and War Diaries, *c.* 1939–1988; HS 8, Ministry of Economic Warfare, SOE and successors, HQ Records; and HS 9: personnel files. Freddie Clark kindly allowed me to quote from *Agents by Moonlight*. Roger Kirkpatrick gave leave to include excerpts from his informative document *Audley End at War*; M.R.D. Foot kindly allowed me to reference his work, and extracts from *The Special Operations Executive, 1940–1946* by M.R.D. Foot (Copyright © M.R.D. Foot, 1999) are by permission of PFD on behalf of Professor M.R.D. Foot CBE. The first two paragraphs of the Preface use historical information that can be found in the Audley End guide books (now amalgamated in one guide), published by English Heritage and referenced in the Bibliography. Other information, not referenced, is attributable to conversation, interview and written correspondence with Messrs Bines, Mack, Nosek and Pospieszalski. Important information concerning training, Polish instructors and other factors was gleaned from Jędrzej Tucholski's *Cichociemni* through translation into English, and is referenced wherever appropriate. Apologies if translation does not adhere to Tucholski's exact wording. Thanks to all the publishers who gave leave for me to reference authors under their aegis.

PHOTOGRAPHIC SOURCES

I am particularly indebted to Dr K. Stoliński and Krzysztof Bożejewicz of *Studium Polski Podziemnej*, the Polish Underground Movement (1939–1945) Study Trust (SPP), 11 Leopold Road, London, 020 8992 6057, a registered charity dedicated to the preserving in documents, memoirs, photographs and archive footage, the activities of the Polish Underground State and the Resistance Home Army during the German and Soviet occupation. Marilyn Dalton gave permission to use the photograph of Val Sandes with Tony Currie and Alan Mack at Audley End House in May 1998 and the photograph of the Polish flag flying from the Jacobean Mount Garden (Audley End House photograph albums). The following photographs were kindly lent to me for use in the book by Ruby Harris: Lieutenant Aleksander Ihnatowicz, 'Ataman', in 1943; Captain Alfons Maćkowiak (Alan Mack), 1943; Corporal Bill Harris in the West Park, July 1944; British Army soldiers on exercise on the Adam Bridge in 1944; and Waldemar Mariusz Szwiec, alias 'Robot' and 'Jakub', on a motorcycle in the yard outside the stables. Every effort has been made to trace the original copyright owners of these photographs, without success. Mrs Harris has kindly donated copies to SPP for their archives. I welcome response regarding sources, at present unknown, for the following photographs: Wanda Skwirut (kindly lent to me by her son, Jerzy Grochowski); the photograph of Józef Hartman, Antoni Pospieszalski and Jan Kazimierski in the grounds at Audley End, and the portrait of Captain Antoni Pospieszalski (copies kindly given by Jeff Bines with permission from Pospieszalski); and Six Gun Salute for Lieutenant Lemme in Saffron Walden cemetery (kindly given by Mr M. Cottiss). My thanks also to those mentioned in English Heritage for permission to use their images, and Pat Payne for photographs of 'ordinary-looking' bare rooms in a country house, rooms that were far from ordinary during the 1940s.

Bibliography

Primary sources

Andersen, Per B. 'Interview with Ralf Hollingworth, 27 December 1966', in *Berlingske Tidende* (BT), Copenhagen, Denmark

Audley End House, *SOE Polish Section in Audley End House 1942–1944*. Polish Home Army Association presentation book, various authors

Bines, J. 'Secret Training Station 43, SOE', article published in *Newport News*, winter 1997 (Bines has comprehensively researched the Polish Country Section of SOE at Master and PhD level)

English Heritage (East of England Regional Office, Cambridge, archive). P. Howe, 'Recollection of Cpl P. Howe, Audley End 1942–44' (1986), Archive HBMC13 CBMAG (2SP) 386 and letter (9 October 1986); A. Pospieszalski (1996), 'Audley End in Wartime, recollections' (uncategorised); A. Watts (1986), 'Recollections, 23/05/86, Audley End 1942–44', HBMC6 CBMAG (2SP) 386; Ministry of Works and Buildings (9.5.41), 'Audley End Palace, Sketch Plans for Proposed Accommodation'. File AA 046205/IIC PE3

Essex Record Office, C/W 1/2/61, Air Raid Damage Report, Audley End Station

Gubbins, Major-General Sir Colin. 'Lecture on Resistance Movements in the War', Wednesday 28 January 1948. Published in the *Journal of the Royal United Services Institute*, volume XCIII, no. 570 (May 1948)

Imperial War Museum, Sound Archive 8188/4, interview with Fergus Chalmers-Wright, 1984

Land, Sea and Islands Visitor Centre, Arisaig, Scotland,

BIBLIOGRAPHY

Exhibition on SOE training, info@arisaigcentre.co.uk 01687 450 263

Nosek, A. Transcription of a speech made by Major Nosek at 'SOE–Polish Section reunion at Audley End House', 24 May 1998

Radwinter Archives, 'Memories of Jim Bacon'. Bacon, J., unsigned and undated.

Royal National Lifeboat Institution. *The Life-Boat Service and the War: Three and a Half Years.* (Booklet, author unknown)

Saffron Walden Town Library archive, V4949, 'Audley End at War' (Kirkpatrick, R., 1992)

'"Scarlet Pimpernels" of the Air. The Secret Out. Tempsford HQ fed Resistance Movement'. *Bedfordshire Times*, 15 June 1945

The National Archives

HS 4/185, SOE training, Poles/Czechs

HS 4/201, Interrogation of agents, Report on an interview with Ryszard Maczinski

HS 4 /253, STS 43, Student Training Reports

HS 5/576, Operation *Bracing*, Poles in the German Army

HS 7/13, SOE History, RAF Station Tempsford

HS 7/51, Training Section, 1940–1945

HS 7/159, Dutch Section History, December 1940–December 1941

HS 7/174, Norwegian Section History, 1940–1945

HS 7/183, Polish Section History, 1941–1950

HS 7/277, Polish affairs in the Balkans and the Middle East, 1942–1943

HS 8/237, HQ files (1941), France, Belgium, Denmark, Holland, Italy, Norway, Poland, Czechoslovakia and Switzerland

HS 8/291, OVERLORD, The Role of Polish and Czech Secret Armies

HS 8/435, SOE Training Section, 1940–45

HS 8/875, Middle East Security, repatriation of displaced persons from the Middle East, 1 January 1945–31 December 1946 (Ryszard Maczinski)

HS 8/960, Special Training Schools (1 January 1941–31 December 1943)

HS 9/1130/1, personnel file, John Henry Oughton.

STATION 43

Secondary sources

Addison, W. *Audley End*. London, J.M. Dent & Sons, 1953

Ascherson, N. *The Struggles for Poland*. London, Michael Joseph Ltd, 1987

Atherton, L. *SOE in Eastern Europe: An Introduction to the Newly Released Records of the Special Operations Executive in Czechoslovakia, Hungary, Poland and Russia*. London, PRO Publications, 1995

Bines, J. 'Operation Freston'. *The British Military Mission to Poland, 1944*. Hart-Talbot Printers Ltd, 1999

Bowyer, Michael J.F. *Air Raid! The Enemy Air Offensive against East Anglia 1939–45*. Wellingborough, Patrick Stephens Ltd, 1986

Clark, F. *Agents by Moonlight: The Secret History of RAF Tempsford during World War II*. Stroud, Tempus, 1999

Jeffrey, K. (ed.). *Audley End* (chapter by D. Church, 'A Tour of Audley End House'). English Heritage, 1999

Foot, M.R.D. *SOE in the Low Countries*. London, St Ermin's Press, 2001

Foot, M.R.D. *The Special Operations Executive, 1940–1946*. London, Pimlico, 1999

Garliński, J. *Poland, SOE and the Allies*. 1st edn, London, George Allen and Unwin Ltd, 1969

Hamlin, J.F. *The Royal Air Force at Newmarket*. 2nd edn, J. Hamlin, 1989

Iranek-Osmecki, G. *The Silent and Unseen*. London, Sheed and Ward, 1954

Mackenzie, W.J.M. *The Secret History of SOE: The Special Operations Executive 1940–1945*. London, St Ermin's Press, 2000

Marks, L. *Between Silk and Cyanide: A Codemaker's War 1941–1945*. London, HarperCollins, 1999

Merrick, K.A. *Flights of the Forgotten: Special Duties Operations in the Second World War*. London, Arms and Armour, 1989

Newnham, M. *Prelude to Glory: The Story of the Creation of Britain's Parachute Army*. London, Sampson Low, Marston & Co. Ltd, 1947

BIBLIOGRAPHY

Ney-Krwawicz, M. *The Polish Home Army, 1939–1945. Polish Underground Movement (1939–1945)*. London, Study Trust (SPP), 2001

Robinson, J.M. *The Country House at War*. London, Bodley Head, 1989

Ryder, S. *Child of my Love: An Autobiography*. London, Colins Harvill, 1986

Suchcitz, A. *Poland's Contribution to the Allied Victory in the Second World War*. Sussex, Caldra House Ltd, 1995

Sutherill, M. *The Gardens of Audley End*. English Heritage, 1995

Tucholski, J. *Cichociemni*. Warsaw, Instytut Wydawniczy Pax, 1984

Waller, J.H. *The Unseen War in Europe: Espionage and Conspiracy in the Second World War*. London, I.B. Tauris & Co. Ltd, 1996

White, M.D. *Saffron Walden's History: A Chronological Compilation*. Saffron Walden, M. White, 1991

Index

INDEX